"This is a fantastic book! Not only is Carla Anne Coroy an engaging writer but also, in our book, she is the expert of experts in relating to all who have ever had an absentee husband. Buy one for yourself and give one to someone you love who is going at it alone."

—Dr. Gary and Barb Rosberg
President and Executive Vice-President,
America's Family Coaches

"Carla Anne Coroy doesn't mince words when she talks about how lonely being a married single mom is! But while acknowledging the bitterness, the fear, and the exhaustion, she also plots a road forward toward peace, a healthy family life, and even a thriving marriage. An honest, hopeful look at one of the loneliest jobs around!"

—Sheila Wray Gregoire
Christian speaker and author of
The Good Girl's Guide to Great Sex

"People learn more from our struggles than they do from our strengths. And that's why this book is an amazingly valuable resource for every mother; it is soul-piercingly vulnerable. I recommend this book to *any* mom because *every* mom will find an absolute treasure trove of wisdom and hope inside— *practical* wisdom and hope that works because it was bought in the fires of real-life stresses and pressures. You will be encouraged and helped if you read this book!"

—Kris Duerksen
Associate Pastor of Southland Community Church,
Steinbach, Manitoba

D0771968

Married Mom, Solo Parent

Finding God's Strength to Face the Challenge

Carla Anne Coroy

Kregel
Publications

Library of Congress Cataloging-in-Publication Data
Coroy, Carla Anne, 1970–
　　Married mom, solo parent : finding God's strength to face the challenge / Carla Anne Coroy.
　　p. cm.
　　1. Mother and child—Religious aspects—Christianity.　2. Child rearing—Religious aspects—Christianity.　3. Parenting—Religious aspects—Christianity.　I. Title.
BV4529.18.C673　　　　　2011　　　　　248.8'431—dc23　　　　　2011024223

ISBN 978-0-8254-2626-1

Printed in the United States of America
11　12　13　14　15 / 5　4　3　2　1

This book is dedicated to
the man who has given me the privilege
of living the life of a married mom and solo
parent, causing me to grow, learn,
and lean on Jesus. My husband's support,
prayers, and pursuit of godliness and
integrity have given me the space I've needed
to share my heart and our story of God's
hope and healing in our life. Not only has he
been my biggest cheerleader and deliverer
of cups of coffee and chocolate, he's faithfully
(and ruthlessly) edited my words to
help me say what I mean.
Trent, I love you.

Contents

Acknowledgments

I always read the acknowledgments in a book because I want to get a feel for the kind of person who wrote it. But sometimes I get bored of the endless litany and skip the last few paragraphs. Now I understand! I'm trying to put my thanks down succinctly and accurately. I don't want to miss any of the amazing people who toiled in this project with me, but I just can't list them all. As it is, this is getting longer than I'd anticipated. I hope what you see is not just a long list of names but a group of people who have come to love you, my reader, through their work on this project.

Trent, you've been more than supportive. I've shared our secrets, our struggles, and so much of our lives, and you've cheered me on the whole way. When I've been discouraged, you spoke just the right words. When I needed a proverbial kick in the pants . . . well, you obliged! You believed in me even before I thought I had it in me. Thanks doesn't quite cut it, but I have no other way to describe how my heart overflows with gratefulness to a man who is so willing to do what you've done for me in the publishing of this book. I love you.

I'd like to thank my children for the back massages, foot rubs, cups of coffee, and encouragement. I doubt any other author has such an incredible troupe of believers cheering her on. You will always be my most favorite people in all the world.

Ahria, thank you for believing in me and giving me permission to share stories from your life. You are growing into a beautiful young lady.

Aethan, I love how you said the other day, "Mom, just keep writing. We never wonder if you still love us . . . don't worry!"

McCaellen, you are the best popcorn maker in the world, and every bowl you brought to my desk while I was in my writing frenzy helped me remember that the most important things in life are enjoying the people around me. So thanks.

Myanna, you have grown into a little girl who can easily see the best things in life and choose to celebrate those even when the "yucky" parts of life are in full swing.

Thanks to my faithful prayer-team members, who have prayed diligently for this project and for every person who will read this book. You are more than friends. You are truly co-laborers in this book!

Thanks to Rebecca Sendall-King, who graciously went on holidays so I could use her beautiful home to rest, write, and rejuvenate.

Thanks to Tamara Inglis, a married solo parent. You've read these words, seen my life, cried with me, laughed with (at) me, encouraged me, and parented my kids when I just couldn't go on. You are a blessing from God.

I'd like to thank the fine people at Focus on the Family, including Larry Weeden and his team of editors, for their encouragement and input on various aspects of this book.

Julie Antillon, of Julie Antillon Photography, made my photo shoot so much fun! Thanks for being a great friend and photographer.

I'm especially grateful to the many women I've interviewed across North America in preparation for this book. Thank you—all of you—for sharing your stories.

There are friends who've helped me become who I am, who have challenged me to grow and become more godly in all areas but are too many to name. I love you and thank you . . . you know who you are!

Les Stobbe, my agent, I appreciate your expertise and sage advice.

And of course the people at Kregel who make things happen like magic behind the scenes! Steve Barclift, Dawn Anderson, and Cat Hoort helpfully and patiently provided the answers to all my "why" and "how" questions. I couldn't ask for a better team to work with.

Jesus, without you I can do nothing. Every word, thought, and idea that I have of my own is worthless. It is only you living in me that has any value. Thank you for giving me your life, your love, and yourself.

What Is a Solo Parent?

I'm not sure when I fully realized it. It took me years, and when I finally got it, I was not at all impressed. I was raising my children as a single mom even though I was married to their dad.

I had dreamed about a happy family, a clean house, a warm and inviting meal with me and the father of my children in that picture. In the midst of my husband's doctoral degree pursuit and all that entailed, his job, his volunteering in church, and his excessive computer-gaming habits, I realized that if I wanted a photo of that happy family, we'd have to fake a pose and snap the picture quickly. This was not the happily-ever-after I had planned on. I was raising my kids alone even though I was married. I was a solo parent.

A What?

A solo parent is someone who is raising children and running a home and family alone. In this book I am primarily writing to the married woman who solo parents. Her husband might be working away from home or putting in exceptionally long hours; he might be captured by the lure of hobbies and interests that eat up his time, addicted to any number of things that impede his ability to be a good husband and father, or hindered by health issues that keep him from assisting his wife in the everyday running of their home and family. She feels fully responsible for how the house and yard are maintained, how the kids are raised, the spiritual well-being of the family, how well the kids do in school, and the family finances—no matter how well or how poorly that is going. She feels like the buck will stop with her for any emergencies, and often all failures as well. She carries a heavy load and falls into bed by herself at the end of the day, exhausted.

My story will be different from yours. Each solo parent has a unique set of circumstances. Your struggles will be different from mine. Every generation has had its share of married solo parents. Yet somewhere along the line, we've forgotten how it is done: how a woman with a husband does the job of raising her kids when he is not around.

Perhaps you are the wife of:

- A man in the military
- A long-distance truck driver
- A busy doctor or lawyer
- An executive, traveling businessman, or workaholic
- Someone who works two jobs to provide for you and your children
- An alcoholic or drug addict
- Someone serving time in prison
- A farmer, fisherman, or oil-rig worker
- A man with gambling, pornography, computer, or online-gaming addictions
- A pastor or ministry worker
- A man with a chronic or terminal health condition

There is no end to this list. Your situation may not be listed here, but no matter how you got here, as a solo parent you have needs, desires, struggles, and frustrations that single parents don't face and that married wives with involved husbands just don't understand.

I may not have mentioned your particular situation earlier, but you know if you are a solo parent. Though everyone's story and situation is different, every solo parent carries a heavy load.

I have carried that load.

Difficult Questions

I've lived this life and have learned a lot the hard way. This challenge has become my passion.

During my years as a solo parent, I've had some hard-to-answer questions. Questions like:

- How do I find time to spend with God?
- How can I honor my husband and teach my children to honor him when there are times I wish he'd never come home?
- How can I raise my kids with consistency when my husband comes home and changes the rules?
- Would it be easier if I left my husband?
- What do I do when my kids are suffering physically, mentally, emotionally, or spiritually because of my husband's absence or lack of involvement?
- How can I love my husband when I feel like a doormat or his servant and nanny?
- Is it even possible to have a happy, healthy home and build great memories for my kids when there is such an obvious hole in our family?
- Is it okay to meet my sexual needs without my husband or outside my marriage if he is never around or available?
- How can I teach my kids about godly marriage relationships if they never see one in our own home?
- Is it okay to pray for my husband to die so that I can respectably marry a different man to be a dad to my kids?

Maybe you've been too afraid to ask these questions out loud. Perhaps this is the first time you've seen your feelings put into words.

I would encourage you to be honest with yourself and God as you read through this material. Some parts of this book lean more toward teaching and training, much like spending time with a mentor. Other parts are practical and hands-on. There is a study guide and a personal reflection journal available at no cost on my website (www.carlaanne.com) if you'd like to go through this with a book club, Sunday school class, or other group, or if you just want to dig deeper yourself.

I'd encourage you to go through this book with a mentor or godly woman in your church. Find someone who is a few paces ahead of you in your spiritual walk, marriage, and child-rearing. Ideally she would be someone who has walked this road of solo parenting herself. Get together with her once a week or so. If you have the study guide, discuss the questions in it together. Pray together. If you have further questions for her, be honest and open, asking even the hard ones. It's when we grapple with the tough things in life that we are often stretched to a new level of maturity and wisdom.

If you don't have a mentor at this time or cannot find one, a friend or group of friends who are in the same stage of life would make a great discussion group. Be sure that you are all careful to respect each other's answers, thoughts, and opinions, while staying faithful to the challenge of being women who seek after God.

You can go through this book on your own. I suggest you download the free personal reflection journal from my website (www.carlaanne.com) to record your thoughts, questions, and answers—keep it handy as you go through the book. You may one day be the mentor of another woman who is seeking counsel.

Dear God, I praise you for the wonderful woman who is reading this book. You created her in such a beautiful way. I pray that you will woo her to yourself, let her hear your voice speaking, and grow in her the passion to take up the challenge you will set before her.

I pray that you will guard her heart and mind, that you will surround her with your presence, and fill her with your power. Holy Spirit, I invite you to lead us in this journey of becoming godly women, mothers, and wives. Through the holy name of Jesus the Christ, I ask these things of the one true God. Amen.

Chapter One

This Is Not What I Signed Up For!

At first I was glad to keep the hearth fire warm and burning while Trent studied for his doctorate, taught at the University of Toronto, wrote his thesis, served on our church board, and spent his free time at home unwinding in front of his computer. I was convinced I was being a good wife, doing what I could to support him in becoming successful. It pleased me to think I was partly responsible for his achievements.

While I was expecting our first child, I began to notice my "support" was not having the effects I had hoped for. It was a rough and risky pregnancy, so I was on bed rest for almost eight months. Things were difficult financially as I did not have any income during this time and Trent was still in school.

We set up a cot in the main room of our basement apartment so that I could have a change of scenery at bedtime. I spent my days in silence reading books, napping, and wondering about the baby. Cell phones were not as common as they are today, so entire days would go by without a chat with Trent. I had nothing to do but worry about him, the baby, and how we'd manage to pay the bills. I missed him. I longed for him to be nearby when the baby kicked or my belly bounced with baby's hiccups. When Trent finally did get home, he would either work on his studies or play computer games.

The following few years went by in much the same way, although Trent was able to study less and work more, relieving much of the financial stress.

He would work, study, attend church board meetings, and then come home to sit in front of his computer, spending time with his thesis or a game. The children were often shooed away from "Papa's room" or office. I'd keep them busy every spare moment I wasn't working so he'd have as much time as necessary to do his thesis well.

I found a group of friends that included other solo parents. We called each other every day, encouraging each other and helping each other out. When a mom began spiraling into a pity party or negative thinking about her marriage and parenting, the others would gather round and set her back on solid ground. I was often met at the door by a friend telling me to get the kids in the van because it was time to go to the beach. Without any preplanning on my part, off we went with only five minutes' notice to spend a refreshing afternoon with friends who cared. They knew that it was a hard life to live because we were all in it at the same time. None of us wanted the life of a solo parent, but we all wanted to do more than survive. We wanted to make a change for our kids, for our marriages, for us.

When Trent completed his PhD, we moved to New York State with our three children, aged three and under. I had hoped my days of taking care of the children alone, eating dinner without Trent, having long evenings to myself, making excuses for my husband's absences, and going to bed alone would finally be over. Now Trent had a "real" job, and I assumed he would be home in the evening, walking in from work happy to smell the home-cooked meal and enjoy eating it at the table with me and the kids. I assumed he'd help out with baths and bedtime, cut the grass, and shovel the driveway.

Instead, I found myself mowing our two-acre yard, keeping up the house, cleaning the pool, taking the vehicle for maintenance and repairs, going to doctor visits with the kids, and grocery shopping with three toddlers and a week's worth of groceries in one cart. (Whoever the brilliant person was who invented a double seated grocery cart with the extra seats attached, I love you and thank you. You made my life so much easier!)

Trent had taken a full-time position spread over four days per week instead of five. On the fifth day of the work week, he served as a consultant for the university he had graduated from. Often one of the two jobs would spill over to take up weekend time. When it wasn't work, he was caught up in a new hobby: online gaming.

I began to feel like a widow or jilted lover. The sadness ran deep, the loneliness was constant, and the sense of betrayal stung. I once told a friend that I would rather he had an affair with another woman because then at least I could compete. Anyone can lose some weight, tone their muscles, update their hair and makeup, or even have cosmetic surgery to fix the genetic flaws. But I could not compete with the prestige offered by a lucrative position or the attraction of on-demand adventure in an artificial, online world and community.

Trent found a new job in Southern California. So we moved across the continent with just a few weeks left of my fourth pregnancy. His new position required him to travel extensively around the world. When Trent was out of town, he was gone for days, sometimes many weeks. At times the kids didn't see or interact with their dad for months. When he was in town, he was at the office about sixty minutes away in good traffic, two hours away in bad traffic. He would be gone before I or any of the kids were up, and he'd be home long after we'd be asleep.

In the wake of the telecom market crash in 2000, Trent encountered pressure to perform at work beyond what seemed humanly possible. We now had four children, ages five and under, and only one vehicle with five seatbelts. Two huge mortgages caused a great deal of financial strain, as we tried for nearly ten months to sell our previous home in a city filled with people out of work and attempting to move away.

Those years were hard—especially when the kids were really little and I hardly slept through one night a month. Someone was always teething, nursing, or getting sick. For a long time I didn't know how to answer when people asked me if I was still married or where my husband was. These people meant well, but they never knew how my heart broke whenever they told me they hadn't met my husband so why didn't I bring him along sometime. I made decisions that I would have never dreamed I would make alone: moral decisions, health decisions, education decisions, parenting decisions, spiritual decisions, and decisions about my future and the future of our marriage. I felt betrayed, resentful, hurt, and angry. It was such a lonely time.

I went to church alone . . . with the kids. I went to my gynecologist appointments alone . . . with the kids. I ate dinner alone . . . with the kids. I went out for dinner alone . . . with the kids.

> When I was in my last month of pregnancy, I paid a visit to my obstetrician. Being full swing into my solo parenting career, I had three other children in the examining room with me. The kids were behind the curtain . . . until my cell phone rang. Trent had been gone long hours so I knew it would be him. I decided to let it ring as I was lying down with my legs in stirrups. The doctor was checking to see if I was "ready" to deliver. Ahria, my oldest daughter, knew it would be Papa. She grabbed the phone to give it to me. She was very excited that he would be phoning, but not understanding that a cell phone conversation in the midst of a gynecological exam was not appropriate.
> She tried to pass me the phone.
> I tried to tell her to put it back in my purse.
> The doctor got involved, and it ended up a flying, ringing, black brick that splashed and then gurgled as it landed in a bucket of green liquid on the floor. Leaving me in my awkward position, curtain now flung back to reveal all to the children, the doctor valiantly tried to fix the cell phone by running it under water. It was almost enough to put me into labor! Sometimes you just have to give in and laugh!

It hurt that the one I gave my heart, life, and love to on my wedding day was not there. I love my children dearly, but children never replace what a husband is meant to be.

The Benefits

Being a solo parent definitely has its benefits. I loved making decisions without having to wait for Trent to agree with me. I could make plans without checking with him first like my girlfriends all had to with their hubbies. There was no one to tell what I had spent money on because I took care of it all. I could arrange the furniture and yard just as I liked because Trent was never there to give his opinion. If I was going out to eat, I had two choices: some kids place or anywhere my heart desired. I could watch chick flicks and cry when I watched them. My girlfriends could come over and even have a sleepover. It was just like college days, except for the diapers we changed while we chatted, the larger-size clothing, and the kids who woke up before we were done talking.

I loved that I had full influence on the kids—until I heard them yelling my words at each other.

I loved that I could make whatever my heart desired for dinner—until I got sick of the leftovers all week.

I loved that I could wear my favorite sloppy clothes and not have to look nice for anyone—until I missed the compliments.

As solo parents, we have a lot to deal with on a constant basis. Sometimes we adapt so well, however, that we're really not sure we'd want anything different. Yet when the house is quiet, the kids are asleep, and we're left alone to our thoughts, watching our dreams collide with reality, we realize . . . this is not what I signed up for.

The Challenge

Solo parenting was not my dream life. I'm sure it's not yours, either. Like it or not, though, this is the challenge that faces some of us.

The challenge for a solo parent begins with just day-to-day living. Getting the house cleaned, the kids fed and off to school, the laundry done, the bills paid, and fitting in a little sleep seems like challenge enough.

The challenge for a solo parent, however, is much grander, much larger, much more complex, and much more rewarding than these day-to-day struggles. I would like to extend to you the challenge that God gave me and that I believe he is giving to all solo parents.

The challenge is simple, but not easy.

The challenge is biblical, but not necessarily found in a particular chapter and verse.

The challenge is noble, but not often applauded.

The challenge is easily undertaken, but needs God's help to accomplish.

The Challenge

for the married solo parent is to be
a woman whose heart seeks after God;
a wife who honors her husband and teaches her children to do likewise;
a mother who teaches her children how to
seek after God, honor him, obey him, and love him in all things
while practically caring for their needs,
all the while leaving room in the family for her husband to be
the man, husband, and father God created him to be.

To run from this challenge is to refuse to see the wonderful purpose God himself has chosen you for.

I didn't see the challenge at first. Maybe I was just too tired. Or perhaps I wasn't ready to face the idea that the God I said I loved might have had this in mind for me. I'm not sure if I just didn't want to, but whatever the reason, I didn't see it. Not until things got rough and tough for me did I even bother to look and question whether or not there was actually a purpose in my situation that was bigger than what I could see from my worn-out vantage point.

I believe God created you and me. It is remarkable to me—completely incomprehensible—how intricate and delicately balanced our bodies are. Add to that a brain that somehow houses our thoughts, controls impulses to our body, and communicates with it without our having to first think the thoughts. And how does our brain communicate emotion to our souls? Wow! I believe that there is one true God who created each of us beautifully and for a purpose.

Each of us has many different purposes for different seasons of our lives. For the solo parent, God has planned a very special purpose . . . one that he chose us for. That's why grabbing hold of this challenge and making it your own is so important.

You may be saying to yourself, "Isn't that what every Christian mother should be doing?"

Absolutely! The difference is that for a solo parent the reasons for being that kind of woman, wife, and parent are different from those of a mom with an involved dad. When fully engaged parents rely too much on the other spouse to get the job done, at least there is a backup. The solo parent has no backup; no one's available to step in when she's having a bad day. The emotions and overloaded to-do list also make rising to this challenge that much more difficult.

Perhaps you are a solo parent who hasn't thought about how God or Jesus could make a difference in your day-to-day life. I'd like to encourage you to read on, ask him your questions, and even test him. The great King David said this: "Taste and see that the LORD is good. Oh, the joys of those who take refuge in him!" (Ps. 34:8). This book provides plenty of tips, tools, ideas, suggestions, and resources that you will find helpful, whether you follow Jesus or not. But the most powerful resource I can point you to is Jesus himself. Think about it.

If you believe in the Lord Jesus Christ and have chosen to spend your life becoming more like him and choosing to obey him in all things, you have at your disposal all you need to succeed. "By his divine power, God has given us everything we need for living a godly life. We have received all of this by coming to know him, the one who called us to himself by means of his marvelous glory and excellence" (2 Peter 1:3). God promises in the Bible that "He who began a good work in you will perfect it until the day of Christ Jesus" (Phil. 1:6 NASB). That means that God is working in you to make this perfect by the end. It doesn't have to be perfect today or tomorrow . . . but he is working in you and me, that we might become the kind of mom, wife, mother, friend, and godly woman that he intends, and he's not going to stop until he gets it just right!

Chapter Two

The Emotions of Solo Parenting

Each person travels their journey differently. There is no formula for preparing for this adventure or doing it well. That's part of what makes solo parenting hard. We often receive little warning before solo parenting becomes our lifestyle. The surprise attack of our emotions can throw us for a loop, giving us an even greater sense of instability and lack of normalcy. We rarely take the opportunity to sit down and evaluate what is really going on inside our hearts.

Grief

I remember when I felt like I was grieving. I told a friend I didn't know what was wrong with me. Never having been a woman quick to tears, I suddenly found they came easily and flowed long. My sadness was deep. My friend told me I was grieving my dreams. I told her flat out that she was wrong.

Over the next several weeks, I tried to pay more attention to what brought about the tears. I realized that my wise friend had spoken truth. As a young bride my dreams of parenting our children together with my husband held hope, love, fun, and success. As a young mother now doing the duties of both parents, I realized I truly was grieving the death of the dreams I'd held.

The truth is many of us are not really sure what we are expecting when we walk down the aisle. Perhaps you went through premarital counseling with a pastor or counselor. Maybe you wrote out your expectations for each other as you prepared for the big day or even as you were deciding if marriage was for you.

The crazy thing about our expectations is that we often don't realize we have them—until they're not met.

It is likely that you have pent-up emotions, or perhaps you find yourself in a state of depression or lingering sadness. I would encourage you to write out a gut-wrenching letter to God. Include in this letter all the things you had dreamed of that have not come to pass. Write out your emotions. Pay attention to all the things that are happening throughout your days this week to see when an emotion flares up. Then stop and figure out if it is due to a deeply seated expectation that has not been met.

Take time . . . get yourself a sitter or make time after the kids are in bed. Take this time to cry. Visualize yourself letting go of the dreams and expectations you have had. You can picture balloons with your expectations in them carried away into the sky. Perhaps writing them out on paper and then burning them in a fireplace will help solidify your act of releasing them. Write a poem, compose a song—however God has gifted you, use that to release your unmet expectations.

While you are releasing these expectations and giving yourself permission to grieve, pray. Ask God to give you something new. Through Jeremiah, God spoke to the Israelites when they were exiled, no doubt feeling hopeless. He assured them that he had plans for them, and we can be confident that God has good plans for us as well. "'For I know the plans I have for you,' says the LORD. 'They are plans for good and not for disaster, to give you a future and a hope'" (Jer. 29:11).

The one true and living God wants to give you hope for your future. He is not excited about the idea of you slugging away, doing things that wear you out and cause you grief just for the sake of causing you grief. He is a God who loves to give good gifts to his children. He wants you to come to him and ask him to give you hope and a future, ask him to clarify what your expectations should be. Ask him to give you a word, thought, or picture of what kinds of desires he wants you to have. Be prepared to be filled with hope, excitement, and joy. Psalm 37:4 says, "Take delight in the LORD, and he will give you your heart's desires."

This means that God wants to give you your heart's desires: the desires that he puts in your heart, not our selfish, sinful ones.

Take time to understand what your unfulfilled expectations have been, and then take the time to grieve them. Don't stop there, though. Ask God for new desires and dreams that come from him. If you have a Bible, make sure you spend a lot of time reading it during this process. If you don't have one, find a Christian bookstore near you or find one online and order it. Inexpensive Bibles in easy-to-understand translations are readily available. This will be one of the most crucial parts of becoming a healthy solo parent. You can't skip over this step.

Loneliness

Loneliness is something we face as solo parents. It's not that we don't have people all around us. It's that we don't have that "special someone" with whom we had dreamed of sharing our thoughts and dreams, our ups and our downs. Girlfriends are great, but they are not there in the dead of night to hold us when our tears are making tracks down our cheeks. At least not very often!

Sometimes our children step in and become our social network. It is important to be our children's parent, not their friend. When we get this mixed-up, we'll find childish expressions and habits developing in our lives. There's nothing more embarrassing than excusing yourself at a fancy dinner function because you have to go "potty"! Being your children's friend also puts a burden on them that they are not meant to carry.

Loneliness is real. It becomes more pronounced when your situation is not recognized by those around you. If your husband has a nine-to-five job but escapes to the computer, newspaper, or bottle when he arrives home, leaving you just as alone as before he arrived, it is difficult to explain your predicament to others without speaking negatively about your husband. It is hard if you have a husband who plays the part well in front of others and in public, but who leaves you emotionally (and possibly physically) when they are gone.

You need to be diligent in building meaningful relationships with other women who can build you up and speak life to you. It is important that the relationships you spend your valuable time on will help you in your efforts to become a parent who has the skills, resources, and tools to do the job well. If you find yourself in a group of friends who speak negatively about their husbands, who complain frequently, or who brush you off as if your situation isn't as bad as you feel it is, I give you full permission to find a new group of friends.

Making meaningful friendships is not necessarily easy, but it is very worthwhile. I've had to start from scratch many times! Here are some ideas that have helped me:

- Look around you to see who speaks positively about life and those they love.
- Look for people who don't gossip or slander.
- Look for women who love to laugh and can have a good time.
- It is important that you feel comfortable around them, so find people who don't mind getting messy or who have no problem plopping down on the grass for a chat.
- Keep your eyes open for other mothers who show up at places you frequent, especially if they show up without a husband.
- Open up yourself and your home, if at all possible, or be prepared to meet at a place that has a play area for children or at a nearby park.
- Invite a mom or two or three over for coffee or brunch.
- Make it simple. Ask them each to bring something to take the pressure off any one person.
- Make what you are looking for clear, as well as why you would choose them. You don't need to sound like a charity case. But who wouldn't want to belong to a group of women who are dedicated to raising all-around healthy kids with a spiritual perspective even if there is not always a dad in the picture?

Remember, there are more of us out there than we realize! Chances are there is a mom you see regularly who is aching inside, wishing just once someone would notice her lonely efforts.

From experience, I warn you against developing friendships with people of the opposite sex. It might feel good and be convenient. They may even seem better at being a friend than the women you know. A relationship with a man other than your husband is one sure-fire way to put the blinders on and find yourself one day having to make decisions you'd rather not make—not to mention the fear, confusion, and guilt you will live under in the meantime.

Fear

Not everyone will struggle with fear the same way. Many will find coping strategies to help live with the fear. I suggest that there is a way to live without most, perhaps all, of that fear.

When life as a solo parent began for me, one of my fears was staying home alone at night with the kids. I'd never had trouble when I was single, but for some reason being alone with the kids gave me a sense of fear I hadn't known before. I was nervous about someone breaking in or hurting the kids. I heard things at night that didn't exist and checked and double-checked doors and windows every night.

I had to learn how to ask God for protection. I would make my rounds once, circling the house, locking doors and windows, and turning off lights as I went. Then I would lie in bed and talk to Jesus. I would thank him for being my protector. I would ask him to send angels to stand at every corner of our property and be a guard at every entry to our home. I learned to read the Bible at night until I couldn't stay awake any longer, and then fall asleep with his Word in my mind. This is a habit I continue to this day.

I also began to fear the responsibility. What if something happened to the kids? Being the only parent on duty so much of the time, what would I do if something happened to one of the kids? I couldn't possibly be there for all of them if one got sick or had to be hospitalized. What if one of them died in my care? Would my husband ever forgive me?

You might not be a what-if kind of person, but many of us are. We cannot live joyfully in a what-if world. We live in a world where God is in control. Not a single thing happens on this earth that God has not somehow foreseen and allowed. No matter how ugly, scary, or unfair it may seem to us, God is willing to breathe life into it and bring wholeness out of it. So with a hopeful end to every worst-case scenario, I would encourage you, friend, to let go of the what-ifs. Every single one of those situations is in God's hands!

I also feared my demise. This affected our oldest daughter. One day she came to me and asked me, "Mama, what if you get in an accident? Who will take care of us until Papa gets here?" "Well, honey, if something happens to me, then your babysitter will take you to Miss Terra's house." (Miss Terra was a wonderful woman who saved my sanity many times and watched my children on top of it all!) "But Mama," my persistent child asked, "what if

Miss Terra can't call Papa?" Her questions continued for several minutes. I realized that I had not prepared myself or her for such an event. I had hoped it would never happen, so I didn't plan for it.

I did some planning after that conversation, though. One of the quickest ways to quiet a fear is to deal with it. Come up with a logical, safe plan for others to work from if you can't. I made a list of all Trent's numbers (including his secretary's and boss's cell numbers), the numbers for my parents and Trent's parents, our neighbors, our pastor, and for those selected in our will to be our children's guardians. I had this all typed out on a sheet of paper. Also on that sheet were all the necessary information bits for our children: ages, birthdates, allergies, doctors' information, likes and dislikes, comfort toys/blankies, medical numbers, and other ID. I had one posted for our babysitters in case of emergency. (It was posted in an envelope marked "In an Emergency" on the inside of our pantry door. I made sure each sitter knew about it.) I also gave one to the top three names on the list as well as to two of our neighbors. That way at least five people had access to information should something happen. I gave my parents the list, as well, so that they would also have the information if someone needed it.

Once that was all done, I spoke with each of the kids who were old enough to understand. This was lighthearted, yet serious. "If something should happen so that Mama can't come home one day like I plan to, then your babysitter will call one of these people. Those people will come pick you up and take you for a sleepover to their house. You will have a really nice time at their house until I come home, or Papa comes home, or until Ma or Pa [my parents] come to get you. But you will always be safe, even if Mama can't come home one day." This did not scare them at all. Rather, it made them feel safe. It also gave me peace of mind knowing that, should something happen, the kids would be safe and secure until someone like Trent or my parents could explain what had happened.

As a solo parent, you need to ensure that you have backups. Prepare your children, those people you've chosen as backups, and yourself for those times when you will have no choice but to lean on them. That may mean allowing your children to have sleepovers for practice or spending the night at a friend's house. Give your children the experience of last-minute changes to bedtime routines. When you have a friend over, ask her to do the bedtime shtick. Nothing is harder for young children than being in a strange bed in a different house and being put to bed by someone who doesn't know the good-night ritual. Give them opportunities to experience change and to learn how to be flexible.

If you have the stomach flu, take that as the perfect excuse to call a friend and say, "Hey, I'm too sick to do the mom thing. Would you please take the kids for the night so I can get more rest?" Watch your kids get excited about the unplanned treat; relax as they pack their own bags with four dresses, a purse, and no pajamas or toothbrush. It's a night they will always remember and will set the happy stage for an event you hope never happens.

Perhaps you fear that your life will never change, never get better. The truth is that none of us knows what lies ahead. Only God does. You may be a solo parent and then a solo grandparent, or the winds of change may blow in your family and your situation may be different next week. There is no quick fix or certain future. What we can know, for sure and for certain, is that if we commit our way to God, he will turn everything to his glory and make our future, even if it is eternity, a beautiful thing. Set your heart on God, and he will give you a hope and a future! Some days, thinking about a beautiful future in eternity seems too far away to matter today. You see, though, that each day in which we choose God's way, live in his power, and allow him to guide our decisions and actions, we are becoming more and more beautiful. Not just beautiful for eternity, but beautiful for now.

I have a beautiful friend. Her circle of influence continues to grow. She's been my friend since 1996, and every time I see her, I see a deeper beauty. She was also a solo parent. There were days she cried because of the pain her situation caused. As her husband lay in their bedroom month after month, year after year, trapped by his mental illness, she made the painful and difficult choice of remaining faithful to him and to God through it all. When her son's aggression caused her heart to bleed, and her daughter's anger lashed out viciously, she carried it to Jesus.

She is not a wimp. Neither is she a fuddy-duddy or genteel grandmother. She stands at least six inches taller than I do. Her Jamaican culture shows through in her gregarious and fun personality. Life with her is never boring or static. When you encounter her, though, you will know very quickly that this is a woman who has spent time before the throne of God. You will hear her sing his praises as she recounts her separation from her husband, his miraculous healing, and their restoration of love—not because God made everything better in the end, but because with God she is better.

The Bible says that perfect love casts out all fear. I wondered about that so often. What I have learned is that perfect love is found only in a Holy God. When I trust in this God and in his perfect love for me, I find there is nothing at all left for me to fear. Nothing.

Insecurity

Many, many times I have wondered what is wrong with me. Why does my husband, who married me of his own free will (I did not have a gun to his head and neither did anyone else!), choose to be apart from me? If he was working long hours, I would wonder how a job or project could compare to a loving wife at home. I guessed I didn't measure up. If he was at home, sitting for hours in front of the computer, I would wonder what I could possibly do to compete with technology and the instant gratification of anything online. I figured there was something wrong with me. When he had to travel again, and again, and again, I would begin to think it was because he was choosing willfully to stay away from me.

It doesn't take much for a woman to feel insecure. A prettier woman makes us feel ugly and shakes up our confidence. Someone with business savvy can make us feel unintelligent or boring. The perfect stay-at-home mom makes us wonder if we're sacrificing our kids and marriage on the altar of a career. A plain and simple woman whose husband loves her dearly makes us wonder if we are even capable of being loved.

Insecurity is an emotion many women face, whether they are solo parents or not. It is also a tool the devil uses to undermine our marriages and our parenting. No matter what you look like; what your IQ is; whether you work for pay outside the home or care for your children full-time at home; whether your house is big or small, pristine clean or well lived-in; at some point insecurity will come knocking on your door. If you are a solo parent, it has already knocked and possibly moved in.

Do you compare yourself to others? Do you avoid people because you're not sure if you'll fit in? Perhaps you dress differently, to see if you've still got what it takes—perhaps if you can catch some man's eye, then you'll know it is not you but your husband who's got it wrong.

There are many signs of insecurity. The questions above highlight just a few of them. It is so very important that you gain a security that is second to none. The rocky years of teenage hormones (your children's, not yours!), the lonely nights ahead of you, and the weariness of doing this solo parenting thing for a long time will eventually require a lot from you. You will need to know who you are, why you are here, and what you are going to do about it. You need a *person*, a *purpose*, and a *plan*.

The *person* you need is Jesus Christ. If you have not already noticed, I am a believer in the one true and living God whose Son is Jesus Christ. He lived on this earth, died on a cross, then rose again from the dead three days later. He did this so that our sins (all of them, big and small, intentional and inherent) could be forgiven. This needed to happen in order for us to spend our eternity (our life after death) in heaven with God. He loves you incredibly. He is holy and powerful. He listens personally to each of us when we pray. His first concern is your eternity. He so desperately wants you to ask for forgiveness of your sins. Then he wants you to commit to obeying him and living your life according to his plan. He has promised to be with us and never, ever leave us. If you go through with these steps, you will always have a person to count on, live with, love and help you. The days may not get easier, but your burden will be lighter because you'll be sharing it with him.

The really exciting thing about being a follower of Jesus is that God has designed a *purpose* for each of our lives. Not a single one of us, no matter what kind of family we are from or upbringing we received, is without a purpose. Listen to what the Bible says in Ephesians 1:4–6: "Even before he made the world, God loved us and chose us in Christ to be holy and without fault in his eyes. God decided in advance to adopt us into his own family by bringing us to himself through Jesus Christ. This is what he wanted to do, and it gave him great pleasure. So we praise God for the glorious grace he has poured out on us who belong to his dear Son."

Even before he made the world! Get a load of that! Your purpose is so sure and so significant that God thought about you even before he made the world. You are not an afterthought, a mistake, or a byproduct of some evolutionary act of combustion. You were thought of and chosen. He thought of you, picked you, then wanted you to be close to him. He wants to see you without fault. To top it off, he chose you to be part of his family. Why? Because it gave him *great pleasure!* My sweet, sweet fellow solo parent, you are beautiful and chosen by God. The simple fact that you exist gives him pleasure. He is fully thrilled about the fact that you want to be in his family. One of your basic purposes in life is to enjoy being part of the adoptive family of God. You were designed to belong to him. He dreamed of you as a daughter, a child, someone he could love even before the Rocky Mountains or the Grand Canyon or Niagara Falls were created. Before the sun shone or the planets spun, God set a purpose for you to love him and be loved by him. Isn't that grand?

There may be other purposes he has for you. I cannot tell you what they are; only he can. He may lay it all out for you one day, but more than likely the plan will unfold before you step by step as you obey him.

You have the person, you know you have purpose. Now you need a *plan.* If you run around throughout your life like a chicken with its head cut off, dashing here and there, doing this and that but without direction, your purpose may not be completed. You don't want that. I know you long for significance, like I do. You want your life to have more meaning than what you see every day, day-to-day in the eyes of those around you. Well, it won't get done waiting around, will it?

In order to know and live the plan you need to do a few things. Read the Bible. Each day read a few verses in the Bible. Read until a word, or verse or story pops out at you. After you've read some, write down what you think God is saying to you through those verses. Then talk to him.

I find it easiest to sit at my computer and type. I close my eyes and write my prayer to God. (I'm so grateful for auto-format and spell checkers!) Then I wait. I just sit there with my eyes closed until I get this sense in my heart that God is saying something to me, and then I type that. Our conversation goes back and forth that way until I sense that he says I am ready for my day or my time is up. I usually end by asking him what he'd like me to accomplish that day, and then listen. He often gives me a to-do list. (He knows I'm a list lover!) Then I set about doing those things. When I live with God this way, listening to his voice, reading his Word, then obeying what he says, I find that I am living with purpose and his plan unfolds before me each day. Find a way to connect with God in your own style. Perhaps you prefer a ring-bound journal for your handwritten prayers. Maybe you write it all out or just jot down points as you pray. When you make a point to connect with God, remember to go "RPO":

> **Reading:** You should always have some time reading in the Bible.
> **Praying:** There should always be some time of prayer (both talking and listening).
> **Obeying:** Make a commitment to obey whatever you read in the Bible or hear from God. (Always check to make sure it does not conflict with anything else in the Bible or the character of God.)

With those three steps in place, you will find that your insecurities will vanish like the wind. You will have purpose and meaning. You will not be looking to others for approval or security. You will have your heart set on the one thing that will last for all eternity.

Jealousy

Many a solo parent has watched another woman's husband interact with his wife or children, and wished that her own husband did the same. It happens. We compare, we see the green, green grass on the other side of the fence . . . especially if Hubby is not watering on this side!

This was difficult for me at certain points along my journey. I would see a man who had a good work ethic with a great nine-to-five job, home in the evenings and on weekends, scheduled holidays, and I'd be jealous of the steadiness and predictability of a relationship with a man like that. Or I'd see a husband who did handyman jobs around his house or cooked dinner, ran for groceries, or vacuumed the carpets, and I'd dream about the loving care his precious wife must bask in. When I saw daddies at the park with their kids, throwing a ball with them or pushing a stroller, I'd be envious not only of the free time that would give me, but of the relationship my kids were missing.

I learned through prayer and some rough lessons that God's plan for me is not to dream about his plan for some other family or husband, but for me to focus on accomplishing the task he has for me to do today. Contentment does not grow by shopping around.

I have a son who loves my cooking. A lot. He tells everyone how great a cook I am. Just last week, he told his cello teacher that I can make a gourmet meal out of tomatoes and three onions. He neglected the other ingredients and the six hours in the slow cooker, but he has great praise for me and I bask in it. The thing that struck me one day is that when he grows up, he better not be singing the praises of my cooking too loudly or he'll never find someone who'll be willing to cook for him at all! Nobody likes to be compared to someone else, especially if they seem to have all the makings of a perfect somebody—all the strengths where I have weakness.

A few years ago I was listing on a piece of paper all the ways Trent did not measure up. (By the way, that is not a good exercise, and I would highly suggest you never do it.) Do you know how I came up with all his faults? By thinking about the fabulous traits of my friends' husbands! As I neared the bottom of the page (apparently I thought I had a lot to complain about), a thought hit me in the gut and nearly took my breath away. How would I feel if Trent had a list like that about me? What if he compared my overweight body to my friend's size 1? What if he compared my stay-at-home job to someone else's CEO position? What about comparing my strong and opinionated personality to the girl at work who is gentle and soft-spoken?

It didn't take much for me to realize I had made a huge mistake. I should never, ever have made a list like that. So I destroyed it. I asked God to show me something I could do to stop the jealousy in my heart that would take over whenever I stepped out my front door.

God pointed me in the direction of Philippians 4:8, which reads: "Fix your thoughts on what is true, and honorable, and right, and pure, and lovely, and admirable. Think about things that are excellent and worthy of praise."

I didn't know if I could. There seemed to be nothing true about my husband that fit into any of the categories. I couldn't think of anything honorable or right or pure or lovely or admirable. Yet I felt God saying to me that was exactly what I was to do. So I asked him to show me something, anything to start with.

I thought about my Trent's hands. He had two hands, and they worked. I thanked God that day that Trent had two working hands, and how honorable it was for him to be working with them, even if it meant he wasn't at home! Oops! No gibes while you're trying to think pure thoughts! This was going to be hard.

First I thought about his two working hands, then his brain, then his back, then the fact that he could drive himself to the airport so that I didn't have to get up at three o'clock in the morning. I kept a cumulative list growing in my journal. If Trent did even one thing positive, I was sure to jump on it so that I could have something else to think about on God's "allowed" list.

Thinking pure, honorable, right, lovely, and admirable thoughts about our husbands will help curb the jealousy. We also need to be sure that we not only cultivate the right kind of thoughts but that we weed out the ones that don't belong there.

There's a verse in the Bible that says, "So if your hand or foot causes you to sin, cut it off and throw it away. It's better to enter eternal life with only one hand or one foot than to be thrown into eternal fire with both of your hands and feet. And if your eye causes you to sin, gouge it out and throw it away. It's better to enter eternal life with only one eye than to have two eyes and be thrown into the fire of hell" (Matt. 18:8–9).

I don't want you to engage in self-mutilation, but I do want you to consider that perhaps there are some friendships that will need to be cut off or at least severely restricted. If hanging out at your friend's house with her family will cause you to be jealous of her husband or his relationship with her or the kids, cut it off. Your marriage, your kids, and your relationship with God cannot grow in that kind of soil. If you are reading books where the romantic hero is available to meet his lover's needs, makes a great salary, and your fantasies about the perfect man begin, cut it off. Stop reading those books or magazines. This is serious.

Your job as the mother of your children is to train them to become godly men and women. To be people who can be strong in the face of temptation and who can find their strength from something eternal. You can't do that if you are feeding your mind with, and spending your time on, thoughts of your husband's failings and another man's strengths. No matter how great your husband's weaknesses and failings may be, your role as your husband's wife is to control your thoughts and attitudes toward him so that he has the best possible chance of making you the happy wife you dream to be.

When you fight jealousy with thoughts of purity, admiration, and truth about your husband, guarding your heart and mind with diligence, you will find that you grow in contentment, in respect for your husband, and in thankfulness toward God.

Fatigue

Anyone who is on duty 24/7 will burn out. Fatigue is part of life for many solo parents. Fatigue may not officially be an emotion, but because it affects our emotions, responses, and overall ability to think clearly, I have included it in this chapter.

If your kids are younger than school age, your level of fatigue may differ from a mom of school-aged kids. But I have found that no matter what stage you are in, there are always new reasons to be on duty both long past bedtime and much earlier in the morning than you would like to be.

Many solo parents do not have the luxury of a live-in babysitter, although some do. If you are part of the majority, you get up at night, in the morning, and all day long when the baby cries or the toddler pukes or the preschooler falls off a bike or the grade-schooler knocks out a permanent tooth or a teenager skips class or any one of them needs you for any reason at all. There are some solo parents whose spouses can and do participate in lifting this load for brief periods, but who are left to deal with these issues alone the rest of the time. Either way, after a while it gets very, very tiring.

Solo parents who work outside the home may experience a different kind and level of fatigue. They carry the burden of being on the job all day, then going home and working full-time until bedtime, knowing that their few hours of sleep can be interrupted at any moment. However, these parents may enjoy adult conversation, external relationships, and a change in routine that their stay-at-home counterparts do not.

The stay-at-home solo parent is often fatigued because she is "stuck" at home in a rut. Her conversational abilities are capped by the age of the oldest child in the family, and her mealtime adventures are as gourmet as her youngest child's palette. There is very little that is rejuvenating in picking up the same toys at eleven in the morning that you picked up at ten o'clock and that you'll pick up again at noon.

Fatigue is an ever-present companion for the solo parent. Is there an answer? Yes and no. At times, no matter what you do to manage your time and schedule, you will simply be exhausted.

But there are ways to protect yourself from burnout and complete exhaustion. These ways do not happen on their own—you need to take control and make them a priority. A tired mom is more likely to snap at her kids, prepare unhealthy meals, discipline inappropriately, allow misbehavior to slide, get sick, and make decisions that are not in the best interest of the whole family. I know you don't want to be that kind of mom. You are reaching for something better. Much better.

First of all, sleep.

The first few nights that my husband is gone after being at home for a time, I simply don't sleep well. I hear sounds I haven't heard before—walls creaking, the fridge motor running, the water softener starting up, a child kicking the wall—and these don't sound friendly in the middle of the night! I've almost called the police to save me from a burglar that turned out to be my sons' bunk bed banging against the wall when they turned over. I also don't like the cold, empty feeling on my husband's side of the bed because his body heat isn't keeping me nice and cozy. I will often let the kids sleep with me those first few nights to help replace Trent's warmth and to give them my security. But once those few nights are over, I love having the bed to myself!

I also have to be careful that I don't stay up later than necessary when he's gone just because I'm a little edgy. It's easy for me to read until the wee hours, or even clean the house instead of going to bed. I've learned that even though I enjoy the quiet house, the lack of sleep will demand a high price the next day.

When I do sleep, I find that my ears are still "awake," listening for noises and things going wrong. My sleep is not as sound and deep when I'm home alone. Over many days and weeks of this, I sometimes crash physically and need to take a few days to nap during the day to catch up. Good, restful sleep is a valuable commodity for a married solo parent.

> Regarding sleep: Most "married single moms" have trouble sleeping when they are home alone. Only 24 percent report that they sleep well when their husband is not around. However, most of them agree that when he does come home they really don't like learning to share the bed again!

Make sure that you set a no-nonsense bedtime routine for yourself and your children. If your kids are old enough to be awake longer, that doesn't mean you can't send them to bed! Set a reasonably early time for them to be in their rooms, with a lamp on a timer that will go out when it's time to sleep.

I had our kids in bed by seven o'clock for years. The problem for me was that my oldest child did not need as much sleep as the others. So we made a rule: she could be in her room, in her bed with toys and books around her, but at lights-out time she had to go to sleep. If ever she crept out of her room, she would face a very serious consequence. (I made the first infraction so tough on her that it didn't happen again for a very long time!)

I had wind chimes on all the doors in our house. I had big, loud chimes on the outside doors. If anyone tried to leave, I'd hear them ring. By the tone, I'd know which door they were trying to escape from! I had them on the outside of their bedroom doors as well—smaller, lighter ones that would ring easily. No one could leave their room or turn the doorknob without me being alerted. This made it much easier for me to get my rest and needed sleep, while at the same time keeping the kids safe.

If you don't need twelve hours of sleep, it is still important to keep that early bedtime routine. You need your quiet or down time. Maybe you want to read a book, take a bath, do a little scrapbooking, catch up on e-mail, or phone a friend. Perhaps evening is the best time for you to spend with God. Whatever you spend your time doing, make sure that most evenings you are spending some time without the kids before you head to bed. Have some time alone doing something that rejuvenates you and prepares you to be a better mom tomorrow. It doesn't have to be hours and hours. Maybe one hour, or even a half hour. Some nights, two or three hours is what you need. Just don't let more than a couple of days go by without getting in some mom time. You'll sleep better, and you'll parent better in the morning.

Don't forget your hobbies. Perhaps you've forgotten what they are, or no longer find joy in them because you don't have time or money to keep them up. Take heart! So many new and exciting hobbies take little to no money these days, and you may find them fulfilling. Take some time each week—or at least each month, depending on the kind of hobby it is—to indulge in hobby time. It is a great idea to connect with others at this time, too. Perhaps photography is your thing. If you can't afford a babysitter to leave the house, find a good and reputable chat room or forum online where you can see the work of others, get ideas, and learn new things. If your hobby is quilting, join a club where you can connect with others who share your passion and where you can show off your handiwork.

I found that scrapbooking was a very important way for me to spend my time. About once a month I would hire a babysitter and go to someone else's house to scrapbook. I didn't know any of the people there to start with, but I enjoyed listening to their banter and getting to know them over time. I chose scrapbooking because I felt like I was accomplishing something useful while also getting "me time" in. I loved the idea of telling the story of the kids' lives in books with pictures. Journaling the love and experiences I had shared with them. Leaving a legacy that would tell them as they grew older how incredible and precious they are to me. I found that many times my days would end and I couldn't be sure if I had said in words how much they meant to me and how much I loved them. Journaling in scrapbooks was one way for me to communicate to them now and forever. It has become a testimony of what God was doing in our lives through their growing-up years.

You will choose your hobby for your own reasons. Make sure you have reasons, good reasons. The days will come when you will feel too tired, or you'll think that the house needs you more than your hobby does or that you should buy a new outfit for a child instead of paying a babysitter while you enjoy your hobby. There may be emergencies, but make sure they are real ones! Taking time for you, your hobby, and your rest and renewal is one way to prevent another kind of emergency. Find your hobby and write down all the reasons why this is a good, healthy thing for you to be involved in. Then when those "give up" days come, read your list and stick to your guns. Your children need you to have a life separate from them and from your for-pay job if you have one. They need to know that you exist apart from them.

The last thing I'll mention here is that you may need to consider cutting back on everyone's schedules. Most of your evenings are best spent at home relaxing and preparing for the next day. If you are involved in a church (and I highly recommend that you are), you may very well find that you could be there every night of the week doing something very worthwhile. The day may come when you can do that. While you have children at home is not that time. Even if you are the pastor's wife. Especially if you are!

Your children's extracurricular activities should not put a strain on the family. If those commitments have you driving around the countryside five nights a week, they are not benefitting the kids or the family. Studies show that children do best when they also have down time to play and connect with family and friends. They need space in their schedules to do with as they like, to explore their own interests without an agenda.

I have to admit, this is one of the hardest things to do. Saying no to our children is never easy. Saying no to them when they enjoy the activities or are doing well? Saying no to the star performer? Then it's even more difficult. Perhaps it is time to be creative.

Are there carpools already running that your child could get a ride with?

Could you schedule all the kids' activities on the same night? You might run around like crazy one night, but that's better than having four or five evenings broken up.

Ask hard questions:

- Is this something I see as becoming part of my child's future, and would that be a healthy thing?
- Is this just for fun, or is it serving a purpose? (Tutors serve a purpose; baton twirling may not.)
- Is this something my child absolutely needs to learn now, or could he/she pick it up as an adult? (Reading . . . should learn that now. Chess club . . . can do that later.)
- Will this activity require long-term commitment?

- If this activity causes our family too much stress, am I willing, as the parent, to cut it out of my child's life?
- Will this affect my child's character or ability to get and perform a job responsibly?
- Will this help my child achieve a career goal that has already been chosen?
- How hard is my child willing to work to make this happen?

It is easy for solo parents to fall into the trap of wanting to provide for our children in extra-curricular ways to make up for the lack that we sense in our homes. We think that if we give them everything they'd like, then they will not miss what they do not have. This is not true.

Your children need your words, your touch, and your time—both quality and quantity—more than ever. You can never make up for what your spouse is not providing. But don't make the mistake of involving them so much in activities outside the home that you are inadvertently not providing for them what they need from you.

Make time for your family to be at home, together, with plenty of down time to talk, play, and just hang out. They are only in your home so long. Don't ever give them the idea that you want them out earlier than necessary!

MEET KAREN

Name: Karen Reader

Location: Georgia

Kids: four (ages 15, 10, 7, 4)

Married: twenty years

Husband: Gary is an uninterruptable power technician. His job often requires him to travel to job sites around the state and the country.

Favorites: Chocolate. Need I say more? People ask me about hobbies and I say, "Hobbies? What are hobbies?" But when I have the time (rarely), I enjoy photography, scrapbooking, and reading.

Longest time hubby's been away: Five weeks. It was supposed to be longer, but I prayed God would shorten it. He came home early because he was injured . . . not quite what I had in mind! Now he's regularly gone two to three days at a time with a few one- or two-week stints throughout the year.

My thoughts on balance: At one point I was completely out of balance—I taught an adult Sunday school class, was nursery director, and taught a girls' class on Wednesday night, in addition to serving on the women's ministry board and being involved in everything else going on at church. The pastor called one day to ask if I could add another job. Foolishly I said yes. Moms need to realize that boundaries are good and important. It is important to have a church home that cares and looks out for the family instead of taking advantage. I always consider these two quotes: "If you have to walk over dirty clothes to go to church to do ministry, then go back home" (Elizabeth George) and "Until you can rule and reign over the dishes in your sink, the Lord will not allow you to rule and reign elsewhere" (Phyllis Rawlins).

My struggle: I would be lying if I said our marriage had not suffered at times because of his job. It has—at times to the point that I could see no way but out. It was during those times that true Christian women came along beside me to talk straight, pray with me, and listen to me vent. Having a disagreement of any level is difficult when someone is in the house, but when they are gone and no quick resolution can occur, it's extremely challenging. For so long I struggled with my anger, trust issues, and what my responsibility was in our marriage. The Lord has convicted me, set me free, and comforted me.

My strength: I tend to cook more when my husband is away to make the meals special for the kids. They miss their dad, and I try to make mealtime fun for them. In our home we all eat together around the table. It is a special time for us, and I want my children to have the consistency of family dinner. It helps to keep their lives in order. When Dad is gone, we do not close the kitchen. If I did that I'd be saying to my kids that Dad is gone so they don't matter.

My hope: My relationship with God is everything. I used to see our situation as a choice by my husband—a choice for a job he liked more than being with us. I was not taking it all to God; I was taking it to friends and to Gary. The Lord has held my hand and led me through some difficult times. God is my Strength, Provider, and Refuge. He has been here when my husband could not be.

Shame

I hated Sundays. There was nothing I got more tired of than trying to come up with good reasons why Trent was not coming to church with me. The conversation would go something like this . . .

"Hi, Carla! How are you?"

"Good, thanks, and you?" That's what I said, but my racing mind was questioning whether I should tell her that I'm exhausted and that I finally got my makeup back on after crying again this morning because going to church alone felt like a reminder of my failure as a wife. I was also hoping she'd stop asking about me . . .

"Where's Trent today?"

"He's recuperating after a really long week. He's been in three different states this week and needs his rest. You know with the flu going around, he can't afford to get sick when things are so crazy at work." Meanwhile my heart is kicking my conscience, reminding me that he'd have had a great rest last night if he'd not played computer games until four in the morning.

"So he's pretty busy then?"

"Crazy busy," I reply, searching frantically for a child to distract me until I'm sure I can keep the tears from streaking my face. My imagination would form a vignette in my mind about what would happen if they found out that he hadn't come to bed last night. Would they think it was because I was not attractive enough to earn his love? Could they see through my story to a marriage that was being held together by my effort and a smoke screen of words?

You see, Trent is a Christian. His heart has always been to follow God and live his life for him. Along the way, though, he has at times been distracted, sidetracked by things that seem harmless, or even good, but are not best. For many years he was unaware of how some of his choices were impacting his life, me, and the kids. A wife can nag and nag, demonstrate and cry, but a husband needs to hear God speak to his heart, as deep calls to deep, about the things that really matter. Only then will we see change as he gets with the program—God's program.

Many solo parents carry the burden of shame. Depending on the situation, we may feel ashamed to be covering up for our husbands. We don't want someone to think we don't measure up and that's why our husbands aren't choosing us. Deep down, we're afraid that we'll become another statistic . . . another failure . . . another docket in the divorce court. So we cower, keep silent, and hide in shame.

> In an online survey, 68 percent of respondents said that they worry about whether they will end up with a divorce. Some worry more than others, but they agree that it is a daily fight.

How does a woman speak the truth without tearing down her husband? Recently I received an e-mail from a woman who wanted to leave a comment on my blog. This is what she wrote:

> I'm sitting here with tears flowing down my face as I was typing a comment to your post. I had to get out of it and hit cancel as I realized that I was dwelling way too much on the bad that comes with the life we are living and needed to stop before I got carried away. God is good and he has shown me things about myself that I would never have learned otherwise. I will post a comment, but I have to get myself into a different space first so I don't find myself putting [my husband] in a bad light or resenting him for a choice he's made. I still need to honor him. I found halfway through that I was not being a terrific support or even fair in the emotions coming out, so I had to stop.

Many solo parents are afraid of being honest, at least out loud, about the situation they are in. After years of hearing that we need to respect, honor, and support our husbands, we find it difficult to speak truth when it does not make them shine in the spotlight. We're afraid of being the woman who trashes her husband with her words or ruins his reputation in his absence. So we carry the shame: shame of being the unsatisfied wife, of spinning a yarn of excuses, of what our situation may symbolize or predict.

It took me many years to learn how to respectfully tell the truth regarding Trent's choices. We have to remember that God calls us to be imitators of Christ. Jesus often offended others. As a matter of fact, he was called the Rock of Offense (Rom. 9:33 NASB, KJV). Naturally, we need to be careful.

The truth we speak needs to always be covered in love. It is possible to give the facts about where our husbands are and what they are doing, without adding color from our emotions or wounded heart.

I learned how to say that Trent had decided to relieve stress by playing computer games when he got home from work, and that he had played until four in the morning. Although it was difficult, and I didn't always succeed, I learned how to keep the edge out of my voice. My facial and body language did not support his actions, but neither did they condemn his character.

Understanding that God was my guard, my protector, and my sustainer gave me the courage to speak words of truth in love. I knew that even if those around me would have minds filled with negative thoughts about me or Trent, God was for me. "If God is for us, who can ever be against us? Since he did not spare even his own Son but gave him up for us all, won't he also give us everything else? Who dares accuse us whom God has chosen for his own? No one—for God himself has given us right standing with himself" (Rom. 8:31–33).

Go to God and speak to him of your hurt and pain, your frustration and shame. Learn from him how to speak truth about your husband and your situation. Learn how much to say, when to speak, and when to refrain. Ecclesiastes 3:7 speaks of "a time to be quiet and a time to speak." Lean on God. Hear from him. Allow the Holy Spirit to move you to know when you should be holding your tongue or speaking the truth in love. Give God every opportunity to stand up for you, and redeem your words of truth.

Pride

Ah, I bet you didn't think this one was for you, right? Well, it might not be. I'd ask you to give it some thought, though. Let God search around in that heart of yours to see if there is some truth in this for you.

As a married solo parent, I've found that we sometimes think single parents get all the benefits while we have to suffer through the same hardships without support. Single parents have whole organizations, support groups, and special services provided to them through churches and community groups. Often they are offered babysitting, meals, and help around the house that a married solo parent doesn't have access to.

Have you ever looked at a single mom and wished you had her life? Have you ever said to yourself that it would be easier to be single than married to an absent husband and father?

Perhaps our jealousy of single parents is from a root of selfishness or pride. If I'm going to have it rough, at least I could have some support!

I'm sure you have listened to your married friends talk about the rough Saturday they had because their hubby was golfing all day. Or a married, co-parenting friend who complained about having to take the kids along to the grocery store because her hubby was home late from work. It might have hit you when your friend was scrambling to find a sitter for her toddler so she could go to the dentist when her husband was called in early to work.

All through those experiences you are thinking, "Hmmm . . . I have all my days alone with the kids, I wonder how she'd handle that. Not only do I shop for groceries, but bras, gifts, shovels, and tampons . . . and I always have to take the kids! What's the big deal about taking a child to an appointment? I have to take mine with me to the dentist, and to the doctor and gynecologist, too."

There comes a point for most married solo parents where they meet those who have never had to handle situations as strenuous as their own. It could be easy to look down your nose at them, thinking you have it all together as a mom. You are capable. When it comes to the SuperMom contest, you are definitely in the running. Not that you'd say it out loud, but you're quite sure you're a few solid paces in front of your married, co-parenting friends.

Sister, this pride will get you nowhere. Nowhere at all. Well, that's not entirely true. It will get you a place outside the circle of friends you are a part of. It might even get you a few stabs in the back. It will not get you the praise and admiration you are looking for. We want people to realize how rough we have it because we'd like someone to notice our efforts and accomplishments.

Be assured that God is watching. He sees it all. The good, the bad, the secret, and the obvious. He sees even the motives behind it all.

God has chosen you for this time and this place for a very specific purpose. Choose to live the life you are in right now, hanging on to him, and living out the purpose he has for you. He will give you everything you need to do your job well. He has not called you to be just like your friend, or the neighbor, or the lady from church. He has called you for this special purpose. If there is something to boast about, it is that God has chosen you, and you have said yes!

Self-Pity

Self-pity is when we decide there is no one who really understands how difficult our situation is. We think we have to feel sorry for ourselves because nobody else will. You may not recognize the self-pity in your own heart as easily as you can recognize it in others. So let's start there.

Some women complain that no one understands them, but when someone shares a story about a similar experience, they shun it because they're convinced it is not as bad as what they live with. Some women complain and complain, but really would rather not do anything about it. In a sad way, being in a solo-parenting position gives them the perception that they don't have to take responsibility for their own actions. People who live in a world of self-pity become pros at blaming others and living life as a reaction to everyone else's actions.

You may or may not live with self-pity, yet all of us are prone to it. You may have heard yourself say (or think) something like: "Yeah, well, if her husband was gone only half as much as mine she'd lose control of her kids, too."

Or maybe it's more like: "I'd be able to keep my house clean and the laundry up to date if only my husband was around to help every now and then."

Sad to say, there are too many women who find themselves saying: "I wouldn't be dreaming about another man (or watching porn, or habitually masturbating, or having an emotional or physical affair) if my husband was home and willing to meet my needs."

This line of thinking comes out of self-pity. We feel sorry for ourselves and give ourselves permission to live to a lower standard. Somehow we think that our husbands are going to see us "suffer" and love us enough to change what they are doing so things can improve.

The problem with that kind of thinking is that we've decided only certain actions or situations will communicate love to us from our husbands. When he does spend a weekend with the kids or helps out with a meal or hangs out at home on the weekend, we still want more. He either didn't make the meal right or roused the kids into such a tizzy that you may have ended up thinking, or even saying, "Why did you bother, anyway?" There are few ways to stifle love for your husband more quickly than to wallow in self-pity and accept (and give) only conditional love: love on your terms.

Self-pity and the blame game are not answers for anything. Even if a problem is somehow entirely your husband's fault, you are still responsible for your behavior in the midst of difficult circumstances. Our actions are entirely within our own control. Someone else's actions (in this case, our husband's) are not an excuse for our poor choices in behavior. We can, and should, choose behavior that is glorifying to God and respectful to our husbands. First Peter 3:1–2 says, "Wives, in the same way be submissive to your husbands so that, if any of them do not believe the word, they may be won over without words by the behavior of their wives, when they see the purity and reverence of your lives" (NIV). Even Christian husbands sometimes get it wrong. They need our prayers and godly behavior to remind them of their calling before God.

By no means am I saying that abusive husbands (whether abusive to you or your children) simply need a quiet and more submissive wife. Not at all. What I am saying is that you are responsible for your own behavior. If your husband is abusing you or your children, you need to take responsible action and find help. If your husband is simply not doing his job as a husband and father because he's choosing a lifestyle apart from engaged family life, you are still responsible for how you act in your situation.

Let me give you a hypothetical scenario. Perhaps a husband works fourteen-hour days, then unwinds at the bar for a couple of hours before coming home. He collapses into bed just before midnight and is up early to leave the house by 6:00 a.m. in order to beat the early traffic rush. Working six days a week is a must. To keep his boss happy, and to keep his job, he even has to work some Sundays. The Sundays he's not working, you can find him snoring in front of the TV, or out fishing or golfing with the guys.

This guy's wife has a few choices. She can nag and complain and let her husband and her friends know that the house would be cleaner and the kids more well-behaved if only her husband was around more—which may, in fact, be true, but focuses on her self-pity instead of her responsibility—or she can explain that she didn't do the housework because she never learned how to do it well, and that she could use a good parenting class on how to raise well-behaved kids.

Did you notice the difference? Self-pity will get her nowhere and could be disrespectful to her husband. By taking responsibility, she doesn't disrespect her husband and instead finds life-giving ways to benefit her family.

Our husbands may never act like we imagine they should. They are their own people and we loved them that way enough to say yes! Yet, our self-pity and blame can be a way of manipulating them to behave the way we like, instead of the way they are wired. If your husband begins to act the way you want only because of your nagging blame, you will find that it doesn't bring the joy and fulfillment you had hoped for and dreamed of.

Your reaction to the difficult task of solo parenting needs to be one of reliance on God for the supernatural strength, wisdom, and love needed to be the woman he designed you to be, the mother your children need, and the wife your husband is one with. Spending any time in self-pity is an incredible offense against God. I say this with a humble and heavy heart as I have so often been guilty of it myself. To spend time in self-pity, however, is to take our eyes off of the only One who can do something about our situation and our hearts, and say that not only is change impossible, but that our God is not big enough to sustain us and give us joy in the midst of suffering.

Is that the legacy you want to leave your children? Is that the testimony and witness you intend to share with friends, family, and neighbors? When you hear your children cry, "But Mom, no one understands!" will they have learned it from you?

The surest way to cure self-pity is to spend time with Jesus. Get to know him through the Word. Listen to the Holy Spirit teaching you and encouraging you. Fix your eyes on him and his sacrifice for you, and you will become less likely to wallow in self-pity.

Find yourself an accountability partner and ask her to smack you upside the head (or remind you gently) the moment you begin your descent into Self-Pity City. Ask God to show himself to be the father to the fatherless, the husband to the husbandless, on those days when being a solo parent seems to be more than you can handle. See what he does! Then remember to do this even on those days when it's not so hard—because that is when things get really good.

Anger

Sometimes our anger is due to the pent-up grief and muddles of emotion that keep piling on our hearts. There are days when we are angry at anyone and everyone. Other times our anger is more focused. Too often though, it is our children who take the brunt of our anger.

I distinctly remember one day when my youngest daughter was just a baby. She'd been up many times during the night. I wasn't sure if she was teething, sick, in a growth spurt, or what. All I knew was that I was very short on sleep. When I went to the boys' room to wake them, I was hit with a smell that told me someone had had an accident. This meant laundry first thing. For whatever reason all the kids were grumpy that morning. (They say if Mama ain't happy, ain't nobody happy, but I wasn't ready to take the blame.) It might have been that I was so tired, but no matter what, we were not exactly a bunch of happy campers.

I went downstairs to get breakfast going and pack up lunches for the day. The older kids were supposed to be getting dressed in the clothes I had put out for them. Before long I was back upstairs breaking up an argument. I left three kids at the breakfast table while I took a quick shower. The baby, in her ExerSaucer, was in the bathroom with me where I could keep an eye on her. She cried the whole time I was in there.

When I got downstairs, having pulled my wet hair into a ponytail, I crunched over the cereal that someone had dumped and which was the cause of the latest fight. I gritted my teeth and sent the older two to collect what they needed for their backpacks. While I swept up the floor, my youngest son took off his socks and pants—again. The realization that I had not remembered to buy something at the grocery store that I would need for today's potluck hit me like a ton of bricks. There was nothing better to ruin my already-running-late morning than the thought of packing four kids into the van, out again at the store, into a shopping cart, quickly picking up the drinks I had promised to bring, waiting in the line to pay while bracing myself for the "I want candy" cry, then rebuckling them into their four car seats. With the added pressure of a grocery stop, redressing my son, and my baby's newly filled diaper (I decided she could wait until we arrived before I'd change her, even though we hadn't left home yet), my anger started to mount.

I was yelling at the kids to hurry, hurry, hurry. I was as impatient as ever with their dawdling toward the van. I yelled at the kids for being slow, for being loud, for talking to each other, for not carrying enough stuff. I picked them up and set them firmly in their car seats, buckling them up roughly and moving on to the next task. By the time I got into the driver's seat, I was steaming mad. I was angry at the kids. I was angry with myself for taking it out on them, for not being able to handle getting four kids ready for the day in record time, and for not being happy-go-lucky on just a few hours of sleep. I was angry with Trent for not being here . . . again! I was angry at God for not bringing him home.

This was one of the times I lost it with my kids and took out my anger on them. I am very sad to say it was not the only time. Until I realized that my anger was not situational but systemic, I was not able to deal with it.

So many of my days I thought my anger was due to the factors and circumstances of that day or even moment. All kinds of things could tick me off: something breaking down, the kids fighting, the cupboards being empty, lack of sleep, or whatever. I had never really thought of myself as an angry person before I had children and an absent husband. It seemed to me that my anger must come from my extenuating circumstances, right?

Wrong. It comes from a much more down-to-earth reality. Our anger comes from not getting what we want when we want it. Another way to say it is that we are selfish; our anger comes out against those who do not cater to our selfish desires.

Now, don't get me wrong. There are definitely a lot of things we need in our marriages. There is also everything right about desiring a husband who partners with us in our family life and marriage. But having that right desire does not mean we are justified in getting angry when it is not met. There are a lot of times when we focus more on what we are not getting and who is responsible for not getting it to us than on serving those in our families.

Our systemic anger (anger that comes not from our circumstances but from our inner expectations and selfishness) will leak out in all the wrong places.

Let me give you an example of both situational and systemic anger.

Let's say you are walking down the street and someone just steps in front of you and punches you in the nose. It is likely that you will have a sudden urge to punch him right back. It is unlikely that you would turn to the tod-dler with you and yell at him. You also wouldn't likely go home to think about it, stew over it, and come back later to get back at the guy. Situational anger tends to be more immediate, focused, and directed at the person, people, or things that crossed your boundary.

Taking a look at systemic anger will hopefully become clear after this example. Imagine that you are punched in the face by this same guy again the next day, and the next, and the next. By the next week you decide that you better choose a different route. This will mean that your walk will be longer and through much more crowded streets. You will have to carry your bundles farther and bring a snack for your toddler. Perhaps you even have to bring a change of shoes to walk that extra distance as your dress shoes will rub your feet to the point of blisters with such a long trek. As you walk along one day, your toddler informs you of his need to use the bathroom. Your arms full of bundles, and your feet sore from walking, you vent your frustration by yelling at your toddler and telling him that he is not very good at choosing when to use the bathroom and that he should have gone before you left.

Are you really angry with your toddler? No. It is inconvenient that he has to use the bathroom now, but no reason to be angry. Is it because your arms are full of extra bundles? No. Your arms may be sore and tired, but again that is no reason to be angry with your toddler's bathroom request. It is not even the extra long walk that put you in an angry mood. Your anger really stems from the "Punching Guy" not allowing you to walk where you want to, when you want to, without hassle. Yet you are taking it out on your tod-dler. That is systemic anger. Some may call it misplaced anger.

I'm choosing to call it systemic anger because there is no area in your life that will be exempt from anger outbursts at some point if the root cause of the anger is not dealt with. Perhaps your root anger issue is with your husband. Then again, maybe it is with God. If the root of your anger is not dealt with, then you will soon find yourself angry with your children, your friends, your kids' teachers, the cashier at the store, the paper boy, and so on. It won't take long before you will find reason to be angry at many people for trivial reasons.

Are you there now? Do you find yourself getting a little hot under the collar when you have to wait in line too long? Or when your order at the drive-thru is wrong? Or the kids track mud into the house? Do you have whole speeches prepared for what you would say if you ever got the chance?

Moms who find themselves angry all the time also feel guilty much of the time. You feel guilty for not being the kind of mom who can laugh things off or who can see your kids' age-appropriate behavior and misdemeanors as a part of life rather than as an additional burden for you to carry. Deep down, you want to be the kind of mom who sits down and plays with her kids or tells jokes with them or shares their secrets, yet you see them closing up in front of your eyes because of your harsh words and actions.

Anger is not healthy. I don't need to tell you that. Anger won't get you what you really want either. As your anger bubbles up inside you, you already know that you are not the kind of person you want to be, and you wouldn't want to be around yourself either if you had the choice. Anger is the emotion that masks the hurt, betrayal, and sadness deep in our hearts that longs to be addressed.

Now, please understand, there are some things that should make us angry—what we call "righteous anger": the abuse of children, rape, murder, and other things where Satan has damaged people and the world through sinful behavior. Anger toward things that offend God is a natural response and should cause us to desire to take holy action to rectify the problem. However, God clearly identifies a difference between the anger (the emotion that rises up in us when we see injustice) and the action (how we respond to that emotion). It is okay to be angry about sin, but it is never okay to sin because we are angry. It is good to be angry when a child has been abused. But it is not good to respond to that abuse by murdering the abuser. Anger that is healthy in the eyes of God leads us and others closer to God and his plan. Unhealthy anger is detrimental in every way, and almost always rises up when *we* are offended, instead of when *God* is offended. Anger in our own defense needs to be removed from our hearts and lives in order to bring healing and freedom.

It is to your advantage, healing, and freedom to deal with any anger. Your children and your marriage stand to benefit. Are you ready?

When I first began to deal with my anger, I have to admit that I focused on Trent as the root cause of all my anger. If it hadn't been for the fact that he had accepted a job that took him away from home, if it wasn't for the choices he made day after day to spend his time in front of the computer instead of with us, if it wasn't for his drive to work more and more hours, then none of these things would have happened to us and we would be a happy family.

Oh really?

You will see in the next chapter how I allowed my anger toward my husband to take root and begin to destroy the family God gave me. I will share with you how God brought me up short, put his face in mine, and gave me a talking to I really needed.

We have to come to the realization that God allows bad things to happen. He allowed you to be the woman your husband chose to love. Was that a bad thing?

It wasn't when you dated. It wasn't when he gave you that sparkly diamond. It wasn't when you saw two pink stripes show up on your pregnancy-test stick. Marrying the man you did, whether you did it for the right reasons or not, is not a mistake you made for which you are living out the consequences.

God has put his blessing on your marriage. His blessing. Not his curse, his blessing. That means the situation you are in is not a sin. We both know that you sin and your husband sins, but your marriage is not a sin. God's heart has always been to dwell with you, live with you intimately, and express himself to you in remarkable ways. Because of our human and sinful nature, we get in the way. He is not as concerned about getting you out of the situation you are in as much as he wants to demonstrate his love to you in it. He wants to show you his power. He longs for you to live in the supernatural, for your life to be a living miracle.

With God all things are possible. It is possible to live as a solo parent and feel God's smile of approval. It is possible for him to take away the hurtful sting of another day alone. God can do all things, even removing the pain of betrayal we feel when a career, pornography, the computer, or another round of golf is the mistress our husbands embrace.

In order to deal with the root of anger we have, we need to come face to face with the emotions we have toward a God who allows these agonizing situations, but then simultaneously offers us hope. We need to escape the clichés of our North Americanized Christianity and encounter the God who is holy; the God who is beyond comprehension; the One whose heart loves us personally and intimately and who sees us in a bigger picture. We have not been taught about the glories of overcoming, about the joy of holiness, about the cost of obedience and the pain of disobedience. It is hard to find a preacher or teacher who will lead us to the Christ who says "take up your cross," "deny yourself," or "submit yourselves one to another."

We have heard about this God of love, this God who is our friend. Without understanding his holiness, his sacrifice, and his call for us to do likewise, we cannot even begin to grasp how incredible he is. It is impossible for us to rely on his strength and power when all we see is a namby-pamby Grandpa in the sky who turns a blind eye toward all the rough stuff of our lives. If he really is that kind of God, then we have every reason to fight for ourselves and feel justifiably hard-pressed.

But that's not who God is. I would like to challenge you to read Job chapters 38–42. (This is reprinted in the back of this book, appendix C, so that you can stay in your comfy spot and read it now without moving a bit!) There's a lot there to read, but there's a lot more to grasp.

After all that Job went through (loss of children, livelihood, and health), challenging God on why things turned out like they did, God expanded Job's view of himself. When our vision of God grows and we are able to see past ourselves and into his immenseness, perhaps we will also be able to agree with Job:

> I know that you can do anything, and no one can stop you. You asked, "Who is this that questions my wisdom with such ignorance?" It is I—and I was talking about things I knew nothing about, things far too wonderful for me. You said, "Listen and I will speak! I have some questions for you, and you must answer them." I had only heard about you before, but now I have seen you with my own eyes. I take back everything I said, and I sit in dust and ashes to show my repentance." (Job 42:2–6)

It is my prayer that you and I both would see God with our own eyes, that our hearts would encounter him like Job did.

God is bigger and more of everything that we can't understand. As we allow ourselves to get closer and closer to his heart, we will begin to see him more and more as he really is. We will learn how to release our pain of today, for the glory of who he is and what he can do.

Jesus is our forgiver, our Redeemer. It is exciting to me that he redeems not just our souls, but our bodies, this created world we live in, and every situation on it. The redemption comes in stages. A little now, a little tomorrow, and by the time eternity arrives, it will be revealed in its all-encompassing perfection. Allow him to redeem your heart, and then day by day a little more of your situation. Ask him for the grace and mercy needed to bring that redemption to your family.

Dealing with your anger as a solo parent is crucial. You are your children's sole caregiver. You are modeling for them how a healthy adult should live. You are also showing them, through your life, the kind of freedom that is possible in Christ Jesus.

It is for your freedom and your children's future that you need—*need*— to release your anger to God. Since you have already figured out what your expectations were/are for your husband and family, ask God to show you his part in all of it. Give God the opportunity to talk to you about your anger and where it comes from. Listen to him. Listen very, very carefully.

Confess your sin of anger to God and allow him to wash your heart free of all of it. He promises that anytime we confess something to him he will always be faithful. He will always forgive us. We need to be genuine. So go ahead. Tell him all about how your anger is affecting you, share your disappointments with him, and ask him for a vision or picture of hope that he can give you.

You may walk around the first few days (or hours) like walking on air with the newfound freedom from anger. Then again, it may not last that long. That's okay. God understands that. Freedom from anger will not change your situation. Remember that! It will change how you feel and how you respond. This is all because of what God is doing in your heart.

There is a list of books in appendix A that will be of help to you as you move toward being set free from the bondage of anger and all the other negative effects of the emotions that you carry in your heart. Find a Christian counselor, pastor, and mentor to pray with you for healing, deliverance, and freedom. Don't settle. Press on toward the prize, because there really is a prize.

As solo parents, we feel many other emotions. There is no way I can cover them all here. Perhaps you will even notice some as you read through the rest of this book. The bottom line is that there is no sense in plowing ahead as worn out, emotionally drained parents if there is a better way. Nobody starts out thinking they'd love to live as close to burnout and nervous breakdown as possible. Nobody does that, so I know you didn't.

Life happens. People make choices. We make decisions and we end up living with the consequences or blessings while flying by the seat of our pants. It is time to change that, to deal with what God has allowed to be served on our plates in a manner that honors him and moves our families into a situation where we can become all God dreamed of before the earth was even formed.

Chapter Three

Emotional Divorce

I prayed and prayed that God would change Trent's heart and give him a desire to be home. I prayed that God would "do whatever it would take" to show Trent how to be more the husband and father I wanted him to be. I bought books for Trent to read. I would write him letters to say how much we needed him and how he was not the kind of man I needed him to be. I thought that this would be a non-confrontational way to show him our pain. I cried. I talked. I nagged. Nothing helped. It seemed that God did not want to answer my prayers.

I began to turn away from Trent emotionally. I decided that if he wasn't choosing us as his family and me as his wife, then I wouldn't choose him either. It hurt too much to keep exposing my heart to his abandonment. Oh, I did all the right and good things. Everything looked good. But I decided that I wouldn't need him. If I didn't need him, I wouldn't be disappointed. If I wasn't disappointed, then there'd be no need to nag Trent, and he could be free to be as separate from us as he wanted and we wouldn't be affected.

God has created us to need community. We need others, period. It's not too hard to find someone to fill the gaps when there are gaps to be filled. And so I did. I allowed someone else to begin to fill those gaps of conversation and friendship. I was finally to the place where I was enjoying life, looking forward to each day, and finding myself excited about the future. The only problem was that this freedom of sorts brought about other bondage.

There is something fabulous about the one true and living God. He loves us! He loves us so much that he will not let us walk away from freedom with him without a struggle. It was this struggle that brought me to understand that it was not only Trent I was angry with, but also God himself.

In the emotional relationship I was in with another man, we seemed ready to move to another level. We had not been physically intimate, thanks to God. Our relationship was getting more serious though, and my heart was definitely given away. I had made the decision on my own to leave Trent. I would wait until my parents came for a visit; then I'd fly back with them and my kids to stay there instead of returning to Trent. I wasn't sure of all the details. All I knew was that I couldn't handle living as Trent's wife any longer.

During all those months of my new relationship, I had been praying. I felt strongly that God had brought this other man into my life to "wake Trent up" since nothing I had tried on my own had worked. I felt God was giving me a chance to be happy. It took only a short time for God to show me that I had been wrong.

I decided I couldn't wait until my parents came for a visit. It was Monday. Trent had been gone for three weeks and would be home on Saturday night. I determined to tell Trent on the weekend that I wanted him to leave. I began to get ready for the "big day."

Looking for Support

Monday night I called a friend to ask for her support and prayers as I prepared to tell Trent that he was no longer welcome as part of our family. She was hard on me. Her words felt harsh, rough, and uncaring. She was disappointed that I would do something like this. I quickly ended the phone call and realized that it would be a difficult road to walk, but I was convinced this is what God wanted for me.

Tuesday I was teaching piano at a student's home. I was acquainted with the kids' mom, but I wouldn't have called her a close friend. After the lessons were over, I walked into her kitchen to explain a change in schedule for the next week. She was cooking when I walked in. She placed her butcher knife down on the counter beside the stove, put her elbows on the counter, looked me right in the eyes, and said, "Carla, how are you?" "Fine," I answered. "No," she said, "I mean how is your marriage these days?"

You can imagine that a question like that coming from a close friend would have been nerve wracking, but from someone who didn't know me very well, it was almost too much. I started to cry. Her teenage son was in the kitchen, so she handed him a wooden spoon and said, "Make supper." Then she ushered me upstairs into her bedroom.

I had never been past the piano room and part of the kitchen. I'm not sure why I had always assumed that her house would be perfect, like a model home. Yet it stuck out to me, as I walked up her stairs past a few piles of laundry and stacks of books into her bedroom, that she cared more about me than about finishing her dinner or cleaning up her house before she brought me to the private parts of her home.

She sat me down on a rocking chair in her bedroom while she sat on the edge of the bed. After asking me what was going on, I spilled the beans. It was like I had no control over myself. I just needed to let someone know about the pain I had in my heart from doing the job of Mom and lonely wife for so long. I told her how I felt God wanted me to leave Trent and perhaps start new with someone else. She asked a few questions to understand me better, then simply said, "I need to pray."

I don't remember everything she prayed. Actually, I only remember one thing. She commanded the Devil to free my eyes and remove the blinders that he had put up. Then she asked God to give me vision to see what I was doing and what part he wanted to play in it.

The thing that surprised me most was that immediately I could see how foolish I had been to think that God would approve of me having an affair, and secondly, that he would use jealousy and infidelity to soften Trent's heart. How absurd it was of me to have believed such a thing! God never sins. He never causes us to sin. So all this time that I had been giving God the credit for my extramarital relationship, he had been grieving. It showed how much I didn't know him and that I had let the Devil blind me and lead me from him.

I don't remember anything else that day except that I was thrown for a loop. I felt like I was in a daze.

The next day was our weekly phys ed day with our homeschool group. I was looking forward to getting out of the house and away from my dark thoughts. We would meet at a local park with many moms and even more kids, a nice place to hide. While the PE instructors ran our kids through exercises, games, and so on, the moms chatted about this and that.

I arrived on time with my crew of four in tow. It was a gorgeous day: perfect weather for the kids to run around and burn off energy, yet not so hot that anyone would likely get overheated, and not so cool that moms would get uncomfortably chilly sitting around and gabbing.

Strange thing was, I was the only mom at the park. Mine was the only vehicle in the parking area. Hmmm. I decided that I would let the kids out and they could play while we waited for the others to show up. There were always plenty of moms, so I was sure they would show.

About five minutes later, the PE instructor arrived. She sat at the picnic table with me for a few minutes and invited me to her PartyLite party that week. She decided to go ahead and teach the class even though it was only my kids. I began to skim through the catalogue as she ran off, calling the kids to follow her around the track.

Moments later, a woman and her son came to the picnic area. "Home-school PE?" she asked. "Yes, just have your son run after them," I responded. Then I went back to my catalogue. I didn't know her, had never seen her before, and didn't feel like I had the emotional energy to make a new friend.

She sat her beautiful, skinny, blond-haired self down on the other side of the picnic table from me, introduced herself, and asked for my name. After some other routine questions, I turned back to my catalogue. She broke the quiet by asking, "So how long have you been married?"

I must have looked like a witch the way I glared at her before I answered. If she noticed my evil eye or rude tone of voice, she didn't let on. She just kept on going, nodded her head, and said, "Man, those are rough years. That's how long we'd been married when my husband found out I was having an affair. That was twelve years ago now, and I'm happily married to my original husband . . ."

For the next hour, without any prompting from me, she told me her story. She shared how her husband had abandoned her for his newspaper and free time, leaving her to be mom, wife, housemaid, cook, and sex kitten for him whenever he was in the mood. She told me of her affair with a man who pursued her and made her feel loved, needed, and wanted. She recounted how her husband discovered her extramarital relationship. Then came the explanations of the hard choices they needed to make and how they still lived with some reminders of her past, such as having an unpublished phone number so her ex-boyfriend couldn't find her. She told me about her anger, her hurt, her choice to stay married, all the hard work, and the reward for it all. This young son she had brought with her was her son from her "love marriage"—same husband, new relationship.

I sat in shock for the entire hour. I absorbed it all. The wind of my soul was knocked out of me. How like God to make sure that I arrived at this abandoned park, on this day, and arrange it so that not a single other home-schooling family showed up except this woman and her son. This messenger was sent by God to shine his light into my heart. I said very little to her. She could see my tears, though. She laughed lightheartedly as she said, "Don't lose this. Remember, I'm not listed," and pressed into my hand her business card with a handwritten phone number on it. "Call me whenever. No matter what time of day or night. Your marriage is worth it."

She left with her son, and I gathered my kids together. I couldn't even speak to them as we drove toward home. I turned on the radio to get away from my thoughts.

It was 11:00 a.m. A new show was starting. *America's Family Coaches* with Gary and Barb Rosberg. I had listened to them before. As a matter of fact, on several occasions I had tried to call in for advice. No matter how early I tried to call, the lines were always full long before the show aired. I heard the co-host share how she had felt abandoned by her husband, how his studies, work, etc., kept him away from the family and the damage it had done to their marriage. I listened for ten minutes to their introduction and testimony. Suddenly I got the overwhelming urge to call. I realized how absolutely impossible it would be to get through at ten minutes into the show. So I made a deal with God: "If you want me to talk to these people, then get me through the phone lines."

With that, I dialed from my cell phone. I got through.

That alone was miracle enough to shake me up a bit. I got no busy signal, I got no switchboard operator, I got straight through to the hosts of the show. I told them my story. I gave them every excuse I knew of for why I should leave Trent and why he should be the one to pay for all my pain and agony.

They spoke clearly to my heart. I was angry even on the phone. They called it what it was. Anger. Hurt. Betrayal. Emotional divorce. They spared no punches and told me that my marriage was my responsibility because I had promised Trent, God, and all those I stood before on my wedding day that I would be there for better or for worse. They called me selfish. I got angrier.

They asked me what I would have done if Trent had become a paraplegic. I answered that I would have nursed him and remained faithful. These marriage coaches told me that being a victim, trapped by my husband's potential lifetime need of me, would have stoked my selfish desire to be everything to someone and would draw sympathetic praise from those who would see my selfless dedication. I was angry with their response. If I thought I would be so dedicated to a man physically incapable of caring for himself or me, why would I be so uncommitted to a man who was not caring for me the way I wanted him to, unless it was not from pure selfishness?

The phone call lasted the entire hour. I hadn't even realized that much time had gone by. I arrived at home partway through the radio program. I left the van running with the air-conditioning on and all four kids buckled in it while I walked into the house. I carried on with the radio conversation inside, uninterrupted by the kids.

When I closed my cell phone at the end of the call, I walked like a zombie to the van to unleash my hungry kids from their seats. I allowed the kids to do what they liked that day. I sat on a rocking chair in my bedroom in a daze. I cried. I tried to pray. I felt the heavy weight of the decision I had to make.

Somehow, in a daze, I managed to take care of the kids, feed them, and tuck them into bed that night. I don't remember anything of it at all. Later that night I sat in that same rocking chair with my Bible on my lap asking God to answer some very hard questions.

I prayed and asked him why? I had kept myself a virgin until I married Trent and had been a good girl and done all the right things, so why, why, why would God not give me a happy marriage? Why couldn't he make Trent love me enough to want to be with me? I asked him why he didn't keep his promise of giving me a happy marriage.

Then I heard him speak to me . . . not in a voice, but very clearly in my heart. "Carla, if you can find a promise in my Word to give you or any other follower of mine a happy marriage, then I will keep it. But my dear one, I have never made that promise."

I cried, prayed, pleaded, and begged God to give me some hope. I pled with him to show me what I needed to see in order to understand what was going on. I yearned to know that my dried out, lonely marriage and father-starved children had a place in this world and in his bigger picture.

Searching Scripture

My mind kept going back to the prostitute Hosea married. I read and reread the chapters, looking at the waywardness of the prostitute wife. I kept asking God, "Do you see me as this prostitute?" He didn't seem to, because his words came to my heart saying, "There is now no condemnation for those who are in Christ Jesus" (Rom. 8:1 NIV). Well, if God was not showing me how horrible I was through the life of the prostitute, then what was he trying to say?

As I read and read and reread the passages, God began to show me something I hadn't seen before. He gave me insight into the life of the "faithful spouse," Hosea. The prophet Hosea. A man whom God loved and had charged with a great assignment. This is how the story unfolded in my mind's eye . . .

In a typical, devout Jewish family lived a son named Hosea. He was like any other boy in his community, full of fun and laughter. As he grew, his parents gave him chores and tasks to help him develop in character. Each day his parents spoke to him about their God, his laws, his ways, and his holiness. They celebrated each of the festivals and made their sacrifices as required by the Law. Hosea grew to love this God of whom he was taught. He feared him with a holy and reverent fear and wanted to serve and obey him above all things. When he reached the age when boys begin to notice the girls, he dreamed of providing for a young Jewish virgin who would be his wife. He dreamed of coming home and teaching his children as his father had done. He dreamed of loving his wife the way his father had loved his mother. He wanted to raise children who would love his God with a deep and reverent fear like he did.

Then God spoke to Hosea.

Now, in this day and age, I find myself wondering when God speaks to me. I wonder if I've heard him right. Often I'm afraid to immediately do what I believe God has said because I'm afraid I might have heard wrong. Hosea 1:2 says, "When the LORD first began speaking to Israel through Hosea . . ." He wasn't experienced in this; he was just beginning, yet he obeyed! And what did he obey? "Go and marry a prostitute, so that some of her children will be conceived in prostitution."

Now, here's a guy, typical everyday Jewish guy, who's been dreaming of a beautiful, dedicated Jewish family of his own, and God tells him to go marry a prostitute. You've got to know some dreams were dashed. There goes the virgin wife—that's at least one dream that won't materialize.

I can imagine Hosea, young and vibrant, ready to serve God and obey him in all things. He may have even been ready to give up his dream of a virgin wife, but do you think that maybe, just maybe, he thought his love for her and, even more, his devoted, obedient love for God would turn things around? We can't know for sure. What we can know is that Hosea was a real live person with real feelings, dreams, hurts, and hopes. I surmise that Hosea was always hoping for a happy marriage.

So Hosea married Gomer, the prostitute. They had children whom God gave names we wouldn't think of burdening our children with. Yet Hosea was obedient. He loved Gomer and gave her a home and his heart. She continued to prostitute herself and was not faithful to Hosea. His heart must have been heavy. More dreams dashed. Betrayal, hurt, and anguish may very well have been his constant companions. Did God ever say, "Okay, Hosea, you know I've been watching, and I see how obedient you've been to me and how you've served me so faithfully. Now it's time for a happy marriage." No. God did not promise Hosea, his faithful servant and prophet, a happy marriage. Instead God said to Hosea, "Go and love your wife again, even though she commits adultery with another lover. This will illustrate that the LORD still loves Israel, even though the people have turned to other gods and love to worship them" (Hos. 3:1).

Don't you think that would hurt? Would you be so willing to obey? I couldn't believe that before my very eyes I saw God plan for his faithful prophet Hosea to have a disastrous (in most people's eyes, anyway) marriage. It was his *plan*! Now, it says further on in the book of Hosea that his marriage was a lesson to the Israelites and to Judah, contrasting their unfaithfulness toward God with God's faithful love toward them. There was a big picture to Hosea's marriage: it wasn't about him; it was about God.

As I sat with tears coursing down my cheeks, this truth was engraved on my heart, and God brought to mind another passage I had memorized just a year before. First Chronicles 29:11–12 (TLB) says, "Everything in the heavens and earth is yours, O Lord, and this is your kingdom. We adore you as being in control of everything. Riches and honor come from you alone, and you are the Ruler of all mankind; your hand controls power and might, and it is at your discretion that men are made great and given strength."

Then a passage in Daniel caught my attention: "His rule is everlasting, and his kingdom is eternal. All the people of the earth are nothing compared to him. He does as he pleases among the angels of heaven and among the people of the earth. No one can stop him or say to him, 'What do you mean by doing these things?'" (Dan. 4:34–35).

It hit me like a ton of bricks: God is in control . . . of everything. God could have given me a different husband, a different set of circumstances, a happy marriage. He could have even changed things up for us as we went along. Instead, he allowed this.

He allowed Trent to mess things up. He allowed me to make mistakes, too. He allowed us complete freedom, and we hadn't handled it well.

I'd spent so many years heaping blame on my husband's head. All the hurtful choices he'd made that put so much strain on our relationship, and on the children, felt like a bag of bricks that needed to be set down somewhere. I'd tried to pass that burden to Trent, but he wouldn't take it. Every time I'd bring up his choices, I was reminded of how his job gave me freedom to be a stay-at-home mom, that we should be thankful for the work God had provided when so many had lost and were continuing to lose their jobs. God knew the burden of blame and choice was heavy in my hand and ripping my heart apart.

That day as God revealed himself to me, he took the load I carried. He accepted me in the midst of my rotting marriage without pointing fingers. He didn't lecture me on my share of the responsibility. God gently and patiently allowed me to bang my fists against heaven's door like a child until my energy was spent and I could relax in his arms of love. He just shouldered all my heartache and weariness without question. It wasn't until my grief had been spent and the healing process was underway that the Lord helped me see how both Trent's choices *and* a few of my own had helped to drive our marriage to the place it was.

But that day God revealed himself as big enough to handle all these issues and problems without any accusation. He was willing to take me and my complete mess of a marriage. I didn't understand that kind of love, nor could I grasp how God could still have everything completely under control despite our poor choices. Could even God make something good out of this mess? So much didn't make sense. My heart hurt so much I couldn't comprehend how deep and wondrous a work God was doing deep in my soul.

I believe it was God's Holy Spirit who protected me at that moment from abandoning all hope, trust, and love of my God and Savior. It is only by his grace that at that point I gave up fighting. I cried and cried as I spoke to God about how disappointed I was. I had not understood that, although he loved me dearly and I was precious to him, I could not be guaranteed a happy marriage. I felt small and tiny in comparison to the accomplishments of Hosea. I was not sure I could commit my life to a marriage of loneliness, heartache, and heartbreak. I poured all this out to God. My heart began to empty out the pain, frustration, and hurt that had been gathering for years.

Accepting God's Plan

God reminded me so gently that I was not ever asked to commit myself to a terrible, lonely, heartbreaking marriage. I was asked to commit myself to him, and to obey him in every step of my life: the way I treated the kids, Trent, and this extra man in my life. God reminded me that what he does, he always does for a bigger purpose. (To be honest, right then I really didn't care about a bigger purpose. I had pain in my heart and I wanted it gone.) I felt like God was asking me to be godly and obedient and to trust him in my marriage.

I fell on my face on the floor. I banged my fists, then my flat hands, as I wailed and cried to God. I admitted I had been so very angry with him for not being my fairy godmother, for not waving some magic wand to make my marriage better and my husband come home to be with us when I had worked so hard to be good. I acknowledged I had nothing in me that wanted this marriage, but that no matter how painful, I would choose God's way, because his way was holy. I knew there wasn't a single thing in life that would be guaranteed except the unconditional love of God, and I wasn't ready to walk away from that.

Nothing in me wanted to stay married any more now than it had a few days before. Nothing in me even wanted to try. There was nothing left in me to try with. I was empty. I felt like a shell of a person crying out to God, saying, "I can't do this, so if this is what you want, you are going to have to do it all for me. I'll only do what you tell me to because I'm so screwed up, wanting things I shouldn't have, I hardly know what's right anymore."

I released my anger, frustration, and shattered dreams to God, feeling completely worn out. At the same time, I sensed a new hope growing deep within my heart: A hope that there was more, something eternal, some-thing significant, something new. I looked ahead, over what I presumed my marriage would look like in the future, and saw continued distance from my husband and tears as my children's hearts broke from missing their papa. But for the first time, I could also see hope. Not hope in myself or in our marriage, but hope that God would not let any of it go to waste. God has a plan and a purpose even for the yucky parts of life.

For the first time, I was willing to walk away from blaming my husband and our circumstances, and instead turn toward a guaranteed stability where God was in control. I couldn't trust Trent to come home, but I could trust God to make sure that none of the pain would be wasted.

The anger that had been building up in me over the past many years was slowly being rooted out by God. I had never acknowledged my anger to-ward God. I didn't think it was appropriate. Yet as I walked through these dark days, the anger I felt toward Trent was mingled with anger toward God as well.

I had to realize I had been afraid to face this God who would allow hor-rible situations and circumstances into my life and the lives of the people of this world. So afraid, in fact, that I was not willing to be honest about my anger, my disappointment. I hadn't realized I was serving a god of my own making: A god who was not big enough to deal with my dreams and desires; a god who was too weak to handle my fears and frustrations; a god incapable of modern-day miracles; a god who couldn't handle evil. Now here I was, face down on the ground, ready to serve this big, holy, untamable, all-powerful God. A God too big for me to understand, yet so loving that his gentle pursuit of me was overwhelming.

I'd always struggled with the tension between supporting my husband and challenging him to become better. Every marriage sermon I'd ever heard preached was about the submissive wife—the woman who would be the silent partner in all her husband's wonderful exploits. I struggled with that as our family's needs and my marital needs grew. Was I supposed to support Trent even when his job was undermining his ability to be a good dad? I could justify the career support because men were created to be the providers for their families, but what about his free time and his emotional connectedness? What about the choices he made, time and time again, that kept him disengaged from our family? At what point should his commitment to our marriage and family come before his career or personal pursuits?

I'd been raised in an environment where women were submissive and supportive of their husbands. I'd met a few women growing up who seemed to have great marriages, loving husbands, and solid families who would "talk straight" to their partners. I admired the freedom I saw in their eyes. But my heart was confused as I heard people say behind their backs, "Anyone can tell who wears the pants in *her* family." I assumed it wasn't Christian to have wants, dreams, and desires and actually talk about them. Yet all my submissive support had dried me up completely and kept Trent separate from us. I knew what he was doing was wrong in at least a few ways, but had I contributed to his distance?

As I wrestled with God that night, I didn't find answers to all these questions. I knew that our tangled mess was not going to be fixed overnight. But for the first time in a long time, I was willing to lay it all on the table and be honest with God about my fears, doubts, insecurities, and anger. I had also finally decided that my relationship with God would be my first pursuit, instead of running in circles pursuing an illusive perfect marriage. I was finally laying down my dreams and hopes for something bigger and better. The settling in my heart confirmed to me that I longed for a solid eternity more than anything else.

A few days after my all-nighter with God, my husband was scheduled to come home. I was still emotionally exhausted. I can't say I had a lot of joy in my heart. It was a commitment to move ahead in what God wanted. There were no bells and whistles of joy, no heartwarming moments of warm fuzzies. The day finally came when I was to pick Trent up from the airport.

I could feel all the anger wanting to build up. I had made a commitment to God, though, and I was not going to quit now. My commitment was for the long haul. So I told God I would need his help and I would not say anything to Trent unless I could speak without anger. So I didn't speak. At all.

I picked him up, and the kids kept him talking all the way home. We got home, and I fixed him a plate of dinner. While he ate, I cleaned up. Then I did the bedtime routine with the kids while he unpacked. He got onto his computer while I got ready and went to bed. I was not asleep when he got into bed, but we didn't speak. I can honestly say, though, that it was no longer anger in my heart. Now it was fear. I knew that my anger was gone because God had taken care of it. Since God had dealt with the anger, I knew I'd have to speak to Trent in the morning. And I had plenty to tell him!

That night as I lay in bed facing the wall, I began a little party in my head. I had gotten through the evening with him and I hadn't said anything out of anger. To top that off I was lying in bed beside him without anger in my heart. Only God could do that!

Facing My Husband

The next morning I got up and asked Trent if he would please get up as well because I had something to talk to him about. Surprised at my request, Trent got out of bed and sat on the rocking chair—the very chair I had sat in just a few days earlier, begging God for a miracle before I'd fallen prostrate before him on the floor. I sat on the edge of the bed. I prayed in my heart, "O God, give me strength and the words to say. I don't want to say things out of hand, but only what you want me to say."

I believe God answered that prayer, because over the next sixty minutes I relayed to Trent how I had been emotionally unfaithful to him, that I had planned to ask him to leave us that morning, but instead, I was choosing to honor God by keeping my word to stay married to him. I explained matter-of-factly that it was not because I felt any sort of love toward him, or because I thought he was a good husband or father, but because God had grabbed me by the scruff of the neck. I was willing to make an honest effort at loving him the way God would want me to.

I spoke to him for one hour. He did not interrupt me. I felt no anger while I spoke. I felt shame, commitment to God, and that's it. Once I was done speaking, Trent said, "Well, thanks for telling me, but I guess it's about time to get ready for church."

Off he went to shower and get ready, while I woke, fed, and dressed four kids and myself.

Oooooh! The anger wanted to come in—anger because I hadn't gotten the response I wanted from him. I had hoped for at least a little something! So I went to God and said, "I've made it through the hard talk; don't let me blow it now. Give me what I need to make it through this." And he did. For the next many, many weeks, nothing was said or done that even implied I had had this conversation with Trent. Yet God gave me grace and love in my heart so that I would not have anger build up in me.

I realized I'd had two emotions in my heart that I'd not recognized. One was fear. Who wouldn't be afraid of telling her husband about her emotional affair? I'd expected an outburst akin to World War III. And when it didn't come, I assumed it was because Trent really didn't care. My mind quickly started working, "Well, if he really doesn't care and if this is really no big deal, then why stick with this marriage after all?"

These thoughts and emotions were birthed from my poor judgment of my husband's character. Again my selfish motives wanted my husband to be my knight in shining armor, to fight for me, and to be angry that some other man had taken ground in his wife's heart. I'd become so distant from Trent though, that I was not taking his heart—or even his personality—into consideration.

Trent is a calm, easygoing guy. His surface emotions are as even-keeled as the prairies are flat. His face shows the same expression no matter what day it is. I have several belly laughs a week that render me breathless, and I end up with a sore face and stomach. But when Trent is truly laughing, a big smile might be all you notice. It's not because he doesn't feel emotion. On the contrary! He feels it so deeply that there is no adequate way for him to display it.

Months after my big disclosure to Trent, I asked him, "Did you understand what I said to you that day? Do you understand that I was essentially having an affair minus the physical intimacy?"

"Yes, Carla, I did. But I was so stunned I didn't know what to do. If I let myself feel the weight of what you were telling me, I was afraid I'd hurt you or say things I'd regret. So I talked myself into believing for the moment that it was no more an affair than if I'd been distracted by a pretty girl walking across the street. My hurt ran so deep and my sense of failure was so strong, I couldn't handle it that day."

It was then that I knew my husband's love ran deeper than I'd ever thought. I'm so glad I didn't get angry, nag, or yell at him because of his lack of response.

Let God work in your heart to release you from the bondage of your anger. It's unlikely that you'll suddenly become a sweet, soft-spoken trill of a woman (and who wants to?), but your heart will begin to change and your actions and reactions will follow. Plan ahead to be a woman who responds to God, not to the circumstance you're in.

Six months passed. I was concentrating on loving God and obeying him. My outlook on life changed. I had hope where previously there had been despair. My friendships became more authentic and my conversations more meaningful. I knew I was working at it. Every thought and word that I expressed with my mouth became a tool I used to reinforce my dedication to serving God regardless of my circumstances. Although I felt changed in my spirit, I wasn't sure it had changed my relationship with Trent at all—until one Sunday morning, six months after my bedside confession to Trent.

After checking my kids into the nursery and Sunday school at church, I headed toward the sanctuary. I didn't know everyone in the mid-sized church and wanted to be sure I sat with Trent. I slowly started down one of the aisles searching for him. I saw a black head of hair with an empty seat beside him, and I made a bee-line for it. All at once that black head of hair turned around, caught my eye, and smiled the smile that had melted my heart and stolen my loyalties just months before. It was not Trent! Unexpectedly, my heart sank. I stopped short in the aisle and held back tears that threatened to become a flash flood. As I realized what had happened, a secret praise and worship service began in my heart! I was no longer captivated by a man who was not my husband. My heart's desire truly was for Trent!

I hadn't realized how honoring God and dedicating my love to him could change my heart so drastically. It hadn't occurred to me that I would ever again long for my husband and be disappointed in the "other" man. The Holy Spirit gave me an encouraging gift that day. He showed me that regardless of the situation I am in, he can change my heart and desires if I allow him to.

He will do the same for you.

Answering the Question: Is Emotional Divorce Okay?

Some married solo parents will wonder at one point or another if it is okay to be emotionally divorced or emotionally separated from their spouses. I firmly believe that when God makes us one, a miracle only he fully understands, there should be no separation of us at all. Being emotionally divorced from our husbands opens us up to believing lies from the Enemy, Satan. It also gives excuse for us to fall short of what God calls us to do. He wants our love, our devotion, and our whole beings—emotions, desires, dreams, and hopes. When we give ourselves to him, we can be assured that even if our circumstances don't change, we will.

Remember, part of the challenge from chapter 1 was to be a woman whose heart seeks after God, all the while leaving room in the family for her husband to be the man, husband, and father God created him to be. Emotional divorce does not bring life to your husband, leave room in the family or marriage for him to engage, or give him reason to grow as a man and a husband.

Our challenge is not to change our husbands. Rather, our challenge is to grow into the incredible women and wives God intended. The exciting thing is as we become those women, in God's hands, we do become effective and powerful influences for change in our husbands.

Speaking the Truth in Love

One of the things we have lost in our culture is the biblical teaching of speaking the truth in love. That alone can be a significant motivator for our men—it can bring light, truth, and life to their hearts and our homes.

There's so much to learn about how to speak the truth in love!

Speaking the truth in love is difficult. By not speaking up with the truth about what is going on in our hearts, our homes, and the minds and hearts of our kids, we are not acting responsibly with the mandate that we speak the truth in love. When we carefully, gently, and with the love of Christ (the kind of love that motivated him to die for us) speak words of truth, we will often be surprised at the response we receive.

Too often we deal with difficult situations out of our emotions. Something happens, we get emotional, and then we respond—out of anger, hurt, betrayal, frustration, impatience, and so forth. When the words we say carry the weight of truth but are delivered with a sincere heart, the listener will recognize the difference. He may or may not actually recognize it immediately, though. Remembering that Jesus says he *is* the Truth, our words should come from him. Every conversation you have with your husband in which you plan to expose a negative impact his actions are having in your heart and home should be led and powered by the Holy Spirit.

If you have carefully prayed through the words God wants you to speak, then trust him and say them with love. Getting your heart in the right place is what will enable you to speak with love. Ask God for his vision of your hubby and your role as his wife. Ask him to fill you with an incredible, supernatural love for your husband.

When you deliver your words of love and truth, you can expect just about any response. If it is a good response, praise God. If it's not, understand that the Holy Spirit may be convicting your husband of those things. Step back and pray like you never have before.

If we look at more of the story of Hosea, we'll see that he didn't just wait until his wife "came around." He was active and proactive in the restoration and redemption of his wife and his marriage.

Chapter 3 starts off with these words: "Then the LORD said to me . . ." This is important. No, this is critical. We need to be listening to the voice of God all the time, every day. It is when God tells us to take action that we can move forward with confidence.

First Hosea had to pay a price. "So I bought her back for fifteen pieces of silver and five bushels of barley and a measure of wine" (v. 2). When we take action—even if it is in obedience to God—it will cost us something. It will cost each of us something different. It might be our reputation, money, friendships, career, dreams, time, energy, or any number of other things.

This cost is not simply a payment, however. It is a symbol of our commitment and dedication. As we indicate with selfless lives our willingness to sacrifice for our marriages, our spouses will see the value we've attached to them. By making the first move, taking the first step, we are communicating our intentions to help create a biblical, strong, engaged relationship.

But Hosea didn't stop at buying back his bride. He took more drastic measures.

"Then I said to her, 'You must live in my house for many days and stop your prostitution. During this time, you will not have sexual relations with anyone, not even with me'" (v. 3).

There are times when we need to set boundaries or take action for the health and well-being of our families and ourselves. Boundaries can be as simple as making a commitment to be involved in a Bible study group, whether your husband is there or not, instead of dropping your attendance when he comes home (or leaves). Or perhaps a boundary might be not to let your husband's absence (or presence) stop you from healthy activities such as scrapbooking with other women, a monthly spa day, movie night with friends, hiking with the kids on the weekend, going to the beach as a family, and so on. Another way to set a boundary might be to assign certain tasks around your home to your husband, and if he doesn't do them, they simply don't get done. Another boundary might be to see a counselor—either together or alone—to help you cope with your situation.

Some situations may call for stiffer boundaries. Perhaps you need to change churches. You may need to insist that your husband not give the kids gifts or treats until he has spent one hour listening to them talk about whatever they want. Or let him know that before you can be intimate together you will need a night out with conversation with him, and until that time together happens there will be no love-making. There may be friendships that need to be cut off, or entertainment that needs to stop. Each situation is different.

Setting boundaries for husbands who are not at home by choice, or who deliberately choose not to engage in family life, will be very different from setting boundaries for husbands who are gone for valid reasons and who make energetic and conscious efforts to enter into family life and to attach their hearts to home. Every situation is so different. Each marriage is so diverse. No two people in the world will rightly handle this boundary setting the same way.

If you have prayed and asked the Lord to give you wisdom and help, then be willing to follow his direction. The Lord will show you if boundaries need to be set and, if so, which ones. Sometimes we are not sure we have properly separated our thoughts from God's directives. Gather godly women around you who are grounded in biblical truth and who practice living in godly obedience. Ask them for prayerful advice.

Setting boundaries "just because," or because you think it will get you something you want, is not necessarily going to "work" for you. Also, while more extreme situations may require more severe boundaries (such as interventions, separations, etc.), more drastic measures should be taken only with the advice of godly counsel, with much prayer (and fasting), and with a network of support. Don't be afraid to follow Hosea's lead in taking action—but don't go there without God's clear direction.

When you enter into boundary setting, if the Lord leads you in that direction, be sure to do so not as a means of punishment for your husband, but rather as a step toward the restoration of the health of your home and marriage. A good resource to consider in this area is *Love Must Be Tough* by James Dobson.

Choosing healthy boundaries with our husbands can be difficult. We want to be their lovers and friends, not their mothers. Sometimes the best way to put up a healthy boundary is to apply it to yourself, like Hosea did. (His wife wasn't the only one who was not going to be having sex.) For example, I encourage you to visit a female biblical counselor for your own emotional health and support. By keeping a counselor in your life, you will be taking a stand to say, "I will not assume responsibility for those things God did not intend for me, and I will seek support to journey through this time in our lives with God's strength."

Healthy boundaries are important in any relationship. For some women the type of boundary setting I have been describing here is simply not necessary. Praise God! There are many men who are away from home for solid, God-given reasons and who engage at least reasonably well when they are with their families. Many others start poorly but respond well as they are presented with and begin to grasp the needs of their wives and children. That doesn't mean that their time away is easy for their wives, by any means. It simply means that these women have the support of their husbands in some of the most critical areas of life—marriage and parenting.

Finally, let me tell you quite bluntly that you do need Jesus in all this. You need Jesus to speak the truth in love. You need Jesus to maintain motives of restoration and not revenge. You need Jesus to be able to take action or to take no action, as God directs. You need Jesus to breathe life into you, into your marriage, and into your family.

Throughout this book you will be encouraged to pray, listen for God's voice, and grow in obedience. An active and vibrant relationship with Jesus will give you what you need to weather the storms of married solo parenting better than anything else in the world.

Grab on to who God is. Be encouraged to reach your fullest potential as your husband's wife and your children's mother. How will their eternities be changed because you were willing, today, to do the work of connecting to God and staying connected in your marriage?

Chapter Four

Life in Community

With so much of our hearts and energies focused on our marriages, our kids, and on deepening our relationships with God, becoming isolated and ingrown is a real danger. We need to live in community with others, receiving from them and giving to them as we are gifted and directed by the Holy Spirit.

Doing this as a married solo parent can be quite tricky. Few churches acknowledge the specific and unique needs of married solo parents. Community organizations and social networking opportunities are rarely designed with us in mind. Our friends and families may not understand or may be too close to the situation to be supportive.

Your social options are much narrower as a married solo parent. You can't simply join in with the couples you once got together with because you aren't a couple. Your relationships change to women-only friendships. Those relationships can be difficult to maintain and develop when your times together include constant interruptions from your kids. What if the women you are friends with don't have absent husbands? They will need time with other couple friends, and as a solo parent, you don't count.

In my situation I found it easiest to build relationships with women who were also married solo parents. One friend's executive husband was home every night but usually so late that she was already in bed. Another's husband was in the military. Yet another had a husband who traveled the United States, selling diamonds. We found ourselves having meals, shopping, and taking the kids on outings together. When a husband came home, though, our cozy coping skills went out of whack. If the diamond seller was home, I wouldn't see his wife until he left again. When the weekends came and the busy executive came home, my friend spent every moment she could with him. And this was how it should be. These relationships that made daily life so much easier had to be held with a loose hand. I needed to encourage these friends to spend time with their husbands even when mine was not available.

There was a stretch of time when Cookie Lee jewelry parties were being held every few weeks by someone I knew. It had been months since I was out, but I still had young kids, and getting out meant getting a sitter. Picking up the sitter was fine; I could bring the kids along. Dropping her off was another story. I couldn't take her home when I had four sleeping babies in the house. Occasionally, a sitter's parent could pick her up, but I reserved those requests for when I had no other options. Although the parties felt like a need (not a want) to me in order to connect with friends, the hassle felt like too much to be worth it. I often felt like I was missing every opportunity to be with other women, get a break from the kids, or even get a glimpse of what normal life must be like for others.

When I did end up going (when my parents flew down for a visit, I finally went to a party), I felt out of place. Some women had brought their hubbies along to help choose their jewelry. Others chatted and joked about how they had left their husbands with the kids and wondered if they'd be in bed when they got home. I remember thinking I had nothing to add, and I feared that if I opened my mouth I'd end up complaining or crying. So I bought my daughter a bracelet and went home.

At church, adult Sunday school classes were filled mostly with couples. When people found out I was married, the next question was almost always, "So where is your husband?" Answering that question became emotionally draining. I got out of those awkward situations by volunteering in the kids area.

Ladies' events usually meant leaving the kids at home, which brought me back to my sitter problem. I learned that there were very few church events or activities I could participate in without feeling left out or having to do a lot of awkward explaining. I found MOPS (Mothers of Preschoolers) to be fabulous. I could be a mom, and the question of who or where my husband was didn't matter. My solo-parent status didn't have to be revealed. I felt at home when I was at MOPS.

As a married solo parent, you have likely had similar experiences. Perhaps you want to attend a Bible study but can find only couples studies or single parent studies. In both of these, we don't fit. It is very tiring showing up week after week at a couples' Bible study and explaining *again* why your hubby is not there, or studying through a marriage course when you have to go home alone.

At one point I decided that my best bet was to align myself with the single moms. The church made Bible studies, support groups, and babysitters available to single moms. For the most part, the only clue that I wasn't single was the wedding ring I wore. Although Trent was a member of the church we attended, few people knew I had a husband because his travels so often kept him from attending with me. The single moms group seemed the right place to be!

We had recently moved to Southern California from upstate New York. I quickly realized that running our air-conditioning through the 80-degree winter meant we would never acclimatize to live through the 110-degree summers, much less be able to pay for the electricity bills! So after inquiring as to how people survived, I learned about the ceiling fan.

I hauled myself and four children, ages five and under, to the store and purchased ceiling fans for our second-floor bedrooms. I got them home and opened the boxes, only to realize that this was going to exceed my skill level. I packed them back up and decided to wait for my husband to put them up. With the lifestyle he was living at work and at home, Trent was not part of our daily lives. When he did come home, he was in no way inclined to put up ceiling fans. So the fans sat on the floor in the bedrooms collecting dust, while our constantly running air conditioner kept the electric company happy.

Once summer arrived, I realized we could not survive without them. Our church bulletin had an announcement for single moms one Sunday. The notice invited them to come to the church to have their vehicles tuned-up or to sign up for a handyman to come do some maintenance around their home. Considering my husband was away more than he was home, I decided to sign up to have my ceiling fans installed.

The phone call came later that week. I was informed that because I was married I didn't qualify for help. The church didn't think it was prudent to send a married man to my house to put up my fans (even though I offered to leave the house and also suggested that the man bring his wife along). I wondered aloud how it was okay to send a married man to a single woman's house but not to a married woman's house. By this time though, there was no discussion happening—I was married and therefore not eligible for help. I felt embarrassed, hurt, and isolated from my church community. I felt guilty for being married to an absent man, and I wished I really was a single mom instead of a married solo parent.

Rejected by the church, I had to look elsewhere. I worked up my courage and asked a neighbor's husband for help. Although this turned out fine for us, it grieved me that the Christian church was not prepared to help me. It is an unfortunate reality that so very often there is no place for a married solo parent to find support within the church.

I share this story not to gripe, but to demonstrate that I understand. As married solo parents we carry a heavy burden of not fitting in.

If you spend any time on the Internet you will know that there are single (unmarried) moms who are very angry with "married single moms." If a married mom vents her frustration about how difficult it is to be alone while raising the kids, it takes only a matter of moments before there is a torrent of comments. Most of these will be from single moms who are upset that a married woman would consider her burden to be as heavy as that of a single mom. On the other end of the spectrum, when we hear married women comment about the difficulty of having to deal with the kids alone once a year when their hubby goes hunting (or whatever), we shake our heads. They generally have no idea what it's like to have a husband who's absent most of the time. Married solo parents don't naturally fit in with either group.

Friends

I remember being too tired and too worn out to even think about getting out to see (or try to find) a friend. The thought of finding a sitter, getting everything ready for her, feeding the kids, bathing the kids ahead of time, preparing snacks or supper, getting ready myself, and getting out the door seemed like far too much work. Friends took a backseat for a time.

If you work outside your home, you'll have even less time for friends. It will seem like a burden some days to even pick up the phone. But God made us to need others. There will certainly be seasons when you'll see less of your friends, but it's never a good thing to walk away from them for very long.

One person you have to take good care of is you. I have yet to see or hear of the child who gets up in the morning and says, "You know, Mom, today I'm going to be taking care of you." There may be a few of those kids out there—and I hope they live in your house—but most children don't think twice about the needs of their parents until they have children themselves.

When we spend time with friends, we connect to a community of people who care about us. A friend will not mind if your nail polish is more worn off than on. She will not care if you did your hair or put on clean clothes. A friend will listen and care about the endless changing of diapers, wiping of noses, washing of laundry, and contending with bags under your eyes.

A friend also gives you perspective when you need it. Those times when you're fed up with your husband, she can talk you down off the ceiling and place you back on your feet where you belong. When the kids have borrowed trouble enough for a whole year, she can point out the humor, the joy, and the good in it. She is the one who will laugh with you when you need a "heart lift," water your prayers with her tears, and tell you to pick up your boots by the straps and keep walking when you need a kick in the pants.

We moved nine times in the first ten years of our married life. Sometimes within fifty miles of our last home, other times across the continent or to a new country. Along with those moves came the painful good-byes to friends and the nerve-wracking search for new ones. Although I like to think of myself as a friendly person, making friends does not come naturally to me. I much prefer to hang out at home with a cup of coffee and a good book. Yet I have learned that I need friends. Friends help me keep (or regain) my perspective and find joy in the mundane things of life.

At times I have felt like a fish out of water in the friendship zone, and I've had to make it a mind-over-matter issue. God has always been faithful. I prayed for friends, and he provided—sometimes only one or two good friends; other times many more. He always answered my prayer for friends who would encourage me and hold me up.

I have had to go on "friend hunts." Sounds crazy, huh? But where does a married woman with kids go to find friends?

I would go to parks, to Moms and Tots groups, MOPS, church, scrapbooking parties, the gym, the Mary Kay lady, and even the grocery store! I made a point of finding some kind of "party" company (Pampered Chef, PartyLite, Tupperware, Creative Memories, Norwex, etc.) and inviting everyone I met to my house for the party . . . no matter who they were. This was way out of my comfort zone at first, but God gave me courage. I made it quite clear that I didn't care if they bought anything, but that I was looking for playmates for my kids and friends for myself. I suggested that this might be a fun way to get to know each other.

You know what? It usually turned out really well. I have actually kept it up; I continue having one party of some kind every year in order to meet new people and encourage those I have not seen in a while. Some years I get just five or six ladies out, other years I get about twenty. I have learned that it really doesn't matter how many when you put it in the Lord's hands. I had one party where only one person showed up. The consultant. That's it. We had a great evening visiting together! I didn't buy a thing. She packed up her nicely laid out display, and we agreed that God must have brought us together for an evening of mutual encouragement.

Spending time with friends gives you a break and allows your children to see how adults deal with friendships. Finding friends with children similar in age to yours is wonderful; while the kids enjoy time with their playmates, you and your friend can enjoy a less distracted "grown-up girl" time. By the time your kids are old enough to stay home alone or babysit younger children, you can expand your circle of friends to include those who either do not have any kids or who are in a different stage of life than you are. Remember that finding friends is not about who your kids like to be with. Although it helps if they enjoy spending time with your friend's family, they will have other friends from school, church, sports, or other activities who will provide their social outlet. This is about finding friends for you.

Make sure you set aside time each week for your friends. It may even be helpful to make a friend connection every day. A phone call, an e-mail, a few texts or instant messages, or Facebook conversations are a good start. But don't stop there! You need the real thing . . . the face to face, the touch, the smile and laughter of your friends. Plan a night when the girls can come over or you can go to a friend's house once the kids are in bed (if yours are old enough to stay alone or you have a sitter, of course). If there is a disengaged hubby in the house who makes things difficult, find a park or a restaurant with a play place to go with your kids.

I met a woman at the park one day. Both of us had a baby. It was her second child and my fourth. We got to talking about how hard it was to get back into shape and discovered that we had each recently joined the same Curves gym. So we came up with a plan. I posted a notice at the gym for moms with preschool kids to contact us. Five or six moms joined our little Curves Club for Moms with Kids.

Every day of the week, from Monday to Friday, we met at a fast food restaurant with a play place. The moms usually bought themselves a drink. We all brought snacks for the kids or bought snacks, depending on what each family could afford. The deal was that everyone showed up at ten in the morning. The first person to arrive would wait until the second woman arrived. The first mom would head off to the gym while the second mom watched all the kids. Then the third would come and the fourth and we would all take our turns going to the gym and watching the kids. There were always at least two moms in the gym, and at least two in the restaurant. We had someone to chat with and exercise with. Our kids got out of the house each day and were ready for naps after lunch.

I was the only Christian woman in the group. It gave me the opportunity to demonstrate my faith in God, build my witness, and sharpen my skills as a friend. The children learned how to relate to other moms and kids in a safe environment that wasn't Sunday school. These women also stood in for each other when someone needed help.

One morning as I was preparing the snack for the diaper bag I sliced the tip of my thumb off. I called one of the women and told her I couldn't make it because I had to take myself to the emergency room to see if they could save my thumb. She told me to bring the kids by the restaurant and she'd watch them there until I was done. With my hand bleeding profusely, the pain almost more than I could bear, I rounded up my kids. My oldest two helped buckle the younger two in the van, and off we went. I was able to have my thumb stitched and arrive back at the play place just before noon. The kids hardly noticed I'd been gone.

Ask God for some creative ways to build relationships with women around you. He created us for community. He knows what you need, and who else might need what you have to offer. Be open to God's leading and be prepared to step out of your comfort zone.

When you are together with your friends, remember your purpose: to build up your friend, to speak life into her life, to encourage her, laugh together, cry together, and share each other's burdens. Sometimes you will seem to be doing all the talking. Other times you will be doing more listening than chatting. That is a sign of a good friendship . . . give and take.

Remember to stay away from "friendship pitfalls." If your friendship with someone is not life-giving, then it may be time to reconsider how much time you spend with this person. Your times together should not be full of complaining, husband-bashing, or gossiping. As a solo parent, you have a heavy burden to carry, perhaps for a long time. What you need are friends who encourage you to do your job as a parent and wife well! You also need to be that kind of friend, someone who looks for what God is doing to bless us and draws attention to those things.

You will need to exercise caution as you choose your friends. I have a dear friend who has spent a great deal of time with divorced women. These friendships may have been fun and exciting. But as she shared difficulties in her marriage and how things were going at home, their advice began to tear her husband down. Within a very short time, she'd become convinced by them that the only way she'd ever be happy was if she left her husband. It became so complicated that she didn't know whether to believe her friends who appeared to have all the freedom that she wanted, or to pursue what she had always believed in—that her marriage was a sacred covenant until death.

Sometimes this is hard—keeping friendships alive and life-giving at the same time. You will need to keep reading your Bible, praying to God, and looking for ways to grow closer to Jesus. Look for his blessings in your life, and you will more easily be able to see them in your friends' lives as well.

Fellowship

At first this may seem a lot like the friendship section above, but hang on! Fellowship is different. Fellowship is when a group of people meet for the express purpose of encouraging each other to become better followers of Jesus Christ. This means that true fellowship can happen within your own family or even with complete strangers.

Many times the word *fellowship* gets thrown around to describe getting together with friends for coffee, dessert, or even a potluck. For some, if there's food it must be fellowship. (Just look at how many churches have "fellowship halls" that are really just large dining rooms.)

Sometimes friendship and fellowship go hand in hand. But some of our friends may not share our faith in Jesus Christ. Those friends cannot fellowship with us the same way that other Christians can. It is imperative that you find those with whom you can truly fellowship.

When you fellowship with others, you should look for ways to share God's Word with each other; pray with and for each other; and speak words of truth, love, and blessing to each other in the name of Jesus.

Wow! You are probably wondering if I really mean that. And I absolutely do.

Many moms can find this in Bible study groups, at MOPS, or with Christian siblings or parents. The rest of us, however, have to make it happen. It is possible and so worth the effort.

Here are a few ideas to help get you going.

Start a "Cuppa Care" with a few Christian friends. Set a time to get together for tea or coffee. Have each person prepare to share something from their Bible reading the previous week. It can be something they learned, are struggling with, or are excited about. Then as you enjoy your tea, let each person share what God is doing in their lives. Pray for them and ask God to bless them before moving on to the next person. The blessings in appendix B may help you get started.

When you are visiting with a Christian friend—either going for a walk, meeting spontaneously at the grocery store, or getting together for a play-date—look for opportunities to turn the conversation to the things of God. Pray ahead of time that God would show you something in his Word that day that you can bring up in conversation with your friend. Then do it. Start with, "You know, I read in the Bible this morning . . . What do you think about that?"

As you spend time with your friend, listen carefully to what she is saying. When you hear something is going well, point out how God is favoring her, or how God is showing his love for her. Be the first one to speak words of life: "I think it is so incredible that God gave you the gift of hospitality. I could learn a few things from you. It is exciting to see you use your gift." Or encourage someone who is down: "Things are really tough right now, but I believe God when he says he won't give us more than we can handle, so this situation tells me you are a very valuable and strong woman in God's eyes. I have a great deal of respect for you; you're going through this difficult stuff but still working hard to keep your eyes on God. I'm proud of you."

Don't forget to give compliments! When your girlfriend is wearing a new color of lipstick or is having a great hair day, tell her. Every woman needs to hear that she looks great. You are doing your friend's heart good and building her marriage at the same time. The more we hear compliments from our husbands and friends, the less likely we are to let our hearts melt for the smooth words of another man.

Dwell on God's blessings and say them out loud. We hear plenty of negative things. It could be how bad the economy is, how much crime has increased, which countries are at war, or how poorly our schools rate. There is enough of that, don't you think? The Bible says we need to "keep [our] minds on whatever is true, pure, right, holy, friendly, and proper. Don't ever stop thinking about what is truly worthwhile and worthy of praise" (Phil. 4:8 CEV). Make it a point to write down the things that fit this godly way of thinking so that you can review them when things get tough. Keep a little notepad in your purse or diaper bag so that you can take "Noteworthy Notes." When you are with a friend and the conversation starts to deteriorate, pull out your purse and say, "You know, I've just about had it with the doom and gloom so I've been practicing what God says about what to think about. Here are some of the things that are in my Noteworthy Notes. Let's change the subject." It can be fun to take a ridiculously difficult situation and together with a friend come up with true, pure, right, holy, friendly, and proper things of note. A friend and I did this as I struggled with an absent husband, and we just about killed ourselves laughing as we came up with some very true things that I could be thankful for: He has two hands, he has never had long fingernails, he showers every day, his legs work, he helped make very beautiful babies, and so on. There are always things to think about and dwell on that fit the bill.

Fellowship is so very important. It keeps our perspective straight on the things that are critical to our well-being. Fellowship with others reminds us that we have something to give and that God has given us gifts for use. God wants to use his people to build up his people. There is a good reason why he says in Hebrews 10:25, "Let us not give up meeting together. Some are in the habit of doing this. Instead, let us cheer each other up with words of hope. Let us do it all the more as you see the day coming when Christ will return" (Nirv).

Fitting In

Just the other day I sat and chatted with a woman whose children are older than mine. She has been a solo parent from day one, almost twenty-four years. Her husband is a long-distance truck driver and actually spends more time out of the country than in it! She shared with me how she didn't attend Bible studies at her church or go to marriage seminars because she was always alone. When she walks into an adult Sunday school class, she is nervous about finding just the right seat. If she takes a seat where there are only two chairs together, she is worried that a couple will come in and want to sit together, pointing out that she doesn't have a spouse along. Who should she sit beside? What if all the empty chairs are beside a man? How will that be seen? To avoid this problem, she has decided not to go.

I'm sad for her.

I have experienced very similar things. On one Sunday I remember well, I decided to attend a church lunch. It was advertised as a family meal: three dollars per person or ten dollars per family. I was really looking forward to this, because when does a solo parent get to go "out" to eat for that cheap and enjoy adult conversation along with it? So I packed up all four kids and headed out to church.

My oldest carried my diaper bag, while my four-year-old helped me get the others unbuckled, locked the car doors, and opened the church door for all of us. I carried my two-year-old on my hip and the baby in the car seat. It was quite a load, but we managed. When I got to the door I paid the family price and went to look for a seat. There were people at most of the tables that seated at least eight. I went to one table where I recognized a woman from the moms group. She asked me not to sit there because she wanted someone with a man to sit there so that her husband would have someone to talk to. The same thing happened at a second table, although these were complete strangers. I found another table with two couples already at it, but they asked me not to sit there because they had left their kids at home and wanted a break. By then I felt like the center of all the negative attention in the room as I paraded with my children between the tables, looking for a place to sit and eat. I was not permitted at the table with the single moms, so I found an empty table at the back of the room.

It was hard not to cry as I put down my sleeping baby in her car seat. I left my oldest child at the table with her so that I could take the two boys through the food line. We were partway through the line when a woman came to me and said, "Your baby is crying, you really shouldn't leave her unattended." I felt so completely abandoned and outcast. I went back to the table and gathered up the car seat and my oldest daughter. On my second try through the line I had a car seat in one hand, my son's plate in the other, and no hand free to fill it. It took us forever to get through the line. I never did eat, as I couldn't leave my children at the table to go get a plate of my own. I cried through the entire meal, quiet tears streaming down my face. Not once did someone come to help, or offer assistance of any kind. It was clear: as a married solo parent I just didn't fit in.

Sometimes you just won't fit in. But there are some things you can do that will ease the pain and make the awkward situations a little more bearable.

MEET JILLIAN

Name: Jillian Mabe

Location: Kentucky

Kids: four (ages 12, 9, 6, 4)

Married: seventeen years

Husband: Tim is an airline pilot. His job keeps him away from home for four to six days at a time with one to four days off between trips. When he is home, half of the time is spent working at part-time jobs.

Favorites: Lori Copeland books, Hearts at Home conferences, *America's Funniest Videos, Extreme Home Makeover,* Pepsi

Longest time hubby's been away: five weeks

My social life: Oh boy, this is a sore spot for me. It is so hard for me to do anything that involves dads because my husband is rarely around. It just seems to be a neon sign that I'm a solo parent. I also tend to avoid doing couple things when Tim's not around. You should see me when he's at church with me. I want everyone to know I'm not a single mom so I hold his hand and stay close to him. I probably drive him up the wall. I do lean on my girlfriends, but not as much as I probably should. I don't want to be a bother to them. So I typically just deal.

My struggle: One of the hardest things for me is having to be the sole disciplinarian, having to be the only one that all four kids come to for everything. This means that every few minutes someone is usually coming to me to chat, tattle, needing help, with a question, etc. This is exhausting and frustrating. I find it hard not to be able to do any of the mom-only gatherings because hubby is out of town and we can't afford a sitter. I also find it hard that when hubby is home he thinks nothing of running to town for three hours while I still have all four kiddos. I find myself feeling resentful and taken advantage of. I struggle with this a lot because I don't get to go anywhere without kiddos—maybe twice a month if I'm lucky. It's hard having to have the kids 24/7 with no help . . . even when hubby is home. I find myself being jealous of my husband's friend whom he goes out to lunch with and hangs out in town with a couple of times a month. I don't get dates with him, but this friend does. Okay, I'm probably going way too deep here so I'll leave my answer at that, but that's how I really feel.

My strength: I attend MOPS meetings, gather with other co-op moms and their kiddos. I dive full force into church. And I simply run the house the way I want to when my husband is gone. I do try to stick to any rules my husband has made, but when he's gone, I suppose I truly treat things as a single mom would.

My hope: Oh, without God I would be lost.

Buddy-up. Find a friend who is in the same boat you are or one similar, and be each other's companion. When she wants to attend a certain Sunday school class, visit her church for those weeks and be her companion. You can always sit in the two-seat zones then. If there is a dinner or event where you suspect you might feel awkward without your spouse, bring your friend. Not only will you get to go to more places, but you'll have great experiences to share and remember later. Is there a marriage seminar you'd love to take in? Go together with your friend, have a blast, and then help each other practice what you learned by keeping each other accountable.

Make reservations. I have several married friends whose husbands are always around. They work nine-to-five jobs Monday to Friday and are very involved in what the family is doing. I know my friends don't try to ignore me or make me feel awkward. They just don't think about my situation because they have never experienced living life alone while married. So don't be shy. If you have similar friends, ask them to save you a spot or get a ride with them so you won't have to arrive alone and find a place to sit by yourself.

Be an early bird. You'll not only get the worm but the best seat in the house. Show up early to wherever it is you are going and then invite people to join you. This gives you the opportunity to surround yourself with people whom you feel comfortable with.

Just do it! Some people are better at this than others, but give it a try. I learned not to ask if I could sit somewhere—I just sat. Remember that there is nothing second-class about who you are. You have every right to stand tall and to be confident in the fact that you are a married mother. Way to go! So when you join a class, find the seat you want and take it with confidence. Join a table of couples, enjoy the company, and participate in the conversation. Your opinion and knowledge is valuable.

Remember that there will be situations where you just don't fit. That's fine! Remind yourself that you have a very special calling in life. Your challenge in these situations is to dig in and find what it is God has for you and to not let your situation stand in the way.

It helps to remember that even the Queen of England doesn't fit in! She can't show up quietly without attention, sit wherever she wants, or even wear whatever she feels like in the morning. She has a special calling. Fulfilling her purpose means that there are some things about her lifestyle that the rest of us just won't understand. Just because we don't fit in does not mean something is wrong with us or our situation. It means we have to stand tall, chin up, our hand in God's hand. We need to acknowledge that with God's help we can and will be the solo parent he purposed us to be. With him, we fit in.

Chapter Five

Discipline Divided

I have had to teach my kids many things. I've taught them how to brush their teeth (although why I still have to remind them I'll never know!) and wash their hair. There have been lessons on vacuuming, sorting laundry, writing their names, counting by twos, and answering the phone without lifting up the receiver and yelling, "What do you want?" I have taught them much of what they know.

I'm not sure how, but they are better on the computer than I am. My son can hook up and attach anything electronic to the TV, and it works perfectly. They were born into a world of cell phones and text messaging and can type with two thumbs almost as fast as I can with two hands.

I have brilliant kids. I hear other parents have brilliant kids, as well. Kids these days are so smart they don't need anyone to teach them how to fight, argue, disobey, pinch, bite, hit, lie, or tattle.

I hope you hear my sarcasm.

As a solo parent, I considered it a successful morning if my kids would wake up happy and we could just get through breakfast without a hitch. Or I would have. I'm not sure we ever got that far. Often it was the bathroom. When four children share the same bathroom, there seems to be a mandatory amount of yelling and pushing and shoving as they loudly discuss who deserves the toilet first and complain about who has to go the worstest. If it wasn't the bathroom, it was someone sitting in the wrong chair at the breakfast table. Should we eventually make it as far as the van, the argument would switch to whose stuff got closest to whose car seat.

(Quite frankly, the benefits of car seats go far beyond mere safety. I am quite certain that the mother who invented these restraining devices did it to end the War of the Line. "You are on my side; you crossed the line!" is a much less frequent war cry now that the little warriors have to be locked into a stationary position for the duration of every trip. This mother was also wise enough to have laws passed requiring the use of these devices so that parents can pull over to the side of the road and truthfully say, "If you don't stay on your side, locked up in your car seat, the policeman might come to get us!" Okay, I have no idea if it was a mother or if she thought like this, but it sure makes sense, doesn't it?)

Solo parents have to fight these battles alone so much of the time. On some days things seem to go more smoothly than others, but string together many days of fighting and chaos and I begin to dream of running away.

> Disciplining children is a heavy burden for more than 95 percent of "married single moms" responding to a recent online survey.

Disciplining my children was obvious. I knew I should. I thought I knew how. Like a lot of parents, though, applying what I knew in my head and what I'd seen in my childhood home didn't always turn out like I had hoped it would.

I picked up a book that said I should reason with my children. So I tried that for a while until I determined that this author had never had a lawyer for a child. If he had just spent one day with mine, he would have never written his book!

Another book said I should give my children an allowance based on their behavior. This assumes, of course, that a child understands the value of money and has some interest in obtaining it. Unfortunately, our children started off with no interest in money at all. As they grew older and started to see some slight value in having money, they found other ways to get it: sometimes earning it, sometimes collecting from other people who said they loved them (also known as grandparents). Our oldest realized she could double her money if she traded a nickel for her brother's dime.

"Look, this is much bigger!" The kids had little desire to be good. "Why be good? If I don't get an allowance, who cares?" My kids were not motivated by money.

I found books on time-outs, spanking, stricter rules, and self-esteem building. Christian books, secular books, magazines, and so on. I finally learned with all this information and much trial and error what worked with each of my kids. I had figured out a good, workable system. Everyone was happy and our house was orderly.

Then Trent would come home.

Unfortunately, he had not read all the books or been in attendance during all the "experimental" weeks, and neither was he in my head as I observed the effects these discipline tactics had on the kids. He'd still be stuck in last month's method.

He would come home and spank when I was giving time-outs. Or he'd give a time-out when I was handing out extra chores. I would get frustrated, and the kids got out of hand. It wasn't pretty.

There were also issues with the differences between us. In the beginning when routines were paramount for the kids, I was like an army major: Get out of Bed! Get yourself Dressed! Eat your Food! Pull up your Socks! Wipe your Nose! Blink your Eyes! Lick your Lips! And Hurry it Up!

Trent, on the other hand, was a walking play structure and bringer of treats and gifts.

Rarely did he get upset with the kids because more often than not he was the one who had gotten them into trouble. He is the kind of papa who thinks it is good to mix up the schedule with a few impromptu movie nights during the school week or with a last-minute, late-night run to the store for junk food. "Who wants to come?"

Trent is also very forgiving and rarely dwells on the negative in situations. So if the boys are fighting, he may let them fight until someone is bleeding hard enough to warrant stitches. "Boys will be boys!" He is not as quick to declare an emergency as I am.

A few years ago I received a phone call while I was on a business trip. It was Monday afternoon. "Hi, honey. I think Aethan broke his arm. I'm going to take him in tomorrow to have it looked at." It was all I could do not to call an ambulance to my house to force Trent's hand. He took him in on

Tuesday, and the broken arm was casted. Aethan survived, and I learned that some emergencies can wait.

As our children enter their teen years, I find that we have reversed roles somewhat in how we deal with them. Now I tend to be the lenient parent while Trent has no problem initiating and carrying through with the tougher line of discipline and consequences. Trent and I complement and balance each other well in a dynamic way that continues to change over time. But when Trent has been absent for a while, his balancing influence starts to feel a lot more like an annoying rocking of the boat!

One of the struggles I have had as a solo parent is dealing with that boat rocking. Trent would come home and the kids would act as if it was a holiday and they would be on "vacation" in our home. Schoolwork would be a fight, chores would fall by the wayside, and routines went out the window. It was like swimming upstream in a flood of mud. I hated it.

It also seemed that Trent was the super parent. He'd arrive home, show his face to the kids for a few minutes, and then disappear again. Yet they wanted to be with him. They loved him. The kids thought Papa brought life at its best. When he was around for a few minutes, they could climb on him, play with him, get tickles from him, and make a lot of loud, fun noises and messes.

I would get upset because I had been the one putting the time, the energy, and the work into raising the kids, yet it was Trent getting all the love and affection from them. To top it all off, it would take me almost a week of him being gone again to get the kids back into a routine. Sometimes it would take even longer to get them back on the track of obedience and respectfulness.

In those days when Trent was home, we rarely discussed discipline issues. Oh, I would fume about how disrespectful he was of me. I was upset that he didn't ask me how he could help or how I would handle things or that he didn't seem concerned at all that how he was interacting with the kids would make the next few weeks so difficult for me. (Of course, I expected him to be fully clued into all this without my telling him. Don't husbands come with mind-reading chips installed these days?) I so dreaded the disruption that I often wished he wouldn't even bother coming home.

Solo parents are usually left to make all the daily decisions about discipline by themselves. This is not an easy task. We worry that we are disciplining our kids too much or not enough and that we are not doing it right. We feel that our kids will see us as the "mean Mommy" instead of the loving, caring, nurturing parent we want and are trying to be. To top it all off, we are often working on too little sleep, overworked minds, and unhealthy bodies. Our tempers are shorter than we'd like, our tolerance is lower than it should be, and we are tempted to punish our children in anger rather than discipline them in love.

Add to all that the strain of raising children together with a husband who is willingly or unwillingly out of the picture for great chunks of time and things get complicated when he does reenter family life. His way versus your way. Is there a right way to do this?

Without a doubt our children need to see us as a united front: Mom and Dad in agreement with what is going on. That is a hard thing to do. You may never come to a complete agreement, but you can take steps forward that will free you to raise your kids in a godly fashion, while at the same time giving your husband the freedom, privilege, and opportunity to be involved in this important stage of your children's lives.

Determine if This Is Something That Really Matters

The first question you need to ask is, What is this really about? Will it really matter once your son is twenty-five years old if you gave him a time out on the stairs for hitting his brother on the head with a metal Tonka truck when he was three or whether you spanked him soundly and sent him to bed? If your daughter lies to you about where she got the new necklace from, will it matter to her at thirty years old if you made her write out an apology to the rightful owner or grounded her from seeing her friends for a week? Not likely.

But it will matter whether or not you have taught your son to settle his disagreements without violence and your daughter to be joyful with others when they have things she doesn't have and how to earn and save for what she'd like rather than stealing them.

This is one of the times when the end is much more important than the means.

Now I'll qualify that. If you handle your daughter's stealing by demeaning her, calling her names, or punishing her beyond what she can handle at her age and stage of development, you may not be teaching her not to steal. Instead you might be teaching her not to get caught and that your love and acceptance of her is conditional. If your child is beaten for his misdemeanor, the injuries he suffers will teach him a lesson that has nothing to do with what he has done—but everything to do with what he wants and doesn't want in a relationship with you.

When I talk about discipline, I am talking about caring, loving ways to guide our children to something or guard them from something, someone, or themselves.

As you raise your children and they grow, I hope you will be looking at the best possible ways to communicate with them the most important things you want them to learn. When your child is three and stomping his foot because he is not getting what he wants, you will hopefully communicate with him differently than when he is sixteen and upset because he can't have the car. You will need to become a student of your children. Learn who they are, what makes them tick, and what motivates them to do well or to do wrong.

Teach Obedience with Rewards and Consequences

God asks for our obedience more than anything else. That is why teaching our children to obey is so important. "What is more pleasing to the LORD: your burnt offerings and sacrifices or your obedience to his voice? Listen! Obedience is better than sacrifice, and submission is better than offering the fat of rams" (1 Sam. 15:22).

Disobedient children fail to follow the instructions of their parents, guardians, or approved authorities immediately and without contradiction or opposition.

You might see disobedience in your children when you call them to come to you and they don't come even though they have heard you. If you have asked them to clean up the toys, get their pajamas on, take a bath, or do their homework and they put it off, regardless of the reason or rationale, they are being disobedient. Perhaps when you ask them to carry in the groceries, they start immediately but don't finish the job.

With obedience, we have to be careful to give age-appropriate assignments in a timely, well-laid-out manner. Asking your five-year-old to clean the house would likely bring about as much success as cleaning windows with butter. Give them the instruction, set the standard, provide a time frame, and motivate them with a reward or consequence.

This is something I might say to my seven-year-old: "Honey, please go put on your pajamas and put your dirty clothes in the laundry closet. If you can be back here in ten minutes with your face washed and teeth brushed, I will rub your back for three minutes!"

My thirteen-year-old might hear something like this: "Sweetie, I would like you to have the kitchen cleaned up and two loads of laundry done before I get home tonight. You can't have a friend over until it's done."

If my daughter had never cleaned a kitchen before and never touched the laundry, this would be too much to ask. Because I have charts that list what needs to be done and I know she has done it before, I can ask this of her.

Once you have made sure that your children are capable of obeying and you have set the time frame, setting the consequences and rewards follows. Children should not always be rewarded, but should be rewarded regularly. While they are young, train your children to obey, reinforcing good behavior with positive rewards. Be prepared to hand out consequences when they don't obey.

Some forms of positive rewards or reinforcement would be:

- Words of praise and encouragement
- A hug, kiss, pat on the back, or high five
- A special treat to eat or drink
- A back or foot rub
- An extra book read to them at bedtime
- Staying up an extra five minutes (or longer if it's a special reward)

As they get older, you should be adding to this list. Recently I sent my son to the store for a carton of cream. Then I kissed him on the forehead as I handed him the money and told him to buy himself a treat with the change.

Positive reinforcement works wonders in training children. Most children, however, also need guard rails. These guard rails are the consequences that they bang up against when they disobey.

Last summer our family took a trip through the Rocky Mountains. I was very grateful for the guard rails along the sides by the steep cliffs. While we were traveling, one of our sons commented that I had better not get too close to the rails. Someone else piped up, "Yeah, Mom, don't get too close to the rails; you might scratch the van."

At first we might stay away from the rails because we might scratch the van. As our awareness of the world around us increases, including its many dangers and pitfalls, our reasons for staying away from the rails deepen. We keep our distance to avoid the much more serious danger of a fall down the cliff.

With our kids we need to provide the guard rails—the consequences that will "scratch the van" of their lives. These consequences will not necessarily keep them from making huge, life-changing mistakes, just as the rails at the side of the road will not by themselves keep my speeding one-ton van from going over the edge of a cliff. They will, however, give guidance and provide a tangible boundary as our children learn to navigate the cliffs of life.

Every family will have a different set of guard rails. You need to work out what works best for you and each of your children. No book can give you the perfect formula. I can give you some supplies, but you have to build the rail.

Make the punishment match the crime. If children draw on the wall, have them wash it off or paint over it. When two siblings are constantly bickering, fighting, and tattling, keep them together until they work it out. (I used to put two of my kids facing each other into one of Trent's large, cable-knit sweaters. Both their heads fit through the neck opening, and both their arms into the sleeves. His shirt kept them facing each other and in a confined space until they could laugh, play, and love each other again. They rarely wore "the shirt" for more than fifteen minutes.) If someone steals something from a store (or a friend) have them make a face-to-face apology and return the item or pay for it if necessary (half-eaten chocolate bars are hard to return, as well as items removed from packaging). In the case of lying, have them write out a Bible verse and memorize it because the Bible is truth—especially if the Bible verse teaches about lying.

Now as our kids are older, we've had to be more creative. When someone gets in later than they had permission for, they lose friend privileges for a week. If their chores are not done willingly (or they manipulate a sibling to do them instead) they are assigned someone else's chores in addition to their own.

Make sure it hurts. The guard rails have to be strong enough to "make a scratch." If the consequence is "worth it," then it is not a consequence. Our oldest daughter has challenged us on this one many times. When we give her a boundary, she will ask what the consequences are. When we tell her, she will weigh whether or not it is worth it. If she deems it worth it, we have to up the ante. We don't do this because we want to control her or be mean. We do this because we would rather have her feel the pain of controlled consequences while she lives in our home as opposed to the life-altering consequences that can come later on.

We have on occasion asked our children if they would rather be disciplined by us now or wait and have the Lord deal with them. Not once have they chosen to wait. If you teach your children that discipline is God's designed plan for teaching them how to be successful, they will receive your correction more readily. They will complain, balk, cry, and get upset. It will not last long, though, if you have corrected them out of a heart and spirit of love.

Make use of natural consequences. If your child steals someone else's candy, make them give theirs to the offended child. Do not replace his candy! When your child lies to a friend, walk with them through the verbal, face-to-face apology. The discomfort and humbling will not soon be forgotten and hopefully will trigger a sharp memory the next time they are tempted to lie. Is your middle-schooler misusing computer time or internet privileges? Cut them off completely for a long period of time. Did someone spend all their money foolishly? Don't give them more. Let them wait and work through the process of earning more. If your daughter hurts a friend's feelings and that friend refuses to spend time with her anymore, don't step in and attempt to clean up the situation. They both need to learn how to navigate relationships.

The school of natural consequences is the hardest school of all. I tend to feel sorry for my kids and want to make things better. I forget that my purpose is not to provide a home where nothing goes wrong. My job, and yours, is to provide a safe environment for our kids to learn how to deal with the stress and hurt that comes when things go wrong.

Not long ago I told the children to clean up the DVDs in the playroom and pick up the CDs off the floor. They didn't obey. The first thing that happened was that someone's favorite movie was lost. I remembered how much I had paid for it as a Christmas gift, and that tempted me to search high and low for it. I refrained and warned the kids that they needed to be more careful. Next thing I knew, a CD had been stepped on and broken. "But Mom, it was my favorite CD! You gave it to me for my birthday." Again, my mamainstinct wanted to rush out and buy a replacement. I didn't. They learned the hard way to clean up their belongings. You can nag and yell, shake your finger, and love them to death, but sometimes the best way to teach is to let them hurt.

As a solo parent, this can be more difficult as we often feel like we need to somehow supplement our love for them to make up for what they don't get from their dad. Your kids don't need you to be both mom and dad. They need you to be the mom who doesn't change, who loves them the same no matter what—and no matter where dad is. What they need from dad, you can never give them. They may always lack that. As much as that may be a pain you carry in your heart, it is not your responsibility to be what you are not meant to be. By making life easy for them, by not disciplining them, and by trying to soften the blow, you will be robbing your children of an understanding of life and God that will ground them as adults.

You love your kids. Now it's time that we as solo parents grow up and become the kind of parents who show our children the love that comes from loving enough. We must love enough to discipline, to hurt, to say no, to be consistent and firm. With God's help and his example, we can do it!

So far we've only talked about disobedience. We need to teach our children so many other things. They need to learn how to be respectful of other people and their property. We need to instruct them on how to handle conflict without violence or running away. We need to teach them to be speakers and believers of truth. They need to learn to forgive and be forgiven.

Correction and discipline are necessary parts of parenting. Remember as you live the life of a solo parent that, although some methods work better with some children and parents and not so well with others, the most important thing is that you truly are implementing a plan to raise them up in the obedience and fear of the Lord.

Remember to be a student of your children. They will benefit from your understanding of how they work, what makes them tick, and what they are passionate about. As you set boundaries, priorities, and strategies in place, keep in mind that these children are yours for only a short time. Take the time and rest you need to be fully prepared and energized to do the job of disciplining well. The foundation you lay in your children today will be passed on to your grandchildren as well, and all the generations that follow.

Find a Vision for Your Children

There will be times, I guarantee it, when you and your husband will deal with your children in ways that are not ideal. No parent is perfect. For some families, harmony in disciplining is more of a strain than in others. But God has not asked us to raise perfect children. He has asked us to do our part—to train them, to love them, and to teach them about him in an environment that soaks them in his love and makes it easier for them to want to obey him.

"Train up a child in the way he should go: and when he is old, he will not depart from it" (Prov. 22:6 kjv). This is a familiar verse for some of us, one that has often been held out as a promise for Christian parents to hold on to. It is not a promise, however; it is a proverb. It's a verse that for many years I completely misunderstood. Let me share with you my thoughts on it.

This verse has often been taken as a formula for pumping out good kids. It's been waved as a blueprint for producing sons and daughters who go to church regularly, do their good deeds, volunteer in the church, grow up, and live as Christians. The implication is that we can train them not to make all the mistakes we made, and they will "turn out"—and if they don't, then we didn't train them well enough. If you can just get them to church enough, buy them enough devotional books to read, stock their MP3 players with Christian music, say grace before every single meal without fail, and teach them how to be good people, then they'll be "safe."

This passage has nothing to do with keeping our children safe. Nor is it a promise that our children will turn out how we want if we push them that way hard enough. It is also not a guarantee that your children will choose to follow Christ just because you do and have taught them to do the same.

Instead, this verse is an invitation to participate with God in raising your kids to become what he has created them to be, and to be successful in what he has planned for them. It is about equipping our children to live a life of purpose and fulfillment based on an understanding of how God has uniquely made each of them.

How many times do we discipline our kids because they are not doing something our way? Too many! Who says my way is right? Let it go if it is a matter of method. If your child has an artistic flair and rearranges the living room when she does her chores, don't scold her or punish her for not getting to task unless it is defiant disobedience. Encourage her to use her gifts within the parameters of the time and task you have assigned to her.

This verse is about getting to know our kids, pressing after God to show us what his plan and purpose for them is, and then raising them to be those kinds of people. If you have a natural-born athlete with no interest in music and you deny him access to physical exercise or force him to forgo sports so that he can sit quietly on a piano bench for hours every week, think about it. Is he really going to grow up and continue practicing the hours it takes to become a master pianist? Not likely. But if God has given him a "way he should go" in his energy and ability, he will find ways to use it. We are to help our children learn to use what God has given them so that they won't have to struggle with purpose, dreams, vision, and choosing between their heart's yearning and our pressure.

So if you have struggled with this verse like I did, wondering how to raise godly children when my husband and I were not "training our children in the way they should go" like I had hoped we would, relax. This verse is about much more than a formula; it is about learning about your children and pursuing God on their behalf.

In that sense this verse is a verse of freedom! You can take the time and energy to get to know your children's likes, dislikes, passions, abilities, talents, skills, and affinities. Find places for your children to shine. Give them plenty of chances to be the "stars" in your family. Knowing which way our children are bent allows us to provide them opportunities to live out what God has put in them rather than fighting with us because they are not suited to whatever our dreams and desires for them may be.

You may have been a high school volleyball star or a tomboy who loved nothing more than being outdoors and getting your hands dirty. Yet somehow God chose to give you a little girl who loves to wear dresses, put pretty things in her hair, decorate her nails, and draw and paint the cutest little caricatures. It is completely within your responsibility as her parent to ensure that she gets outside and gets enough exercise to keep healthy. But if you keep her from her art, or sign her up for soccer instead of painting classes, you may have a very belligerent, grumpy little girl on your hands.

What a privilege God has given us as parents to equip and affirm our children while they are in our homes! If you have sons who can design gorgeous websites, or daughters who can fix any motor, or sons who easily pick up any instrument invented, or drama-queen daughters who steal the show every time . . . encourage them! Give them wings and let them hear your blessing while they live with you. How many times have you heard some grown-up friend of yours wish that she could have had her parents' blessing? You don't know how long you'll be around, so learn about your children, encourage your children, and bless them in the way that God has created them. Then watch them thrive in that way when they are older!

Object Lesson: Coffeepot Macaroni

Gather around the kitchen counter or table. Take out your coffee-maker and set it nearby. Ask your children, "If I wanted to make macaroni for supper, what would I need?" Their answers should include macaroni, water, a pot, and a heated element—you can help them along with any parts they miss.

Now tell them, "Okay . . . I've got a pot, water, and a heated element. While you are talking to them, fill your coffee pot with water and put it on the element of the coffeemaker and turn it on. Give one of your children a measuring cup full of macaroni and ask them to add it to the coffee pot because you want to have macaroni for supper. Watch their response!

If your children pour it in and don't notice anything, then just wait to see how long it takes for the macaroni to get done. Encourage your children to be patient!

If your children tell you that you can't cook macaroni in a coffeepot, then ask why.

Once the macaroni is done or your kids have realized that coffeepots don't cook macaroni very well, explain that coffeepots are for coffee, cooking pots are for cooking; coffeemakers get to only a certain temperature, and stove elements can get much hotter.

God made each of us for a special purpose just like the manufacturers made coffeemakers and cooking pots for special purposes. Yes, it is possible to cook macaroni in a coffeemaker, but it will take longer, possibly not taste as good, and will mean that nobody can have coffee while the macaroni is trying to cook.

If God gave you a brain that loves to think about numbers and adding and subtracting and working on a computer, and legs that trip when you run, do you think that God planned for you to be a professional baseball player?

If you can't tell the difference between chicken and tuna, but God made you to love music, singing and worshipping him as you play an instrument, then do you really think he planned for you to be a gourmet chef?

What kinds of things do you hate to do? What do you love doing? What are you really good at?

Together with your children, ask God what special purposes he created them for. Then thank God for how he made them and look for ways to encourage them in that.

Is Dad On Board?

As you learn about your children and set your priorities and methods in place, you will find opposition. Your children will balk at the new rules. Friends and family may give you negative feedback. Your husband may not support you.

That last one is a toughie. What do you do when Dad comes home and the rules change?

Let's say you have been spending time in prayer over your children and how to discipline them. You develop a plan, and you and the kids are on track with it. Now your husband comes along and administers a consequence or punishment that you would deem too great for the crime. Your first and most important step is to support your husband.

Ugh, that one hurts, doesn't it?

Your children need to see that their parents cannot be pitted against each other, and trust me, they can tell you are a solo parent even if they don't have words for it. They know you are on your own. Don't let a difference in disciplining methods become a wedge that your children can use to further separate you from your spouse.

If your husband is abusive in his discipline, that is a different story. This requires a different kind of love. In the event that you sense or know this to be the case, I recommend that you visit your pastor, who will know how to help you protect your children. If you do not have a pastor, you can call a shelter, a women's or children's help line, or talk to the school counselor (although I still recommend finding a solid church and pastor).

Please be careful that you do not overreact when it comes to accusing someone of abuse. There is no doubt that physical abuse is a terrible reality in too many homes. Abuse occurs when someone physically, emotionally or sexually does damage to a child or spouse. This includes things like biting, punching, shaking, burning, or any other action that causes injury or leaves marks. Emotional abuse can include things like constant yelling, demeaning, and threatening to the point where it affects the person's daily life. Neglect of a child would include not supplying the basics of food, shelter, clothing, medical care, and supervision. Sexual abuse occurs when *any* adult has *any* type of sexual contact with a child under the age of eighteen (sixteen in some countries). These types of abuses *never* constitute discipline.

But a disagreement over how to discipline or a difference in style does not constitute abuse. If you think a child should sit in time-out for ten minutes but your husband thinks a week of grounding is more appropriate, it might seem like too harsh of a consequence to you, but it is not abuse. If you know your husband prefers a particular form or method of discipline, and you don't share that feeling, it would be best to communicate together to find balance and agreement. However, if that agreement proves impossible, give your husband room to parent the way he sees fit. Some parents have more lenient styles or personalities, others have much stricter guidelines. Be very careful that you don't pull the abuse alarm unless it is truly abuse. If you really believe your husband needs help in this area of parenting but is unwilling to communicate with you about it, pray hard and then seek advice from your pastor.

Remember, as wives we need to give our husbands room to be the best fathers they can be. They'll need practice. They don't get the same amount of practice we do because they are rarely involved. Give them grace to make mistakes and learn from them.

As I mentioned earlier, I have become more lenient in my style of disciplining the children over the years. One day I felt that my husband had given our daughter too much consequence for her "crime." I would have likely given her just a reminder or word of caution, whereas he saw her actions requiring a much stiffer penalty. I was furious! Thankfully, I kept my thoughts and words about it out of her hearing. Later I quietly discussed this with a few others to get their opinion. (By the way, I would not recommend doing this. It was a very bad decision on my part.)

Sure enough, the opinions ran the gamut. Some agreed and some disagreed. Some cheered him on and some were pushing me to make sure it never happened again. I decided to let the situation rest for a while. After a few days, Trent and I discussed it, and after hearing him out I agreed with him that she had needed the discipline more than I had originally thought. I told him I would not have responded the way he had but that I supported him wholeheartedly because I knew that his heart was for his daughter, to see her grow up in character and maturity. His methods were definitely not my methods, but his heart was in the same place as mine, and he had disciplined her in love. There had been no breach or even momentary lapse in her love for him and his for her. Interestingly, although this was a very big deal to me, she doesn't remember the consequence or even what she did to deserve it!

Disciplining our kids is a tricky business. But we are promised in the Bible that we can ask God for wisdom. James 1:5 says, "If you need wisdom, ask our generous God, and he will give it to you. He will not rebuke you for asking."

Prayer will be your number one tool, your most needed resource as you solo-parent your children and deal with their misdemeanors, mischief, and mistakes. Be prepared at all times to put the discipline on hold in order to get your heart right with God before you deal with your children.

If your husband is gone a lot but has a heart for his family, you are in a beautiful position. Pray for several days or weeks on how to approach him. When you have heard from God and have come up with a plan for disciplining the kids, go on a date with your husband when he's home next or set aside some quiet time for the two of you alone, and lay out your plans. Tell your husband what your heart for your children is. Build a vision for what kind of children you want to raise. Ask for his input. Then come up with guidelines that you are both comfortable with, and ask for your husband's blessing to discipline the kids this way while he is gone. Creatively ask him to make the transition home easier on your relationship with him and his relationship with the kids by implementing a "Dad's home" plan.

A plan like this could mean many things. Maybe you'll agree that he will refer the discipline to you. Perhaps you'll agree to discipline together. Another option is that you are hands-off about discipline when he's home, and he'll do it his way. If this is what you choose, remember to honor him and actually stay hands-off!

Keep praying for your husband. Allow him the room to make mistakes. You've made them. He'll make them. Give him the grace he needs to become the dad God made him to be. We're all growing. Allow him that space.

For others, the discipline situation is not so pristine. I'd like you to remember the story of Queen Esther. I believe that, like Esther, you have been created for such a time as this.

Esther's people were in danger. She loved them. The Jews were about to be annihilated because Haman had convinced King Xerxes to sign a document with his seal, ordering their slaughter and the plundering of their goods on a particular day.

Esther's uncle, Mordecai, asked her to do something about it. She was to approach the king and ask him to spare their lives. Yet to approach the king uninvited was against the law and could very well cost Esther her life.

Esther fasted and prayed. She got her people to fast and pray. Then she humbly approached the king. She knew that it was against the law, but her faith in God was stronger. She was willing to lay down her life for her people rather than to sit back and allow the king to destroy them. As she humbly and quietly approached the king, he held out his golden scepter to her. It was a sign that she was accepted. He offered to give her whatever she asked, up to half of his kingdom.

She could have right then and there asked for the lives of her people. She didn't, though. Instead, she asked for another meeting where she could honor him with a meal. He came to the meal and brought Haman with him. At that meal she could have asked for anything in the whole kingdom. But she didn't. She asked for a second meal.

Esther was obeying the leading of God. We know that God was directing her and the events surrounding her request because that night, between her first meal with the king and her next meal with him, the king had an encounter with Truth. Because of insomnia, he asked someone to read to him from the documents of the land. This was likely supposed to be boring enough to put him to sleep. Instead, he was reminded that Mordecai had saved his life and yet had never been rewarded. His heart softened toward Mordecai and, by extension, the Jews, and he was made ready for Esther's request. God was on the move.

The next day at the meal, Esther asked the king to save her people. Not only was the king mortified to hear that someone (Haman) had engineered a plan to kill her and her people, but when he returned from taking a breath of fresh air, he found Haman on top of Esther in the chair she'd been lying in! As you can imagine, King Xerxes was not a happy camper and had Haman executed with the very tools Haman had prepared to kill Mordecai with.

As you can see, the king's heart was changed. Impossible circumstances were changed. It had nothing to do with what Esther said or what she wore or how beautiful she was. It was because Esther had spent time talking with God. She had listened to his voice. She was willing to obey regardless of the cost to herself. Her commitment to obeying God must have been difficult when she turned down the king's offer for up to half the whole kingdom not just once, but twice! What if time ran out? What if this was her last chance? What if, what if, what if?

God heard her pleas and the prayers of her people. He changed King Xerxes heart. Proverbs 21:1 says, "The king's heart is like a stream of water directed by the LORD; he guides it wherever he pleases."

If God can move the hearts of kings and uses the prayers of an orphaned, adopted young Jewish girl, then he can use your prayers to move the heart of your husband.

Spend time in prayer. Consider fasting and praying. Follow the Lord's direction as he speaks to your heart. Obey immediately and do what he is directing you to do. If you get a sense of something or a feeling that you should do it, commit it to the Lord and go for it. Where Esther prayed for the sake of her people, you must pray for the sake of your family, your legacy, your children, and grandchildren.

For Esther it all happened quickly. Three days of prayer and fasting. A few meetings with the king. Then it was over. You may find yourself praying for much longer. Remember, though, that God is working. He is never idle or sleeping or too busy elsewhere.

Commit your discipline to the Lord; commit your children to him. Ask him to teach you how to love your children enough to discipline them and your husband enough to keep praying for him.

When it comes down to daily routines and everyday life, when the rubber hits the road, life can be very hard. Yet God has not given you more than you can handle, provided you are leaning into his strength. So count on him for what you need to do the job he has set out for you. Without that, without obeying him in it all, you will not succeed.

Whether your hubby is open to discussions or not, your job as mom is to take each situation to the Lord. Ask for wisdom. Ask for insight. Obey His leading.

If your husband does not allow you to discipline the children freely or without his prior consent, pray. Pray, then honor him. Remember that God has placed the responsibility for your children's eternal well-being on his shoulders, as well.

One day he will stand before God and have to give an account of how he has raised his children. What will that look like? As you stand beside him that day, will you be cheering at his sorrow? "Yeah, now you'll get what you deserve!" No. Oh, my friend, my dear, dear solo mom, that will not be your song.

As you stand before a holy God with your husband at your side, God will ask you what you did to make it possible for your husband to be the incredible dad he was created to be. What did you do to smooth the road for him, to allow your love to cover a multitude of his sins?

When it comes to parenting your children, you need to do it in light of eternity. Will my actions today lead my child or my husband closer to God, or will they push them away? When my husband does not support me, how can I love him through the pain so that his eternity, mine, and the kids' can be affected for the best?

For solo moms the job is more than just parenting. The task includes giving your children the foundation they need to become leaders in their world and their homes. It includes giving your husband every opportunity to honor God with his parenting. He may not be a Christian. He may not want to engage. He may throw every obstacle your way. Those are his choices, his mistakes. Separate yourself from that and ask the question: Can I trust God so fully I can obey him completely and give him control of my children's lives no matter the outcome, so that my husband and children can have the freedom to choose God?

The biggest turning point in my parenting and marriage was when I wept before the Lord. I lay on my bed for hours one day after Trent left for another trip. He had greatly offended the kids and had pushed me away with his words and actions. Although he had a good-willed heart, he was not engaged enough to know how deeply what he'd done would affect us all. I could see how the hearts of the kids had been cut, but he couldn't see it.

I asked God to give me a picture of what he saw, because I could see nothing redemptive in the situation. In my own strength, what I saw was that the only way to protect my children was to leave with them so that they couldn't be hurt anymore by their dad.

God gave me a picture of Trent standing before him, head hanging and tears flowing down his cheeks. He showed me the pain in Trent's heart as the movie of his life played before us. I ached deep in my soul for him. It was like Trent was bound up somehow, unable to do the things his heart had desired. I had a picture of the chains around Trent's arms whipping here and there, cutting into the kids and me as he tried to wrap his arms around us. His attempts at loving us were good and true, but the chains around him were tearing us apart.

Then I saw myself. I was weeping. The heart-wrenching sobs were because I saw how I had stood back and let Trent fend for himself. I had not softened the blows of disappointment and heartache for the kids or given Trent the opportunities he needed to love them without fetters or obstacles. Instead of bringing the kids to him to love him, honor him, and cherish him, I had stood my ground apart from him, letting him stumble about on his own.

At first I was angry. I questioned God: "Why should he get credit for good kids if I'm the one who's done all the work?"

Then God spoke clearly into my soul: "My dear daughter. Why should you get the credit for all the work my Son did on the cross?"

Ever since then I have been convinced that my role, and all of our roles as women, wives, and mothers, is not to produce good kids or Christian kids or godly men. Our role is to live a life that is in obedience to Christ and that paves the way for those around us, especially our husbands and children, to experience Christ's redeeming love and to choose to obey him as well.

We do our husbands a disservice if we just stand idly by and let them make mistakes. Our role of finding the delicate balance between giving them room to parent in their own daddy style and yet be their helpers in learning about their children and staying engaged with the discipline we are enforcing can be tricky. The art of walking that fine line is never perfected. Occasionally we will do it well, other times we will look back and see that a different method may have worked better. Parenting and discipline changes continually. Just when we've got the naughty words under control, someone begins back-talking—and by the time we finally have that taken care of, a teen has been abusing internet privileges.

Many moms find that their husbands don't appreciate their parenting advice. It is difficult for men to think that they don't understand their own children, and they balk at the idea that parenting is not instinctive to them. It's a rare dad who picks up a parenting book to learn how to raise his kids. And I have yet to hear a group of men chat about what they've recently found that works in the discipline department. Don't be offended if your hubby falls into this category. It may mean that you need to be creative in your attempts to be his helper.

Many men really have few clues on how to parent well when they first become fathers. My husband was one of them. Even if they grew up with an involved dad, they may have been so involved with the fun of growing up that they didn't stop to notice what it was that the men in their lives were doing to help them become the men they are. And sadly, many of them are following in the footsteps of disengaged fathers—doing exactly what they saw their daddies doing.

Each man has a few things in his mind that make a father great. One man might believe that as long as his kids can play every sport and attend every football game he's being a great dad. Another might bank on his more-than-sufficient income to satisfy whatever needs his children might have. I know several dads who believe they are doing their best fathering when they work on a vehicle with their boys. All of these can be really good for your children, but being a great dad takes more than entertainment, extra money in the pocket, and a couple of hours tinkering under the hood. Parenting involves the emotions of decision-making, heart-to-heart talks, boundary setting, the teaching of values, wrestling and playing for fun, and even snuggling on the couch.

As you pray for your husband's parenting and your ability to let him be the dad he was created to be, it might be necessary to look for some outside assistance. Often a pastor, a godly friend, or even your husband's father can become your ally as you pray for your husband. Promise Keepers has great information, magazines, books, and conferences that help men become great fathers and dads. Perhaps a few men from your church can attend men's conferences together, or you and a bunch of your friends could plan to send your hubbies to a great Promise Keepers weekend.

Praying for your husband to be part of the discipline in your family will include asking the Holy Spirit to give you wisdom on how to walk that fine line of helping and letting go.

Chapter Six

Those Should Be *His* Chores!

Discussions about roles in the home for husbands and wives are really an exercise in futility if you are a solo parent. If there is a job to be done, someone's got to do it, and it most likely is going to be you.

This was one of my big hang-ups when my journey as a solo parent began. Coming from a home where Dad did the outside work (the yard, the home maintenance, the tools, and the vehicles) and Mom did the inside work (the cooking, cleaning, mending, laundry, and shopping) I was unprepared for the multitude of tasks that waited for me to tackle them. I had been taught how to keep a yard, change a tire, and use the odd handy tool. I had never anticipated, though, that I would use those skills on a day-to-day basis once I was married.

This is not an issue of women's rights. This is also not an issue of women's capabilities. This is an issue of who is taking care of whom. I had no problem cutting the grass or taking out the trash to show my husband how much I loved him. But force me to be the one to do it all the time and I start feeling like the slave, the housemaid, and the taken-advantage-of wife.

Every married woman wants her man to take care of her, protect her, and help her to feel secure. When the burden of child rearing and homemaking is made heavier by the load of whatever tasks our brains consider "his" chores, we can burn out very quickly.

So let's take a fresh look at this whole household chores and roles situation.

How Is Your Husband Wired?

Each couple has their own ideas of what "his" and "her" chores should be. It could be that even between husband and wife that line is blurred. I know many couples where the grocery shopping is done by the husband. Not in my house! Then again, in some homes the ironing is done by the wife. Not in my house! Regardless of what our preconceived ideas and expectations are, we can take steps to have a healthier perspective on the roles we have to play.

First of all, if your hubby is open to a discussion, talk about it. Perhaps there are tasks he would prefer to do or not do. Maybe some chores can wait until he has time for them . . . like cleaning the car, changing the furnace filter, or tilling the garden. Some men would be happy to take over certain chores when they are available. When my friend's husband comes home from his month on an oil rig, he does more of the cooking, takes care of the home and yard maintenance, and ensures that the kids get a healthy dose of outdoor adventure. During the in-between times, she and her son take care of the mowing, snow shoveling, and car cleaning. They've worked out a system where he gets to do the chores he can do and enjoys doing during the days he's available, and she does what she can while he's gone to ensure that nothing gets out of control.

For many couples, though, this type of discussion just simply won't happen. Your challenge is extra special. The task ahead of you is to see if there is anything your husband naturally gravitates toward doing or even noticing. Does he drive into the yard and say, "Man, it's too bad I don't have time to get that lawn cut"? Or does he call you from the road to remind you to take the trash out? Maybe you notice him tinkering under the hood or tightening a few screws in the house as he walks through. Pay attention to what your hubby does without being asked. Enjoy that! Then leave those things alone. They are things that he will likely enjoy doing if he can. If it is getting past-due the time to accomplish these things, ask him politely if it would be okay with him if you tackled the job, reminding him that you so appreciate him doing it, but you would love to show your support of him this way.

My situation is different again. My husband just doesn't notice many of the tasks that need doing around the house. By the time something starts to bother him, it's been driving me insane for days or weeks. He's not a handyman; he doesn't enjoy tinkering with things on and around the house the way some men do. (House repairs aren't rocket science, but if they were, mine might get done a lot faster! He has a PhD in aerospace engineering. He still wears a T-shirt from his university days that reads "Will build planes and rockets for food"—and he's not kidding.)

Over the seventeen-plus years of our married life, he has definitely improved in this area. He recently spent an afternoon fixing the lawn mower, another working on the air conditioner (notice I didn't say *fixing*), and has repaired a few cupboard doors, sink pipes, and window grilles. His strengths, however, lie in his communication skills, his technical and problem-solving expertise, and his business savvy, not in his ability to perform household chores.

For those of us whose husbands cannot come home, choose not to be involved, or are simply not wired that way, the job is a little trickier. We've got to come up with a strategy.

How Can You Get It Done Creatively?

When it comes to things like the lawn care, or snow shoveling, you can do them yourself provided you are healthy. If you are working outside the home as well, your time may be limited. If you decide not to do them, the next place you should look is to your children. Are they old enough and mature enough to handle a mower or shovel? If they are not now, they soon will be. Be prepared to spend a few evenings and weekends teaching them how you want it done; then pass the baton and let them at it. It may not be the best-manicured lawn on the street, but who said it had to be?

If your children are too young, consider hiring a young teenager to do it for you. Set your price in advance and lay out your expectations clearly. Depending on the age of the person you hire, you may want to meet with his or her parents, as well. The other option, and obviously the most expensive option, is to hire a yard-care company to handle your lawn and yard maintenance. Sometimes the cost is little in comparison to the stress of doing it yourself.

We live in Canada, where getting three feet of snow overnight can be exciting and a lot of fun. That fun all ends if I'm supposed to leave the house at six fifteen in the morning to attend a meeting at seven and it will take me three hours to shovel the driveway. The twenty dollars it costs me to have the driveway cleared by the time I leave the house that morning is more than worth it to me. But if it is a lazy day at our house, the kids can dress up warmly and attack it with their youthful energy.

One of the more difficult problems I have run into as a solo parent is vehicle maintenance and repair. I probably know as much about vehicle maintenance and repair as my husband does, but the guys at the shop don't know that and treat me as if I don't know anything at all. I have received really bad and expensive advice that might not have been given to my husband. There is also the issue of logistics, especially when your children are very young. It is frustrating to drive to the mechanic shop, with four kids in tow, and stay there, with four kids in tow, because they do not have a courtesy car for a woman with four kids in tow! Few things match the experience of spending three hours in a mechanic's filthy waiting room with children who want to touch everything, need to use the hasn't-seen-a-cleaning-person-in-years restroom every twenty minutes, and want to eat the stale peanuts from the vending machine. I know because I've done it.

First, you have to find a trustworthy mechanic. It may take some time, but this is more than worth it. Ask around. Find people who are meticulous with their vehicles and find out where they go. Ask some car buffs where they go. If you have a friend whose husband does most of his own repair work, ask where he takes his vehicle for things he can't do himself.

When you are looking for a mechanic, ask if he offers a courtesy car or a ride home in your own vehicle. This is important if you have children, especially if they are still in car seats.

Take your vehicle for regular maintenance and tune-ups. This will cost you less in the end and keep your visits shorter. This will also give you a heads up for when things are starting to wear down so that you can price out parts, save up some money for the repairs, and even do some price shopping for labor costs. It also allows you to plan your schedule in advance rather than have an abrupt interruption in your plans because of a car problem.

Don't be afraid to ask a friend if her husband would take the car in for you. Many men would like to help, but are not sure how. I have often asked my dad for advice and a referral to a good repair place. When we've lived close to my parents, my dad even came with me if Trent was not around. If you know someone who can do oil changes or other smaller maintenance tasks at home, don't be shy in asking. Be prepared to pay them for the work they do, or at least the materials needed. (So know your prices ahead of time, because work at home is not usually under any warranty.)

> Did you know that 84 percent of "married single moms" find vehicle maintenance and repair a difficulty? Most leave the job for hubby when he gets home or ask a friend or relative to help out if there's an emergency.

Women can be very industrious. Likely you are one of these women. If something needs doing, you can figure out a way to get it done. Perhaps you can learn how to do some of those jobs yourself if you really want to.

You will need to hire someone for some things—or at least ask for outside help. My ceiling fans were one of my big ones. I also had problems with my patio door. I had to ask for help with that. Hiring help is an honest way to achieve a goal. If you cannot afford to hire someone, perhaps you can trade services like babysitting, baking, cooking, sewing, accounting, organizing, or whatever else you can do. Asking for help is a perfectly good and respectable way to make sure things get done well.

In your quest to get it done, let me remind you that you are not your husband. It is perfectly okay for there to be some things that just don't get done because he can't or won't. When others mention them, let it roll off your back. Do not take offense. There may even be some things that you choose not to do.

For me, I decided I would leave taking out the trash for Trent. I didn't do that because I was angry or feeling resentful. The amount of time that Trent was gone necessitated that I take care of all the yard, home, and vehicle maintenance, as well as all my homemaking and childcare tasks. There came a day when I sadly realized that I no longer needed him. There was nothing left that I couldn't handle, do on my own, or find a way to get done. I asked myself, "If Trent wanted to walk into our home right now and do something, is there anything I would need him to do?" The answer was no. I no longer needed him for anything.

It's stunning how quickly and easily we can go from simply not being around each other to not needing each other. I had to stop the spiral that was moving us further apart from each other. I chose a task (the trash) to be that one thing I would give to Trent as his necessary contribution to our family. It would not get done unless he did it. At first I didn't tell him what my plan was. Our large city-provided trash cans were at the side of the house, and I just kept putting bags from the house into those large cans. They piled up and piled up. We were paying for weekly trash pick-up, but our bins weren't making it to the end of the street. It was weeks before it finally got taken to the road—partly because he didn't know and partly because it hadn't bothered him enough. After that, he set an alarm on his Palm Pilot and started making sure it got out. If he wasn't home, he would call and ask me to do it—and I would, because he was still taking care of the task by delegating it. From there he went on to assume (or resume) other responsibilities as well, but the trash was our turning point. These days our boys usually take care of it well in advance, but it is still "Papa's job," and his trash alarm still goes off each week to remind him, even after almost ten years.

Taking responsibility for the tasks around your home that you would consider "his" job does not mean that you have given up on your husband, your marriage, or the dream you have for what your family will look like some day. When you carry the load, you are showing your children that doing what is best for the family comes first. God has called us as women to be our husband's "helpers." We are to help them be the kind of men God created them to be. So when it comes to chores, remember that you are helping, not necessarily taking over. You are teaching your children how to work hard and have a good attitude about it. Remember that the tasks you complete are of no value unless you do them out of honor toward God and your husband.

I've never fallen in love with the Proverbs 31 woman. She seems like Superwoman to me—although I have to admit I love the fact that she has servants. Three cheers for her! Never, ever, ever has God asked you to do it all alone. The idea that asking for help, hiring work out, or having a house-keeper means you are somehow not measuring up is a lie from the Devil. God has given each of us gifts and abilities. So what if he didn't give you the gift of cleaning and organizing, or of welding and automotive repair? Learn to enjoy your strengths and live in them. Give others the opportunity to live in theirs.

Be sensitive to how your boys may be able to take part as they grow older. Lovingly place a mantle of leadership on their shoulders when you think they are old enough. The idea isn't to have them replace their dad, but to empower them to be men and take on responsibility for things wherever they go. Boys do this naturally because that is how they've been created. Sometimes our sinful world and culture tears it down and out of them. You can reverse that. Build it up in them.

When our oldest son was still quite young, I noticed him walking around the house in the dark after I'd gone to bed one night. I called quietly to him, and he came to my room.

"Son, what are you doing out of bed?"

"Well, Mama, I had to check to make sure the doors and windows were locked."

"But, honey," I said to him, "I already did that."

"Yeah, I know," he nodded and looked down at the ground. "But that really is a man's job. You're not a man, and I'm the only one at home that's old enough, so I had to do it."

I gave him a big hug, the dim light hiding my tears, and told him he'd make a great husband and papa someday. I prayed a blessing over him and asked the Lord to strengthen his little heart and give him the training and security he needed as a child to be the man God wanted him to be as an adult. He walked back to bed a confident boy.

They may be "his" chores, but for now they are your responsibility. Be creative and find ways to get it done. Ask for help, and bless others by giving them the privilege of using their gifts. Pass on the baton to your children when they are ready. And always honor God by the way you serve your husband and your family.

Chapter Seven

Keep My Mind *and* the House?

I used to have a comic on my fridge. In the center of the picture was a woman at the kitchen table trying to read her Bible. A stack of dishes sitting in the sink had a voice call-out with a comment that said something like, "We're going to have to soak until Christmas to get all this dried stuff off." A call-out from the fridge made a remark similar to, "You won't believe what's growing in here!" The counter was full of papers, books, dishes, and food. Cupboard doors were left open. The table around the woman's Bible hadn't been cleared or wiped. Drawers had been left open. Her husband is walking into the room with question marks over his head because of her comment, obviously a scream because of all the capital letters. Evidently frustrated she was yelling, "How am I supposed to have quiet time when it's so noisy in here?"

Even without a peep in the house, mess causes stress in our lives. And our lives are about more than just mess, right? Think about all the other things we do as well.

We work full or part-time; bathe the kids; serve nutritious meals; do the laundry; drive the kids around; clean the house; teach them manners; instruct them in spiritual matters; referee disagreements (or fist fights); and try to be kind, courteous, gentle, full of grace, and soft-spoken. In our spare time we have to pluck our eyebrows, do our nails, lose some weight, work out at the gym, and whiten our smile. And if you can't, well, just fake it!

One of the stressors of a solo parent's life is taking care of the house. It is one of those tasks that never really ends. Unless you all go naked for a week, more laundry will be in the hamper by the time you finish the current loads. If it's okay with you that your kids can't find the homework they are supposed to do and you have to eat straight off the table because the plates are all dirty and stacked up in the sink, then life might be just grand. Maybe you have to wear shoes in the house because you don't want to get your socks dirty. Or perhaps your carpet is clean because the clothes covering it keep it from getting soiled. Your closets are booby traps waiting to empty their contents on the next unsuspecting victim who opens the door.

Okay. Maybe it's not so bad, but there are days when it sure feels like it, right? No matter how you try to ignore it, the stress from your environment will spill over into the rest of your life and make things much more difficult.

My mom loves a clean house and loves cleaning a house. Not me. Oh she taught me well—I know how to clean *thoroughly* and keep it that way, but my priorities are not the same as hers. Therefore my house is never as clean as hers. I used to feel trapped by this. I believed I was a failure if I didn't keep house like she did. I worried that people would think my mom had failed to train me to keep house properly. Not anymore.

I know now that God has not called me to be SuperMom. And he hasn't called you to that either.

Sure, we need to have clean homes. But perfect? No.

In this chapter you will find many ideas to help get your housecleaning done and your home organized. The point is not to help you be Missy Prissy in the housekeeping department. I want you to be free for more important things than chasing stuff around the house. I dream of you working alongside your kids as you train them to work with a godly work ethic. In no way is this about getting a perfectly clean or tidy house. It is about putting systems in place that lighten your workload and help you be more strategic in training your children.

To ensure that you don't lose your mind, it is important that you keep the easy stuff easy and the simple stuff simple.

Get Vicious

To begin with, we need to become vicious. Not with the kids, of course, but with our stuff. There is a saying that goes something like this: A place for everything and everything in its place. It's an important principle to learn and to pass on to your children.

The way to make this happen is to start in one room. Choose a room that you use most often . . . like the kitchen. Start by going through each cupboard and drawer. Remove all the things that don't work, are broken, you never use, or you have duplicates of. Put them in a box (or a few of them) marked "To Go." If you plan on having a garage sale, you could even be pricing them as you put them in the box.

Some of you are already hyperventilating. Take a deep breath—this will take more than one day. Plan on a room a month. If your house has three bedrooms, a kitchen, a dining room, two bathrooms, a living room, a laundry room, a storage room and two halls (including entrances and their closets), that's twelve months. You can take a whole year to do this, maybe even a little more. Just do one room at a time.

Once you have decluttered your cupboards and drawers, go back through each one and make it work. Try to keep like things together. Put all your baking supplies together. Keep your measuring utensils together. Your lunch bags/boxes and water bottles should be kept in the same place. Paper plates, napkins, and plastic cutlery are easiest to find when you keep them in the same place.

Making your cupboards work for you also means considering your usage of each item. I very rarely use my punch bowl, so it is in a corner cupboard in my kitchen that is very awkward and difficult to get into. I don't want to be going in there often so I would definitely not keep my coffee mugs there. Use the very top shelves for things you don't need as often, and the lower shelves for things you use frequently. It makes sense in most kitchens to keep the dishes you use all the time close to the dishwasher. When it comes to plastic margarine, yogurt, and sour cream containers, use your viciousness! Do you really need forty-five containers? Could you keep just five or so? Maybe get rid of them all and invest in some clear, see-through containers. This also helps avoid opening all five sour cream containers in the fridge only to discover that you actually don't have any sour cream at all but you sure do have a lot of leftovers that have gone bad.

When our children were little, I used a cupboard under my kitchen counter to keep our plates and cups. I did this so that my kids could help set the table and empty the dishwasher more easily because everything they needed access to was within their reach. There is no rule for what has to go where in your kitchen, so be the boss and make it work.

And give yourself freedom to change things up as you go. It is not uncommon for me to change around a cupboard or two every six months or so to keep things fresh and working well for us.

Once you've gotten a drawer or cupboard set to work for you, invite the kids and your hubby, if he is around, for a tour and explanation of the new space. Make sure you tell them why you changed things around and how you think this new system will make things smoother for the family. Do this for each cupboard or drawer, or room, or closet. Encourage them to keep it up.

If you have children who are natural organizers, boost their confidence by recruiting them to be your helpers. My oldest son is gifted at organization so we work together on many things around the house.

The next rooms you may want to be vicious in are the kids' bedrooms. These rooms have to work extremely well. Make sure that you have a place for dirty clothes and a place where clean clothes can be "deposited." Together with each child, go through the clothing, and be vicious! If it is not a favorite, put it in the garage-sale or giveaway box. If it has stains or holes, out it goes. Cut down the amount of clothing drastically. And don't replace it. The less clothing everyone has, the less there is to wash, put away, and pick up off the floor when it's *not* put away. The same thing goes for shoes. If your teenage daughter (or you) want to own twenty-seven pairs of shoes, make sure she's aware of what she will have to sacrifice to find the space and place to keep them all. If the stress of keeping more than what you need outweighs the benefit of having it available, it needs to go. Be vicious!

School backpacks and sports bags are notoriously dropped at the front door. Put up hooks near the door and encourage the kids to use them. Your encouragement may come in many forms. You could set a price per backpack, and what you find on the floor is yours unless the "fee" is paid. Feel free to make it a per-day charge. Or hang it up for them, along with a little note that invoices them for your effort. Make sure the invoice is large enough to be a strong encouragement. Do the same with jackets, hats, and other items that habitually aren't taken care of. If everything has a place and is returned to its place after use, you will have less stress running out the door because someone can't find what they need.

Remember that lunch bags and boxes that are not removed promptly from backpacks are also a source of stress. Make it simple and keep it simple. Let your children know that if they do not bring their lunch containers to you or their designated spots by the preset time, with all the leftovers disposed of appropriately, then you will not make them a lunch for the next day. Either they will have to do it themselves, or they don't get lunch. If your children make their own lunches, make sure this gets done the night before.

Set a time, and make it the same time each day, to go through the kids' backpacks together with them. This will give you a chance to connect with them about what happened at school, sign notes, read agendas, and take care of all the other things that can be forgotten otherwise.

Dirty laundry can cause stress for most families. In our house that stress often takes the form of one or two people without clean undies on a morning when we are all in a rush. Simplify your laundry system so that it is easy to stay on top of and you know what has to be washed next.

Find yourself five plastic bins; lids are not necessary. Label the bins: Whites and Bleachables, Light Colors, Darks, Reds, and Rags and Towels. Put these bins in a location that is easily accessible to each family member. In one house we lived in, each bedroom had its own set of bins. Sometimes the bins have been kept in our laundry room. In the house we are in now, the laundry bins live in a closet under the stairs. When the kids put their pajamas on, they are to put their clothes either back into their drawer to be worn again, up on their wall hook for the next day, or into the right laundry bin. (Go to my website, www.carlaanne.com, to download your free fully color-coded laundry bin labels.)

If you do a "flip 'n' fold" (put a load in the washer, flip a wet load to the dryer, and fold what was done in the dryer) at breakfast, another at lunch or just after work/school, and a third before bed, you will never, ever have large loads or many loads to do. You will even find at times there is no laundry waiting to be washed. (That is the perfect time to strip a bed!) You will always know which load is the most needed by glancing at your bins and choosing the fullest one.

Again, this is your opportunity to be vicious! If someone needs an article of clothing that has not been washed because it wasn't in the laundry bin, too bad! If there is enough time to get the item washed, you can set a price to do the job. But remember, you are not a housemaid, slave, or laundry service. You are a parent. Your time is valuable. Set your price and stick to it. Maybe the cost is not money, but other chores, tasks, or services that your child can perform.

After several reminders to our daughters to clean up their clothes from the floor of the room they share, they still had not done so. I let them know that I would be doing impromptu visits. If I saw something on the floor, I would collect it and they could only buy it back for a fee. They agreed. Within two days, the floor was covered again. We collected the clothing (enough to fill a large black garbage bag) and removed it. It took a few weeks of them wearing the same old outfits day after day before one of them finally decided she wanted her stuff back. She paid the hefty fee (with a few complaints about how it was more than what we originally paid for her clothes at Value Village) and has kept her floor much cleaner since.

Find a bag to keep music from lessons in. Keep it close to the place where practicing happens. Train your children to always put the music back in the bag after each practice session. This way you will not have the stress of "lost" music, and you will save time getting ready to go because the music will always be in the bag, ready to travel.

Library books can cost a lot if there are overdue fines. Set a day as the library day. Our library day has typically been on Tuesdays. We only take out books or renew them on Tuesdays. That way I only have to do an on-line check for due dates on Tuesday mornings to see what is due. I save my time and reduce my stress. Keep all the library books in a bin or box that is easy to carry. When someone wants to read a book, they get it from the bin. When they are done, it goes back to the bin. Train your children to always put their library books back when they are done. This makes it quite simple to grab the bin and return books without having to go searching the house or van for books.

Be sure your children are paying the fines for books that are not returned on time. This is another natural consequence for their behavior. Don't teach them that you will bail them out for their lack of responsibility or their failure to be respectful of other people's property. Once they enter kindergarten and understand how a library works, they can start paying fines. Remember, your job is to help your children learn this when they are young. When words don't teach, consequences will.

Labeling doors, drawers, boxes, and bins will be helpful for both you and your family. In our garage, duct tape along the bottom of each drawer and door has a list of what is stored inside. My labels say things like: Paint Supplies; Nails & Screws; Handy Tools; Canning Jars; Rope, Bungee Cords, & String; and Light Bulbs. When a bulb burns out in the house, I can ask my seven-year-old to run and get me one because she can read which cupboard it is in. This saves me time and stress. In my coat-closet-turned-pantry, I have labels on my shelves and containers. I tend to empty things from boxes into clear containers so that I can easily see how much is left. That saves me time and stress. There is nothing more frustrating than making dinner, only to find that the cornstarch container is empty when my gravy is on the stove boiling and we have twenty minutes to get to an evening appointment or lesson. All it takes is a glance into my closet to see what I am low on and what needs refilling.

These clear containers don't have to cost you anything up front. Use empty peanut butter containers or canning jars. When I can, I choose to buy groceries that come in clear, reusable containers, preferably square. When they are empty, I wash and stick labels on them, and my cupboards are much more organized. Take advantage of your local thrift shop and garage sales to find clear containers. I've found whole sets for less than a dollar. Dollar stores are also great for finding containers for storage.

What do I keep in the containers? Short of saying "everything," here are some things I have in my pantry in clear containers: flour, sugar, cornstarch, egg substitute, salt, spaghetti, macaroni, rice, dried peppers, spices, beans, lentils, chickpeas, cold cereal, cream of wheat, other hot cereals, popcorn, baking chips, rice flour, raisins, nuts, seeds, baking powder, baking soda, yeast, and crackers.

I much prefer getting rid of the boxes and packaging and keeping everything in the containers. It helps me stay organized and on top of my grocery list.

All the things I have mentioned so far in this chapter are systems that you can put in place to help you run your household more smoothly. In appendix A at the back of this book, you will find books and websites that are chock full of other systems and ways that you can incorporate organization into your life and home. I'm always happy to answer any questions that you e-mail to me or post on my blog.

Train the Children

You can do more to help your home run smoothly than just install systems. It's important that you train your children to contribute to the family. The best way to give them a place of belonging and a strong work ethic is to give them chores and tasks to complete on a regular basis at home.

Children as young as two years old can start doing chores. Here are some tasks your children can be taught to do, and a guideline for what age might be appropriate. Remember, this is a guideline. Adjust the list to fit your children's abilities and gifts.

Ages Two to Four

- Picking up toys
- Bringing trash cans to a central location to be emptied
- Bringing dirty dishes to the sink, counter, or dishwasher
- Putting dirty clothes in the laundry bin
- Helping to put clean clothes in the drawer neatly
- Making their bed (pulling the covers onto the bed and putting the pillow in place)

Ages Four to Seven

- All of the above, plus . . .
- Setting and clearing the table
- Emptying the dishwasher
- Wiping the table and counters
- Dusting flat surfaces (fragile objects toward the seven-year mark)
- Washing and drying dishes by hand

- Sweeping (with a few touch-ups by Mom)
- Cleaning mirrors
- Vacuuming central areas
- Washing vegetables
- Emptying trash cans into larger bags or cans
- Folding socks, underwear, towels, rags, etc.

Ages Seven to Twelve

- All of the above, plus . . .
- Cleaning the kitchen completely after a meal
- Cleaning the bathrooms: toilet, tub, shower, and floor
- Vacuuming well along baseboards, central areas, and stairs
- Washing, peeling, and preparing vegetables for salad and/or cooking
- Some baking, cooking, and frying
- Following a recipe
- Mature and strong kids may be able to mow the grass
- Shoveling snow
- Cleaning out a vehicle
- Helping to wash a vehicle
- Washing a floor with a mop or on hands and knees
- Washing the inside of windows
- Using the washing machine and dryer: A complete flip 'n' fold.
- Folding clothes well
- Preparing a bagged lunch
- Preparing a snack or light meal

Ages Twelve and Up

- All of the above, plus . . .
- Preparing cooked and cold meals
- Putting together a grocery list from a meal plan
- Making a meal plan (according to budget and dietary needs)
- Cleaning and organizing the vehicles
- Preparing the house for overnight guests
- Setting up and taking down Christmas decorations/tree (indoor and outdoor)

- Cleaning out the fridge
- Defrosting a freezer
- Barbecuing safely
- Shopping for groceries (with money supplied)
- Shopping for appropriate clothing
- Organizing the bills and incoming mail

If you are looking at this list and wondering if I'm off my rocker, you are not the first one to think that. But this is the list I have used to raise and train our children. Don't get too worried yet. Keep reading!

All of these things need to be taught. You can't celebrate your children's seventh birthday and then send them out to cut the grass. Take enough time to pre-teach each task. That means that for a while before you ask them to try something, they should be helping you, watching you, asking questions, and playing games with you.

When I was teaching our kids to fold socks and underwear, I taught them to fold well enough so that the items would not come apart if tossed like a football. First they watched me to see how I was doing it and would guess if I had done a good enough job to pass the toss test. Occasionally I would do it poorly, and they'd get all excited about my "mistakes." We then moved on to having them fold them on one side of the room while I sat on the other. They folded socks and undies and tossed them to me. It became a competition between the kids to see who could fold and toss the fastest. Just last night our eleven-year-old son showed me that he has learned to fold underwear better than anyone yet. It's still a game. My husband says when Aethan folds underwear, it lends new meaning to the term *tighty whities*.

When it comes to helping with food prep, I started with shredding cheese. I gave the kids each a stool to stand on and a clean oven mitt on their shredding hand. That way they could shred away at the cheese and not cut themselves. It didn't take long before they asked to do it without the mitt.

MEET TRISH

Name: Trish Isaac

Location: Alberta

Kids: Three (ages 15, 12, 11)

Married: sixteen years

Husband: My husband works on a gas drilling well and is gone for four weeks at a time and then home for two.

Favorites: I love sleeping, Coke, eating what someone else cooks, and nothing that has anything to do with gardening.

Longest time hubby's been away: About six weeks. It was from early October to just before Christmas.

What I'd like others to know: I get very tired of comments like, "Why doesn't he just get a job in the city so he can be home more?" I can't answer that. People demand to know things that they really have no right knowing, yet I feel obligated to defend the life we live. Do I want him home more? Usually. Do I want him following what he feels is God's call? Absolutely. But if this is where God has called him, I want him no place else. I just wish others would understand that.

My struggle: There have been times when I have wanted to give up and start over with someone else. It is hard to walk this road of marriage alone. But God has called me to a standard above my own. Some days it is only this standard that keeps us married.

My strength: I'm not what people would call organized, but I do have some things that I do to make life simpler.

I don't make breakfast. My kids are old enough to pour milk for cereal, make porridge (instant or other), make toast, and eat on their own. I sleep in, and they get their own meals made.

I have the kids do chores and rotate each week so they get experience in different areas of housecleaning. They do the laundry, vacuum, wash floors, and clean the bathrooms. I will help if it's needed, but I don't do the work.

I don't feel bad about picking up fast-food pizza when we have a busy evening or have to be out of the house quickly.

My hope: Because of my husband's absences, I have had to rely on God to be my strength and fortress. I have learned things about God that I could not have learned if Henry was home all the time. God has shown up and been so real to me that I would have trouble trading my spiritual life and growth for time with my husband. Maybe Henry is gone so that we each can learn to love and rely on God more, so we are stronger when we come together. Whatever the reason for frequent time apart, God has our life mapped out. We feel we are following where he has called (as hard as that is for others to understand) and we are living in the strength of the Holy Spirit.

You may wonder, like I have, How can I ask my kids to do chores that they don't see their dad doing? Ideally, our children would see their fathers working around the house and yard, passing on their skills and talents to them. But that is not the case in many of our homes.

I'll venture a bold statement: To *not* teach and *not* expect our children to work around the home would be telling them they are not capable of contributing to the well-being of the world around them.

It is God's plan that work is a blessing. If we don't teach our children how to work and to do it well, we are depriving them of a blessing God has created them for. Whether their dad works around the home or not, God has designed our children for work. Allowing them to get by without working at home will hinder the relationship with God they could be having.

If the subject comes up—and it will—and our children ask why they have to do something that Dad doesn't have to do, fall back on the Word of God. God said it should be used to teach and train: "God has breathed life into all of Scripture. It is useful for teaching us what is true. It is useful for correcting our mistakes. It is useful for making our lives whole again. It is useful for training us to do what is right" (2 Tim. 3:16 NIrv).

Be honest with your children and explain that God has given you the responsibility of training and teaching them. Work is a blessing from the Lord. We need to live all our lives in worship to God. You will give an account to God for how you raised your kids. You will not have to give an account of what your husband did, but you will have to give an account for your actions. Deuteronomy 6:7–9 explains how we need to teach our children God's principles for a godly life: "Repeat them again and again to your children. Talk about them when you are at home and when you are on the road, when you are going to bed and when you are getting up. Tie them to your hands and wear them on your forehead as reminders. Write them on the doorposts of your house and on your gates." Do not be afraid to let your children know, no matter how old they are, that your goal is to raise them, love them, and train them in such a way that you will one day hear Jesus say, "Well done, my good and faithful servant."

We need to speak to our children about our dreams, goals, and desires for them. Help them catch a vision for themselves of what is possible for their futures. Explain how everything we want in life that is good takes work and effort.

If Dad is not doing chores around the house that perhaps he could, be honest in telling your kids that moms and dads don't always choose what is best. Use examples from your own life of when you knew what was right but chose not to do it, and how you paid the price later. Be sensitive. Encourage them to love and respect their dad even though he may make poor decisions that are not to his benefit or theirs. Where possible, and as God prompts you, allow them to bring their honest questions to Dad directly at an opportune time—you may be surprised at the honest replies they receive.

Demonstrate to your kids that, with God's help, we can be honest, hard-working people, regardless of our situations. Teach your children not to compare the amount of work they do to what others do. If at all possible, have your children read biographies of men and women who became successful because of hard work. Give them a high standard to live up to without tearing down your husband.

It is hard to know how to answer those tough questions. At times I have hugged a crying child and cried myself. I've wondered what kind of men and fathers my sons will be when they have homes of their own. Will they leave the work to their wives because they didn't see Dad involved? Will they be more apt to help around the house because they know how heavy the load is?

God knows. He has set before you the task of teaching your children to work. He has not asked you to make excuses for your husband or even give explanations. Take your children, your tasks and chores, your concerns to God. He will give you the answer when you and your children are ready to hear it. Ask God to give your children eyes that see your husband and his contribution to the family in the best light possible.

It may be true that your husband is not doing what he should around the house. Maybe he's not working for income, but is hanging around the house without pitching in. Then again, maybe he's working sixteen-hour days and crashing into bed when he gets home, exhausted from a full day's work. Either way, when your children don't see an example of a man in the house working at home, the job falls to you.

It is your job to train them, teach them and set an example. And yes, it is your husband's job, too. But only God can change his heart. Ask him to. Bring the situation before him. Then relax.

If you burn yourself out working like a madwoman "because somebody's got to do it" instead of doing what you can with the time and energy God has given you, you will be teaching your children a lesson they shouldn't learn. They don't need to learn how to be martyrs. Your job is to teach them to be servants.

Train them to ask the question, How can I best serve the family today?

This may take years. But if you keep at it, saying it out loud for yourself and for them, eventually they will ask the question themselves. It will release them from the pressure of feeling like they need to work hard to replace Dad.

Remember not to place the burden of their father's absence on their shoulders. If you need help from them, ask them plainly. Do not manipulate them. "If your dad wasn't gone all the time, I wouldn't have to do all this work and you'd have more time to play. Sorry you can't go out, but you'll need to vacuum so I can pay the bills that your father didn't take care of before he left again." Words like that are never life-giving. Guard your heart and your tongue. Check your attitude at the Cross, and leave it there.

Training your children will take some time and quite a lot of effort, but you will reap rewards quickly.

If you are interested in other ways to teach your children how to work at home as well as how to implement systems to make your home life less stressful and your housework get done more smoothly, please check my website at www.carlaanne.com. I have materials, ideas, and suggestions that you might find very helpful.

Chapter Eight

Make the Most of Mealtime

I'm not sure who decided that the time between four o'clock in the afternoon and six in the evening was happy hour. It sure isn't at my house!

"When are we eating?"

"What's for supper?"

"Can I have a snack?"

"But, Mom, I don't want to practice now, I'm hungry!"

Happy hour at my house is right after the last child has fallen asleep (or when I have, now that they're older).

Mealtime can be a real struggle for solo parents, and with young kids, it is even worse. When they are hungry it is *now*, not in ten minutes. All of them need everything cut into miniscule pieces, and by the time you've spoon-fed them all, wiped up four spills of juice, pulled a lima bean out of someone's nose, and reheated your food in the microwave twice, they are ready to get down off their chairs and go play. That's when you get to eat. So much for a family dinner, right?

> More than three-fourths of "married single moms" choose less healthy, less nutritious meals when hubby is away. The main reasons? It's simple and the kids won't fuss.

I realized one day as I was making chicken fingers and carrot sticks for the third time in a week that I hadn't cooked a "real meal" in a really long time. I knew my kids loved pork chops, roasted chicken and mashed potatoes, homemade soup, and bread. Come to think of it, so did I! But it was too much work. My kids would inhale most of it in just a few minutes and promptly disappear. That left me to eat the cold remains by myself.

One day our daughter came home from a friend's house and recounted the glorious meal she'd had. Spaghetti with pork chops, vegetables, and juice. "Mommy, there was even dessert!"

I called my friend later to thank her for having my daughter over and inquired about who else had come for dinner. She informed me that it had been just herself with her daughter and mine. "Then why the fancy meal?" I asked.

"Because my daughter needs to know what it is like to have a sit-down family dinner even if my husband never joins us."

Wow. She had prepared this meal because she wanted her daughter to have a family meal and she was worth it. It was normally just the two of them, and I found out she cooked "real meals" then, too. Here I was with five people around my table, yet I had neglected to cook real meals and make an emphasis on family dinner because Trent was gone.

The next day we made a trip to Costco. I bought pork chops, chicken breasts, sausages, roasts, and fish. I made a decision to have a family meal whenever we ate. I would cook healthy, nutritious meals and sit down to share them with my family. I wanted my kids to have the experience of sitting around the table, laughing and joking with each other and fighting over the last piece of choice meat. (Yes, even that is a memory to cherish!) It is important to me that they have favorite recipes that only mom can make. I wanted to build that connection time with them when they were young so that I could count on it when they were older.

The first meal went great but I had to eat like a madwoman to get hot food in my system before the kids were ready to run again. I found I had enough leftovers to last a year. And, quite frankly, there were way more dishes to do when I cooked a "real meal." *Why was I doing this again?*

It just so happened that I went to hear a speaker that weekend.

She spoke about how she set the table with a tablecloth every night, with candles and fancy dishes, because the most important people in her life were coming to dinner: her family. She was talking about her kids and her husband. It floored me. I had always thought that the fancy stuff was for guests and strangers. I had a set of everyday dishes and a set of good dishes. She challenged us to treat our immediate families as guests of honor.

The next day, I went about getting a tablecloth on the table, setting it really nicely, and making a great dinner. It failed miserably. For all my good intentions, my toddler thought the tablecloth was a great pull toy. A "good" plate was dropped to the floor (and although it didn't break, the ensuing crying from the sound of the crash just about did me in). Once again, by the time I had everyone's plates ready to eat, and the babies fed, my portion was cold.

Should I give up on the dream of a family dinner? Or should I fight to keep it?

I decided that it was worth it, but I had to make it work for me. So I began a system of trial and error that has evolved over time. We have found our family meal, and it's become a staple in our home. Whether Trent is home or not, the kids can count on sitting down as a family for our meals. When Trent is home, he joins us. (We just have to remember to set him a place at the table.)

A few months ago, someone dropped in during the day. It was just past noon, and she was on her lunch break. We invited her in, and in a matter of a minute or so had a setting for her at the table, as well. She joined all six of us around our table. We enjoyed a nice visit before she left for home. Later she commented that she had no idea families still ate sit-down meals together, especially at lunch time.

I was thrilled! Our family meals have become such an important part of our lives. We eat breakfast, lunch, and dinner together. Whoever is home, that is. When the kids are out with friends, we miss them. Friends that are at our house during mealtime join us at the table even if they're not hungry. Our meals are not fancy, we don't use a tablecloth, and I usually put the cooking pots on the table so we can serve ourselves. We're down-home-type folks.

Why the Family Meal Is Important

Child Trends Data Banks reports the following based on a 2003 Child Trends Survey:

Like other forms of parental involvement, research shows a positive relationship between frequent family dinners and positive teen behavioral outcomes. Teens who regularly have meals with their family are less likely to get into fights, think about suicide, smoke, drink, use drugs, and are more likely to have later initiation of sexual activity, and better academic performance than teens who do not. Even after controlling for family connectedness, more frequent family meals have been found to be associated with less substance use, fewer depressive symptoms, and less suicide involvement, and with better grades.

Eating with parents is also an important factor for the nutrition and eating habits of adolescents, with research showing that family meals and parental presence at meals is associated with higher intake of fruits, vegetables, and dairy products. In addition, family mealtimes may influence whether an adolescent develops disordered eating. One study found that adolescents who reported frequent and structured family meals and a positive atmosphere at family meals were less likely to have disordered eating habits, with the association being stronger for girls.[1]

Shirley Dobson, wife of Dr. James Dobson, founder of Focus on the Family, cites a 1996 study done by Harvard Graduate School of Education professor Dr. Catherine Snow that revealed similar results: "By following 65 families over an eight-year period, it was determined that dinnertime was of more value to child development than playtime, school and story time. Clearly, there is power in family fellowship."[2]

As a solo parent I often struggled with fatigue along with the overwhelming frustrations of raising little children. The end of the day would come, and I'd remember all the good intentions I'd had in the morning that had not been realized. I wanted to read stories, snuggle up on the couch, and share tender moments with my babies. Other moms seemed to find time and energy to get down on the floor and play trucks and Barbies, but not me. If I finally sat down and it was quiet enough to read or play, I either fell asleep, the phone rang, or the kids were already in bed.

Realizing that the family meal was more important than all those things put together, I had new hope. I want to raise kids who are healthy, well-adjusted, and bolstered against the harsh winds that will blow against them. I'm sure you do, too.

The effort required to make the family meal a priority in your home will be more than worth it. Your children will benefit. You will get to know them more and more. Building memories around the table will give you all a sense of belonging and a place to fit in.

How to Establish the Family Meal

Choose Your Meal. Start by deciding which meal or meals of the day you will designate as family meals. We started with supper. Your family might choose breakfast or lunch. What happened in our family is that as we began the routines around the table, we naturally gravitated toward doing those same things at every meal. Now as my kids approach their teens, they still often think that we haven't had a real meal unless it's been a sit-down meal—even if they've had more than enough food already on their own.

Breakfast can be easier to have as a family meal because most people are in the same place at the same time, especially as the kids get older. This may mean getting up a little earlier than usual to make sure that you have that extra time together. If the first person is out the door by seven thirty in the morning, you may want to be at the table by seven, planning to be done in half an hour or less. Some people can get ready before breakfast; others can get ready after the meal.

Lunch works well only if your kids are at home all day or come home for lunch. If your hubby is around, that's even better. At our house, our lunches are almost always just the five of us. Even when Trent is home, he often doesn't eat lunch or eats in his office. That does not deter us. The rest of us still sit down together.

Suppertime can also work well. Plan it early enough that no matter what scheduled evening events take place, your supper hour can stay fairly consistent. Earlier is also good because if you can curb the after-school snacks, you will have hungrier kids to eat your nutritious cooking. Sometimes this can be an easier time to get conversation going because you've all just come from your busy days, and your activities are still fresh in your minds.

No matter which meal you choose, be consistent with it and keep it up for a long time. Feel free to add flexibility as needed, but communicate to your family that this meal is a non-negotiable. They may only be excused for certain reasons, approved by you of course.

Make Easy Meals. Unless you are a gourmet cook or have endless hours to spend in the kitchen, the family meal can become a burden. That's why it is of utmost importance to keep the meal simple. The purpose of the meal is not to display your prowess in the culinary arts, but to establish a tight connection with your family. Remember, the goal is not to be SuperMom. Be all you can be, but only ever be yourself.

Breakfast can be cold cereal, oatmeal, toast and jam, eggs, pancakes, or a gourmet quiche. Plan ahead to make it easy. Know the night before what you are going to put out and make sure you have all the ingredients. Nothing's worse than getting everyone to the table only to find your plan for cold cereal won't work because you are out of milk, there are only three slices of bread in the bag, and you haven't left enough time for pancakes.

To help our family budget, our morning time constraints, and the decision-making process, I came up with a very simple plan. Mondays, Wednesdays, and Fridays, we have hot oatmeal. I sometimes make baked oatmeal with cranberries and cinnamon for a special treat on those days. Tuesdays we eat Cream of Wheat, and Thursdays we have Red River Cereal. We have cold cereal on Saturdays, and I often prepare a hearty brunch on Sundays. We have two people in our family with allergies, so they eat alternate foods such as rice cakes or buckwheat porridge.

You need to find a system that works for you. Don't follow mine unless it fits your family. The whole point is making this easy for you and sustainable for a very long time.

For our family lunches, we have regular lunch foods. Some of our regular options are sandwiches, soup, salad, or leftovers. Our children are all home-schooled at this point, so we are all at home for lunch. Most days I put a bag of bread and a selection of toppings such as peanut butter, tuna, sandwich meat, cheese, lettuce, and tomatoes onto the counter. Then I call the kids to make their own sandwiches and put them on their own plates. They sit down at the table and wait for everyone else to join them. Once we've all been seated, we pray a blessing over the food and dig in.

During busy periods in our life, the kids make themselves bag lunches the night before. They eat out of the bag at lunch, but all together at the table or in the van or wherever we are. What you eat for these meals and how it is packaged is not important. I can't stress it enough. The whole point is that you connect as a family.

Our suppers are usually fast and easy. Although I like cooking, I don't have the time in my schedule to spend preparing gourmet meals. My slow cooker is my best friend, and tied for second are my microwave and pressure cooker. I'm all about quick and nutritious.

A few years ago I started taking meat out of the freezer on Sunday nights. I put it in the fridge where it will take days to thaw. I never have to worry that I don't know what to make because I have plenty of ready-to-go options in the fridge. In the mornings, usually just before breakfast or while the kids are cleaning up their dishes, I'll fill the slow cooker with ingredients and turn it on. Then I can forget about it until suppertime.

I also learned to cook enough for two or three meals at a time. My plan is to have enough leftovers at every meal to supply my freezer with "fast food" options. Stock up on freezer containers or foil containers with lids, and put your leftovers in them after dinner. Label them with the contents and the date. That way if ever you need a quick meal, it's ready. Pop it in the microwave or oven, and away you go! (Foil containers can't go in the microwave, so if you plan to use one, consider getting some reusable, freezer-to-microwave containers.)

Sitting down for a family meal doesn't mean that you have to have made it from scratch, either. Give yourself a break: throw a pizza in the oven, throw a bag of premade salad in a bowl, and there you go. A great meal in minutes. Reduce your stress by giving yourself the freedom to do what is easiest on you, while still allowing yourself to feel comfortable that your family is eating healthy, nutritious meals.

Because of our budget and the allergies of some of my family members, I do end up cooking more "from scratch" meals. There are many days, though, that we fall back on easy food. We make fried eggs for supper sometimes. Recently the day ran away with me, and the beans I had planned to throw in the pressure cooker were still on the counter, dry, at six in the evening. I hadn't taken any meat out of the freezer (because I had planned on beans), we were out of salad fixings, and the kids were hungry *now*. So I threw a few potatoes in the microwave, and twelve minutes later we sat down to a simple baked potato on each plate.

The point is not that we had an extremely simple meal. The point is we sat down and ate our simple meal together. As the banter of "pass the salt" and "I need the sour cream" was volleyed over our table I also heard about their days. I learned that one friend has a cousin moving here from another country, and that my daughter needs a new swimsuit. One of the kids told a joke we'd all heard a hundred times, but we laughed again.

Our daughter had a little friend over last week. She is from a family of five children and a great home. She arrived to play just as I called the kids to the table. I told her she needed to join us because our family rules were that everyone sits at the table when we eat. She sat between my daughters and watched while we ate. (I did offer her food, but apparently she'd already eaten.) She smiled the entire time. Her eyes danced from person to person as the conversation jumped around the table. As they left the table after being excused, I overheard her say to my daughter, "Your family sure talks a lot at supper."

It's true. We do talk a lot at supper. That's how we stay connected. Your family needs that connection, too.

MEET LISA

Name: Lisa Riley

Location: North Dakota

Kids: two (ages 4, 1)

Married: seven years

Husband: Gary is a field technician who does on-site program-ming, installing, and maintaining of equipment in three states.

Favorites: I love Mexican and Italian foods, but I especially love try-ing new kinds of foods, Ted Dekker books are among my favorites, and chocolate milk is my drink of choice.

Longest time hubby's been away: two to three weeks (sometimes over holidays!)

My cooking tip: My children are so young that they hardly eat any-thing, so making a full meal is pointless. I'm the one who will end up eating most of it. Sometimes I prepare a large meal the night before hubby leaves so we can have leftovers for a couple of days. It's my way of getting food while he's gone without having to cook every day.

My struggle: Discipline is a real struggle for me. My four-year-old daughter has attitudes that I understand are typical for her age but can be very challenging—especially when jealousy of her baby brother rears its head. I'll express my frustration on the phone to my hubby, and over the phone he will start telling me what I should do to discipline. It's frustrating for us both. He wants to help, especially when she is disrespectful to me, but without him actually being there during the "incident" it's all up to his interpretation of what I've told him, and we both end up being frustrated.

My strength: My four-year-old and I kind of have a special tradition that makes things special when Daddy is away. Part of our bedtime routine is to read stories. We read one or two books when Daddy is home, but we read five to six when he is gone. When he's gone, we also watch videos and I snuggle in bed with her while we watch. If my two children wake up in the night while my husband is gone, I let them sleep in my bed with me.

My hope: Because we both have Christ in our lives, we have the same foundation for all things. Our decision making, our disciplining, our relationship choices—they are so similar because of that foundation. We know if we keep him the center that the rest will work itself out. We have our disagreements, but because of our love and commitment to each other, we always seem to get things worked out.

Connect at the Table. Because the family meal is not about the food or its presentation, your greatest efforts should be spent on the most important thing—connecting with your family. If you are not used to it, it can be an intimidating idea.

My husband can attest to the fact that I'm not a natural encourager. I'd sit at the table during our family meals saying things like: "Chew with your mouth closed." "Use your fork." "Cut your meat properly." "Get your feet off the table!" I'd be left at the table wondering what was supposed to be so great about eating dinner together.

At that point I picked up a book on parenting. I can't remember which one because there have been many. This particular book stressed how parents have a unique opportunity to speak blessing and encouragement into our children. I read how each negative comment needed seven to ten positive ones to counteract it. I tried to think back to how often I had said something encouraging to my kids that day, or that week. I was ashamed to find none at all.

My daily communication with the kids tended to center around instruction and correction. "Please pick up the toys." "Go wash your face." "What do you say?" "Eat your food." "Do you need to go potty?" "Are you done yet?" "Don't hit your brother." "Put your shoes on." "Who wants to go to the park?" "It's bedtime!"

So I set my mind to be more of an encourager.

Right. You can guess how that worked out. I didn't even last a whole day! Frustrated with myself but not willing to give up, I developed a plan.

I assigned each person in our family to a day of the week. It just so happened that we were all born on a different day of the week, with one day left over to give to God. Wednesday was my youngest daughter's day. So on Wednesdays after everyone was seated at the table and before we said grace for our food, everyone would take a turn telling her what we loved about her and encouraging her. She also had to say something about herself that she loved.

This quickly became a loved tradition! Who doesn't love hearing those kinds of things from the people they love? It gave me a time during the day to look my kids straight in the eyes, use my words to express love and encouragement, and then say, "I love you."

I also used those moments to cut up food, fill plates and cups, and tie on bibs while we all sat around the table. This meant that by the time we were all done encouraging each other, it was time to pray. After we prayed, everyone could eat at the same time, including me! This practice slowed down our mealtime and gave us a bit of a release from the pressure of the hours before it.

Use your moments at the table to encourage your family, listen to them, and enjoy them. Don't be too worried if there are quiet moments. That's good. Hopefully it means that people are thinking or enjoying their food. Plan a few good questions and have them up your sleeve. Ask them at the table and make sure everyone answers them! Here are a few I've used:

- If you could have any career in the world, what would it be?
- What are two of your strengths and weaknesses? (Mom goes first on this one!)
- What foods do you think should never be served together?
- What is your favorite shade of blue (or green or red or yellow)?
- Where would you live if you could take all your best friends and family with you?
- If you could make a movie of your life, what would you call it and who would be the lead star?

Come up with your own, or check back on my website for other great questions. The best questions don't have one-word or yes-or-no answers. Find questions whose answers require an explanation. You should always be able to ask "why" or "explain what you mean by that" after someone gives their answer.

Talk about what's happening and what's coming up. Ask specific questions about certain friends or teachers. Watch for pained answers or a look of hurt in their eyes. Gently draw out the information that they desperately want and need to share, but are not sure how. Be prepared to put your fork down and keep your eyes on the one talking. This may be a moment you would regret if you simply let it slip by. Your sensitivity in this hour is crucial.

Keep your laughter near the surface and your words to a minimum. Your eyes and ears should be working overtime. This is the perfect time for you to follow the example of Mary, Jesus' mother, as she "kept all these things in her heart and thought about them often." Soak in what is happening around you. Savor the moments.

Not every meal will be full of depth and substance. Some will have more bickering than talking. Other things, such as a knock at the door, a spilled casserole, a screaming baby, or an incessantly ringing phone, can keep the environment anything but calm. That's okay. Let your children know that this is not about performance. It is about connecting with them in the midst of life, and things don't have to be perfect in order to build better relationships.

Guard the Family Meal. Setting the time for your meal is important. If your kids know the family meal is at five thirty every evening and that they are expected to be in their seats or helping to prepare it by a certain time, it will be easier for them to plan their time accordingly. Little children's tummies will get accustomed to a certain eating time. If your time has to change daily, then as soon as you know what time supper will be, let everyone know. If you have made them aware that supper is at six, there can be no complaint that they are not finished with their video game when you call them to the table. Be firm. You are doing what is best for them now and for their futures. This is important.

You may want to consider allowing the answering machine or voice mail to pick up your calls during this meal. If your phone has a ringer volume or switch, turn it off or as low as it will go to minimize distraction. Depending on how old your kids are, this may work best. When you have toddlers, any moment away from the table or with your ear on the phone brings you one moment closer to disaster. When you have teens who seem to be attached to the handset permanently, you can have them answer as long as they are answering only to give a promise for a call back. And as for texting or messaging on iPods or phones at the table? No sirree! Even cell phones go off. This is family time!

I have found that answering the phone during a meal can distract my mind from paying attention to the people with whom I am trying to connect. If you have asked your kids to give their undivided attention and make the family meal a priority, it is important that you do likewise! Treat your time with them at the table as something special. Let them know that even business calls and urgent matters can wait for thirty minutes.

Help your kids get to the table and stay there. We've made a rule at our house that nobody eats until we've all said grace together. This keeps us from having some start before others and being finished too soon. We began holding hands to pray because we had some "food grabbers" in our family. There seemed to be a faster-than-the-speed-of-light-prayer-amen and before anyone could take a breath, hands were flying to the serving dishes to get the best portions. When the kids were little, we said our prayer holding hands, then we had to squeeze after we said amen. It helped slow them down.

As they've gotten older, we've given them more responsibility with this prayer time. I will ask a person by name to pray the blessing. I've encouraged them to talk to God about the day, the blessings he's provided, and the meal before us. I've discouraged the use of memorized graces for the meal. I want them to slow down enough to think and be grateful.

Once the meal is over at our house, no one can leave the table until everyone is finished eating and they've expressed their thanks to the cook and been excused by me (or Trent when he's home). I noticed how books, computer games, friends, and any number of other very interesting things can motivate children to gobble their food faster than is healthy so they can escape to their fun. Since our kids can't leave early to go play, they have learned to eat more slowly, take their time to enjoy the conversation, and are much more relaxed at the table. When we have guests (even now that our kids are older), as soon as our guests are done, I politely say something like, "I hope you had enough to eat and that you'll join our family tradition to stay at the table until everyone is finished eating." It is rare that a guest will refuse the invitation.

Train your children's friends to follow your house rules. They will respect you for it, and it will ease the stress for your child. Set the ground rules at the first visit (or the next visit after you get your family meal established), and then keep it up. We've had to tell one of our daughter's friends that if she can't follow our meal rules, then she can't come over for supper. She hasn't been over for a meal in a long time. At her last visit, she informed me that she is ready to try again.

Take Time for the Family Meal

The average fine-dining establishment will allow about an hour per reservation when they book meals. When people make a point to have dinner, it takes time. You can't just gobble your food and guzzle some conversation and expect that you've connected. Open up your mealtime schedule. Breakfast takes less time than lunch and supper. The other meals can easily take forty-five minutes to an hour. You might be done eating in twenty minutes, but you might not be done connecting.

When you are finished with your food, push your plate up onto the table, lean back in your chair (or if you're like me, you prefer to set your elbows on the table and rest your chin on your hands), and assume a posture that says, "Although my plate is empty, I'm not finished enjoying my family." Work hard to get away from the rush and bustle of your to-do list for this hour, and focus on being a connected family.

The family meal is an investment in your family. If my suggestions don't work for you, then don't use them! Find something that works for you, but whatever you do, find something.

Just because you are a solo parent does not mean that your children don't need the stability and security that the family meal provides. Actually, they need it so much more. We've all heard statistics about how difficult it is for kids to grow up without the positive and consistent influence of a dad. The family meal will not replace him. It will, however, give them a strong cord of family ties binding them to those who share the table—including their father when he is around. It will give you a doorway into their lives and give them a significant sense of belonging. The family meal can weave you closer to each other than you ever imagined.

Chapter Nine

Celebrations Wrapped in Loneliness

The first birthday parties, Easter Sundays, and anniversaries that you spend at home with your kids and without your husband are hard. Marriage is about sharing joys and exciting moments. It's about building memories together. Marriage affords you the privilege of engaging in life's pleasures with someone you love in order to enhance not only the experience but the relationship. That's why it hurts to celebrate alone.

Just like we never planned to do the solo parenting thing—and if we did, it was not supposed to last very long—we didn't count on celebrating alone, either. Every time we build happy family memories without our husbands, it becomes more difficult to connect deeply with each other. We get closer to the path that takes us away from here, where we are happily married, to that place where it's not so happy and maybe we're not even married.

Some authors have likened marriage to bank accounts that receive deposits of love and from which withdrawals are taken. For most moms, any celebration that Dad is not a part of is equivalent to a massive withdrawal from her love account. We can smile at the day and give lip service to how we understand his absence. Yet if our emotions were evaluated honestly, we would have to say it hurts and makes us feel lonely.

There are times we plan our children's birthday parties and special events when Dad is not around. We do it on purpose because it fits our schedules better. But that's not what I'm talking about. It's when every possible opportunity is given to make it feasible for Dad to be there, but he can't or won't be. It's when your mom calls to wish you a happy anniversary, but he forgets. Those times when Christmas trees are set up, lights are hung, candles are lit, and you snuggle on the couch by yourself in the dim light, remembering Christmases past and wondering if they will always be like this. That's when it hurts.

Holding back tears as you see your daughter's overflowing eyes because Daddy missed seeing her dance her first recital. It's hard to fight against the resentment in your heart as you watch your son throw his baseball bat in the dirt with anger after hitting a home run because Dad wasn't there to see it . . . again. It's the feeling you get when you catch your child showing your husband what he got from him for his birthday because Dad didn't know what was in the package from him.

We may try to convince ourselves that celebrations are not a big deal or that having them on the exact day really doesn't matter. Deep down, though, we are not fooled. We want someone to remember. We want someone to care. We want someone to make it special. We want it to be our husbands.

Chick flicks are full of those perfect moments when Prince Charming arrives just in time. Or the heroine gets a surprise bouquet of balloons and flowers just when she thinks everyone's forgotten. We watch as the good-looking movie star turns down the lights, strikes a match to start a fire, hands his love a glass of champagne, and snuggles beside her for an intimate anniversary celebration together. Why do we like these movies so much? Because we wish our lives were just like that: perfect!

But because they are not, because the men we married are not around, we are disappointed. Deeply disappointed.

We could just throw in the towel. The option is open for us to say, "This is just too hard. I give up." Or we can call on God to show us, teach us, and grow us in the art of celebrating—even when we're lonely. That is the higher calling.

I believe you are the kind of woman who is going to choose to reach for that high standard. With God all things are possible!

Involving Dad

One of our goals as married solo parents is to involve our husbands in our children's lives. We can't assume that they will catch up on their own when they are able to engage with us again. As a matter of fact, leaving it up to them to ask about the details, inquire about how things went, and want to see pictures sets them up for failure and sets you up for a grave letdown.

We need to give our husbands every opportunity to shine, to get it right. That means we have to go the extra mile when it comes to special events. Even as we prepare and plan, we need to be searching out ways to involve and include them in the event. There may be some events where the only way to include them is to show them the pictures after it's all said and done. No matter how much participation they are willing or able to give, it is most beneficial for you, your children, and your marriage to make available for him as many ways to connect with the event as possible.

There are ways to invite your husband to your family celebrations without insulting him or accusing him of past absences. See if any of these might work for you:

- Tell him about an upcoming event (birthday party, family gathering, some other special occasion) and ask him to tell you which days he can make it. Have him write it in his schedule. Let him know you are counting on him.
- Ask him what he would like to be responsible for on that day (such as barbecuing, driving, or refereeing the water-balloon fight).
- Offer to have a back-up plan in case he can't make it at the last minute, and have him plan it with you.
- Have your children invite him personally or with a written invitation card.
- Ask him or his assistant to reserve that spot on his calendar.
- Ask him to make the phone invitations.

You can also involve him by having him call at a strategic moment (just like in the movies). If it is difficult for him to remember to call, then arrange with him that you will call him at an important point in the celebration, fill him in on the details, and offer to give the phone to the special guest of honor or broadcast your husband's celebratory words over the speaker phone.

Webcams are great! If your husband is away a lot for work, invest in a webcam system that you can both operate. Our son's last birthday supper was made extra special as my parents came over and, together with Trent on the webcam, we lit the candles on his cake and all sang "Happy Birthday." It took less than ten minutes out of Trent's schedule, but it was worth it for McCaellen.

Take a lot of pictures, and then make a scrapbook for him or e-mail them to him. If he'll be home shortly, make a date to hang out on the couch so you can show him the photos and explain what is happening in each of them.

Make a point not to purchase any gifts for your kids or other family members without talking to your husband first and giving him the opportunity to be involved in at least the decision making. You'd be surprised how generous he might be if given the chance! I remember one year when I wanted to get something in particular for my daughter. There was the generic brand or the brand name. When I called to talk to Trent, he got quite excited about getting her the "real deal." We spent the extra money, and I made sure that she called him immediately after she opened it when the excitement was still fresh.

Perhaps he has ideas that you would not have considered. One year when planning our son's birthday party, I had decided on a Spiderman theme. When I talked on the phone with Trent about it, he suggested a Bibleman theme. He remembered we had gotten our son a Bibleman movie for a gift earlier, and that he'd been thrilled with it. I looked into it, and he thought the extra money for the specialty party would be worth it. He missed most of that party. He arrived home just as the last person was leaving. But he heard all about the fun and excitement, and he saw the messy evidence that it had been a success. He was proud to have come up with such a great idea.

Involve your husband as much as you can. If he doesn't enter into the celebrations of your family on his own, bring them to him. This takes work and is not fair. We know, though, that anything worth something is going to take work, and that life is not fair. We also know that the effort to love our husbands and keep including them in our lives is one more way to honor the men God has given us.

Giving Dad Every Chance to Succeed

My husband has forgotten my birthday many times. Last year I reminded him a week after it was over that he'd forgotten . . . again! Some years, he's remembered and given me birthday blessings. It helps that I now schedule reminders into his Palm Pilot starting a few months before my birthday. I'm shameless. The entries read: "Reminder, go shop for that beautiful wife of yours. It will take you a long time to find the perfect gift so start today!" Memos like this and others pop up with alarms every week or so at random times. It's become a happy little tradition for us. He'll call home one day in the middle of May, and I can hear the smile in his voice as he says, "Someone's been tampering with my Palm Pilot again. So what do you want for your birthday this year?" Seeing how my birthday is in August, I can dream big in May.

I have a friend who has three children, and all their birthdays are within two weeks of each other. Another friend has four kids whose birthdays all fall within ten days of each other. If you have a stretch of time where celebrations are happening left, right, and center, considering asking your hubby to take vacation time for a few days during that busy week annually. It will guarantee he's home and will hopefully lend even more of a celebratory feel to the week.

We've done that around Christmas. Not only do we celebrate the birth of Jesus, but we also have a Christmas Eve birthday boy, and two January birthdays. For several years now, Trent has been taking the week between Christmas and New Year's as a vacation. He helps me with the celebrations at the beginning and end of it with the understanding that all the days in between are truly "off": no guests, no plans, and lots of pajama days.

Buy a couple boxes of all-occasion cards and birthday cards to have on hand. As events are approaching on the calendar, fill out the cards to the appropriate child or family member. You can ask your husband to sign them if he is around (or have him sign the whole box before he leaves or when he has free time). Address the envelope (even if it is your address for one of your children). If your husband is traveling away from home, ask him to drop the cards in the mail, or do it yourself. Your children will be thrilled to receive a card from their dad, letting them know that he's thinking about them. They don't need to know he was prompted. Make sure they call him immediately to tell him thanks and let him hear their enthusiasm. It will pave the way for the next card.

It's Okay to Be Sad

We all know, though, that no matter what we try, there are times when our husbands just won't be there. That is when we need to become women of character, strong and creative, ready to face the lonely moments head on.

Your children may cry and wish Daddy was there. Moms are often willing to sacrifice their needs and wants so that their children don't have to suffer. You may feel like raising your fists and yelling, "I don't care if you don't show up for my birthday, but you're breaking your child's heart. Can't you see that?!" We all know that doesn't help though, does it?

The breaking of a mother's heart often starts with her arms wrapped around a little body shuddering with sobs. That mother realizes there is nothing—nothing—she can do to fix things.

When you see your children hurting and missing their dad, it is the hardest thing to not allow a root of resentment, anger, hurt, and betrayal take residence in your heart. It's those times when we need to hold our children close and pray. Pray for them. Pray for ourselves. Pray for our husbands. Pray for hope.

It's at times like these when each of us will need to be prepared to hear the still, small voice of God. Escaping to his presence is the only way to guarantee keeping our heart soft toward the man who has hurt our children's hearts, and ours. Allow the Holy Spirit to wash over you and give you strength. He is our only hope.

As you answer your children's questions, tell the truth. It is okay to tell them you are also sad that Daddy can't be there. Explain to them that even though it is hard, the celebration can still be good. Give them permission to enjoy themselves. Some children find it difficult to fully engage in a celebration if they think they are betraying a parent who can't be there. Teach your children through your words and actions that celebrating is important and that it is possible to enjoy the day even when you miss someone. If there are tears, allow them. Dry them with your love. Then teach your children how to step forward into what the day holds for them.

Let the Old Pass and the New Begin

Our children used to watch Donut Man movies when they were little. One of the episodes had Duncan the Donut and a group of children singing a song based on 2 Corinthians 5:17. The words to the song are: "If any man is in Christ, he is a new creation. The old has passed away; behold the new has come!"

This verse in the Bible is referring to us. We are new creations, new people when we have traded our sinful lives for the sacrifice of Jesus on the cross.

Yet there may be a deeper lesson for us as solo parents.

We hold tightly to the past so often. We love tradition. It is comfortable and safe. We know what to expect and how to respond. Yet when our husbands are not with us, our lives are shaken up. What we knew and expected from the past is gone. It has passed away.

As a solo mom you have a choice. Do you want to hang on to what could have been, what once was, or what you had dreamed about, consequently living in disappointment and the shadow of the past? Or are you willing to let go of the old and grab hold of the new that's coming your way?

You can do it! You can lift your chin and look forward to the new that is waiting to arrive in your heart and in your celebrations.

Think about all the celebrations that you have as a family now. Many times we don't even realize how we are setting ourselves and the kids up for disappointment because we are stuck in the old way of doing things. Have you traditionally planned your kids' birthday parties for when your husband is home? Change it around if he can't be there, anyway. Plan the celebrations for a time when you are definitely going to be home alone. You can still involve your husband in many ways, but why not remove the opportunity to have him miss it?

We changed around our birthday celebrations five years ago. The effort and loneliness of planning and carrying out four birthday parties a year was an emotional drain on me. I used a friend's plan as a guide, and we switched to a once-a-year birthday party for all the kids on the same day. We invite all the kids' friends and their families for an afternoon. I plan games and snacks. The invitation I make on the computer asks them to please not bring gifts, but that if they so desire they can bring money to put toward a family gift. I plan it for a time of year where we can celebrate outside.

I have one day for this massive party. The yard is full of guests in lawn chairs and loud, rambunctious kids. We celebrate with a cake, chips, and treats. Games are in stations around our yard. It lasts about three hours, and everyone leaves happy and exhausted. I have only about one hour of cleanup, and then it's over for another year.

Then as each child's birthday approaches, Trent and I plan one afternoon to spend with just that child doing something that would interest them specifically. It is not always on their exact birthday, but as close as our schedules will allow. We've asked our kids if they would like to go back to "regular" birthday parties and the answer is a resounding no. It has become a tradition they cherish. They know that no matter what happens throughout the year, they are guaranteed at least that one afternoon to have both parents' undivided attention. It speaks volumes to us about how important our time and attention is to them.

Then there's Christmas. Do you wait for the perfect day when your husband's home to set up the tree and find that you are doing it in a rush and with bickering and arguments once you finally get to it? Is that the tradition you really want to keep? Why not choose a day to set it all up, decorate it with the kids, and build the suspense by not "flipping the switch" on the lights until Dad is home? Maybe you can convince him to drive through the doughnut shop on his way home and pick up a treat of peppermint hot chocolate and doughnut holes to make this tradition extra special.

When we lived in the United States, we began setting up the tree right after Thanksgiving. While living in Canada, I began setting it up even earlier. I usually aim for the weekend closest to Remembrance Day (November 11). It is a calm, relaxing effort. We untangle the lights and set up the bare, artificial tree on Friday night. The next day we decorate it and usually someone does some baking. Then over the next few days, we spread the rest of the decorations through the house. We do this whether Trent is there to help us or not. He enjoys doing this with us when he's here, but he's realized that the pressure on all of us to wait for his schedule to work is not worth the stress.

We have had to make changes for other celebrations as well. For many years when the girls played at a violin recital, Trent would get them each a rose for when they were done. If he couldn't make it, I'd take it for him, having signed his name to the little card. This last year Trent was away, and although we talked about it, I neglected to order the roses and pick them up. Our girls said nothing to me, but they cried when they called him that evening, asking why he hadn't sent the flowers. His little note—signed by me—indicated to them that Papa was not forgetting about them, even in his absence.

Start new celebrations. When Trent leaves after having been home for a while, we do something special. It often can feel like such a downer for the kids to say good-bye to their dad again. I usually get tired just thinking of all the weeks of flying solo ahead. So we usually get in the van and go someplace special. The kids usually find out what the special event is once we arrive. We've gone to have picnics in the park, to cheap theaters to see old movies, to a friend's house for supper and a playdate, or out to a restaurant for supper.

There have been holidays and other special occasions when Trent's not been home. One particular Thanksgiving I was pretty wrapped up in a pity party of grand proportions. If Trent wasn't going to be home, why should I cook a turkey dinner and have all the mess and clean up? My attitude was terrible, and although I knew it, I wasn't very excited about changing it.

Then I realized that my friend's husband wasn't going to be around, either. So we put our heads together and planned a dinner for the two of us and our six children. We baked a turkey, had sweet potatoes with marshmallows, potatoes, green bean casserole, Jell-O salad, and pumpkin pie for dessert. We were both cooking up a storm in our own homes and then planning to put it together at her house. At the last minute, Trent walked in the door. I had been so caught up in our new Thanksgiving plans that I was almost disappointed! When I called her, I found out her hubby had taken the afternoon off, after all. In the end we ate together as families. Our Thanksgiving turned out perfectly, not because our husbands joined us, but because we were grabbing onto something new with joy and excitement in spite of our circumstances.

Although our husbands can never be replaced, there are times when a substitute is a good idea. If a grandparent or uncle is available to sit in the stands and cheer at a game or to present a bouquet at the end of a performance, your child will know the feeling of being valued and loved. Recently, my husband was commuting from Manitoba, Canada, to Dallas, Texas, for his full-time job. He was supposed to be home for our son's cello recital. McCaellen had worked especially hard at the pieces he was playing and was excited to show off his skills. Two days before the big day, Trent called to say that his boss needed him to stay longer. That meant he'd miss the cello performance. After I hung up I sat my son down and explained that Papa wasn't going to be coming to his concert after all. He threw up his hands and stomped down the stairs shouting out that he had no reason to practice or perform if Trent wasn't going to be there so he wasn't going to play.

After calming myself down, I called my brother to ask him if he could come to the concert. He was busy. So I called my brother-in-law and sister-in-law and invited them to come with their son. I called my dad and mom as well. Everyone gave me a maybe. There was no way I could convince my son to play for a "maybe."

My husband's parents live ten hours away. As it turned out, they were coming through our city that week. I called them to ask if they could please adjust their visit to take in the cello concert. They arrived just an hour or two before it.

After telling McCaellen that very special guests were coming to see him play, he donned his concert attire and packed his cello. The excitement of seeing his relatives there gave him the adrenalin he needed to play like a pro. He told me later he really wished Papa could have seen how well he played, but that he was so glad Grandma and Grandpa had watched him.

We can't always step in and soften the blow for our kids. The disappointment cannot be avoided. But we can acknowledge that it hurts and teach them how to surround themselves with people who can support them.

When I get a blister on my heel, I put a bandage on it. It doesn't make the blister go away. What it does is protect it so I can keep walking.

We cannot prevent our children from experiencing the sadness that comes from celebrating without Dad. What we can do is give them the tools—the bandages—they need to keep living life and celebrating what God has done and is doing even when Dad's not around.

When You Are the One Who Is Lonely

It really is amazing how much one person's absence can affect a whole family. We miss our husbands. At least at first. I remember when I realized I didn't miss him anymore. I could call a good-bye from the kitchen without running to the door and watching him drive away, tears in my eyes. We may not miss him in our daily routines after a while, but special occasions add a twist.

Those special occasions that we celebrate alone hurt us or harden us it seems. We either try not to care, or we make a mark in the concrete vowing to never let him forget it. Some of us are strong enough to comfort the kids and smile all day long. Yet at night when the lights are down and the house is quiet, the loneliness and sadness creeps in.

I can't tell you your husband will choose to come home again soon. I don't know if he'll be freed from his addictions and learn to love you well. He may begin to engage tomorrow or it may not happen for years, or ever.

That may feel like a death sentence, but it's not. It's reality.

You cannot survive in a married mom, solo parent lifestyle if you are living only for your dream to come true. You have to base your life on Truth. When you do that, you will find your heart filled to brimming with all the love and security you need.

Jesus wants to be your best friend. He wants to court you, whisper in your ear, and love you. His passion is to see you set free from chasing after your husband's affections and release you to soak in his affection for you. God wants to fill you with a love so pure, so unconditional, so complete and never-ending that your longing for your husband will pale in comparison to what God is offering you.

Learn how to pray. Learn how to listen for his voice. Become friends with his Word. Spend time with him every day. Search for him. The Bible promises that if you search for him with all your heart, you will find him:

I love all who love me. Those who search will surely find me. (Prov. 8:17)

And if you search for him with all your heart and soul, you will find him. (Deut. 4:29)

Learn how to cast your cares on God and allow him to minister to you. The Bible calls the Holy Spirit our Comforter. Let him be just that. It's not your job to be your own resource. God said he'd do it, so give him room and an opportunity. You will still miss your husband, but the ache in your heart will be healed by the presence of the Lord.

Chapter Ten

Give Me a Break!

M cDonald's has registered a slogan that you may remember: You deserve a break today! Then a new one came out that asked the question: Have you had your break today? Many of us would answer, "No, I haven't had a break for months, never mind today. That will happen when someone finally realizes I deserve a break!"

Most moms find taking breaks a challenge. Solo parents have an even harder time. It's hard enough to find time for each child, their activities, and the housework. Making time for ourselves is rarely the priority it should be.

> Less than 10 percent of "married single moms" take good care of themselves so the kids will have a healthy mom while dad is gone. More than 80 percent try to do something but know it's not enough. Almost 10 percent just don't have the energy to try.

Hopefully you've already made the changes necessary (or are well on your way to making them) in your daily life to reduce fatigue after reading chapter 2. This is about taking a break not just to keep you from being burned out and tired, but to go the next step and become rejuvenated.

Taking a break means giving you a release from the normal, everyday stressors. You need to be filled up so that you are ready to carry your load again when your break is over.

Babysitters

One of the main ways to get a break when you have younger children is to hire a babysitter. If you are fortunate, your parents or in-laws live close enough, are healthy enough, and are willing to take care of your children. Build a relationship with them that would allow this, if at all possible. Perhaps you have brothers or sisters who would be willing to watch the children. Don't be afraid to ask. If you can afford to pay them, make that clear at the outset. If they don't want to accept payment, bless them in other ways—a batch of cookies, a surprise frozen meal, a gift card on a busy weekend, or watch their children another time.

If you don't live close enough to family to have them babysit (and even if you do) give yourself permission to hire a babysitter. Don't let anyone try to tell you that because they've never had babysitters other than family, you shouldn't either. There is nothing about statements like that that is life-giving.

Finding a babysitter can be a scary and frustrating business. But there are several ways to go about this.

Talk to your friends and family. Ask them who they use as a sitter and if you could get their names and addresses. If you have friends whose children are old enough to babysit, are responsible, and have taken a babysitting and first-aid course, perhaps you could hire them. Talk to a youth pastor at your church or another local church. Ask for referrals or who they use as a sitter if they have young kids. You can call babysitting services or hire sitters for the summer through a Youth Job Center. Connect with the local community college and put your name on a list or put up a poster in the area where the students are taking training to become daycare workers or early childhood educators. Taking care of your kids will give them experience, money, and something to add to a resume.

Find more than one good babysitter. Having two or three, even four is a good idea. Make sure you rotate them so your children get used to all of them and so that all the sitters stay current and updated with your family policies. You don't want to find out thirty minutes before you walk out the door that you have to cancel because your sitter has the flu. Having other sitters you can call last minute is wise.

Find babysitters who don't all attend the same church. One Valentine's Day my husband and I had a great evening planned, but every single sitter we had ever used attended the same youth group. It just so happened that the youth group was having a banquet that day and none of the girls were willing to miss it. So we stayed home.

Babysitters are not just for when you go out on a date. Use them when you need to have a nap or want to walk the mall for a bit. Call on them when you want to spend extra time with God, want to get your nails done, or just want to hang out with a book at Starbucks. Be creative with how you use your babysitters.

I've often stayed at home while I had a sitter. Sometimes I just need to crawl into bed and sleep until I wake up. There have been times I've left the house only to sneak back into my room with a drive-through cappuccino in hand, then spent a few hours of uninterrupted time with God or made a few long-overdue phone calls with long-distance friends.

Pay your sitters fair wages. Remember that they are taking your place for a short time. If your children are an active bunch, you may have to pay a higher rate or hire two sitters at a time. Babysitters who arrive after your kids are in bed and sleeping may be willing to work for a lower rate. If you are hiring older teenagers, remember that they are comparing your rate to a part-time job where they can make minimum wage. You don't necessarily need to pay that, but be sensitive to the amount of work you are requiring of them and what would encourage them to come back regularly.

Some women will boast about the fact that they never felt the need to have sitters or that they loved being with their children so much they wouldn't think of hiring a sitter. Be on your guard. There is nothing spiritual or even incredible about a woman who doesn't take a break.

Not all women have the same need for alone time. Some women can seemingly go for weeks on end without a break and not suffer for it. Others need breaks more frequently. I propose to you that it's not that some women don't need breaks, but that they are perhaps more efficient in securing them in the bits and pieces of their day.

My mom's sister can be exhausted, lie down or sit quietly in her car for ten minutes, then wake up completely refreshed and ready to go for hours. My mom, on the other hand, can sleep for an hour or more and still get up groggy some days. I've learned that if I don't have at least an hour, there's no point for me to try! It takes me fifty-five minutes to turn my brain off! Every woman is wired differently and is refreshed in unique ways.

Find which ways refresh you. Then stand your guard as you do what it takes to get it!

Bitty Breaks

As a mom of four very busy children who are home all day, I have had to learn to take bitty breaks. If I don't have little escapes throughout the day, I'm beyond worn out by suppertime. This is one of the ways you can extend your time between the real breaks that babysitters afford you.

I keep a book in every bathroom with a paperclip on the page I'm reading. These are not usually theology books or in-depth teaching books. Sometimes they are short stories, easy-reading how-to books, or novels that have simple plots. Currently my bathroom books are *Disconnected: Parenting Teens in a MySpace World* by Dee and Chap Clark and *The ADHD–Autism Connection: A Step Toward More Accurate Diagnosis and Effective Treatment* by Diane Kennedy. Other recent books included a book on questions teen girls wish they could ask their moms, a novel by Karen Kingsbury, and a compilation of short stories by Canadian authors called *Hot Apple Cider.*

I also keep magazines beside my bed. I like to read those at night because the articles are shorter and I'm less likely to read until four in the morning. A short article can get my mind off the worries of the day for a few moments.

The kind of books I do sometimes read at night are light-hearted books full of humor. For a bitty break, if you would like some great books that you can read just a chapter at a time and that will have you laughing till you cry I would suggest checking out the following authors: Dave Meurer, Phil Callaway, Barbara Johnson, Karen Scalf Linamen, and Liz Curtis Higgs. There are many, many others. Go to your local Christian bookstore and ask for some comedy books or search for them at www.christianbook.com.

Occasionally I'll pick up a comedy CD and plunk it into the player and listen while I peel potatoes, wash the floor, or clean out the storage room. I love the Bananas series audio CDs. I also enjoy listening to Mark Gungor from "Laugh Your Way to a Better Marriage." Not only do I get a good chuckle while I'm going about my day, it gives my spirit a lift and I learn valuable lessons while I'm at it.

Other bitty breaks include sitting down for a cup of coffee and drinking it while it's still hot. Some people find tinkering in their gardens refreshing. (I don't, but you might.) A quick call to a friend can be a super pick-me-up. My favorite of all is washing my hands.

Not just any hand wash, mind you! Let me give you the cheapest recipe for an incredible bitty break experience.

Buy yourself a liquid hand soap with the most incredible scent you've ever smelled. I personally like the scents at Bath and Body Works. It doesn't have to be pricey, just something you love. Then keep it hidden somewhere in the kitchen so that nobody else can use it. When you are ready for the Hand Wash Experience, put one tablespoon of table salt into the palm of your hand, add two tablespoons of any vegetable or cooking oil, and one or two pumps of that decadent hand soap. Don't add any water yet. Just rub your hands together for five minutes or for as long as you want. Wash up to your elbows if you're not wearing sleeves. When you are done enjoying the scent and the oily, rough scrubbing feeling, then rinse it all off with really warm water. Your hands and forearms will feel gloriously soft and refreshed. It's way better and cheaper than paying for a manicure at a salon.

Breaks That Don't Break the Bank

As I mentioned above, you can take breaks at home. I also mentioned a few ideas in chapter 2. Here is a list of ideas to consider and try out:

Read a book.

Read a magazine. (Get a subscription and save it until the sitter arrives, then escape to the tub.)

Surf the net for interesting blogs or visit the ones you've subscribed to and read the archives you may have missed.

Stroll the mall, planning birthday and Christmas gifts in September or July.

Rent a movie you've been wanting to watch.

Write a letter by hand.

Write a letter to each of your kids to read when they are older.
Talk to a long-distance friend on the phone.
Browse some catalogues you've been saving for this time.
Attend a craft class.
Knit or crochet.
Learn another language.
Take an adult elective at a local college, like history or journalism.
Swim.
Go to the gym.
Ride a horse.
Ride a bike.
Do a video Bible study by yourself.
Watch a comedy video, listen to a comedy CD, or read a comedy book.
Take some pictures.
Get a manicure/pedicure.
Learn how to do your own mani/pedicures.
Make some jewelry.
Draw or paint.
Suntan—safely.
Do some people-watching at the park, mall, or airport.
Take yourself out to dinner and bring along a magazine, book, or doodle
    pad.
Go walking, running, rollerblading, or skiing.

The list could go on. The point of your break is not just to get you away from the everyday grind and to take your mind off the cares of today, but to remember who God created you to be. Although you can certainly take a break with friends (and for some personalities that is very refreshing), I have listed things that you can do alone. It's important that you can leave everything behind, even the concerns of a friend.

MEET AMBER

Name: Amber Jenkins

Location: Tennessee

Kids: three boys (ages 7, 5, 3)

Married: ten years

Husband: He works in retail grocery. The store is open seven days a week, and he's the manager of his department so he's got to be there whenever! He doesn't know his schedule until the night before, and even then it's never set. He's gone when the kids get up, and they are asleep when he gets home.

Favorites: I love the color purple—indigo purple, brilliant purple, whatever. But I never wear it because it makes me look like my liver stopped working! I like coffee in any form—on ice, latte, with half and half and a bit of sugar, or with some of that froo-froo creamer. My favorite movie is the 2005 version of *Pride and Prejudice*. God knew to put me in this day and age. Unlike the women in my favorite movie, I like to speak my mind!

Longest time hubby's been away: He was gone for four months when our first baby was three to seven months old. Other than that, it's usually a week or two at a time.

My self-care: Coffee! Coffee is good. Coffee is your friend . . . and not decaf! Exercise helps me have energy and feel better. Take a walk. Be in the sun. Weights help me feel better about myself. I'm here to say, "Yes, you can exercise if you have little kids at home." Stairs, whatever . . . it doesn't take much! And on those days when I really don't want to be a mom, I say to myself, "Pull up your big blue panties and get your butt out of bed and be a dad!"

My struggle: Some days I'd like to send out a Public Service Announcement: "Your children are very well behaved or well dressed" are *the only* appropriate things to say to moms. Don't point out how hard it is to parent alone. I know it too well. Say something nice or walk away quietly.

I let him do the mowing and weed whacking, mostly because I unintentionally broke three Weed Eaters. I also let him clean out the gutters. My hubby brings home the paycheck—otherwise I do it all!

My strength: I take a lot of vacations by myself to visit family. I will go to strange and unfamiliar places with my kids. U-pick farms. Libraries. So far everything has turned out well. I just need to have my game face on and a back-up plan in the back of my mind.

My hope: Without God I'd be in an insane asylum and my kids would be taken from my home. I don't have all good days, but I know that God loves me even on my bad days. Often on the worst days the smallest thing will remind me of how much God loves me and change my perspective. I don't know how you can be married or parent without God. I just don't know how people can do it without. I kind of have a running dialogue with God all day long!

The Ultimate Break

The best and most important break you can ever take will be with the best Friend ever. Throughout this book I've expressed how critical it is that you spend time with God, talking to him, listening to him, and obeying him. It's the most important break, but the hardest one to make happen.

Spending daily time with Jesus is necessary for solo moms to live the lifestyle they are in with success. So many of us, though, can hardly drag ourselves out of bed in time for school or work, much less for a few chapters of Bible reading and prayer. Planning to connect with God before bed often gets derailed by sheer exhaustion at the end of the day. So how then does a solo parent make time for the ultimate break—time with Jesus?

First of all, evaluate your schedule. Find all the spots in your schedule that have "dead" moments in them. This would include waiting in line and sitting on a train, subway, or bus. It could include your lunch break at work. If you are a stay-at-home mom, then perhaps you could grab a few moments during your children's nap time. You may have to look carefully to find these moments.

When I had just two children, I found myself one day sitting on the floor in front of the toilet in our bathroom. Both kids were in the tub and having a ball. I wanted to take them out of the tub because they were clean, but they wanted to stay and play. So I gave in and settled in front of the toilet, bored. I wished I had brought a book or magazine, but I didn't feel comfortable leaving them unattended. That's when it dawned on me that playtime in the bath might be the only uninterrupted time I had all day.

The following morning I tossed my happy children into the tub with bubbles and a few extra toys. I had brought myself a cup of coffee, a candle for the counter (there's nothing quite like a bathroom for ambience . . . a vanilla scented candle helped me feel like it was *my* time), my Bible, a pen, and a notebook. I settled in on the floor in front of the toilet again and enjoyed my devotions for the first time in a long time. When I began this practice, we didn't own any cordless phones, so if the phone rang I couldn't answer it because I wouldn't leave my kids alone in the tub while I ran to the phone.

I did my devotions in the bathroom for years. Sometimes I sat in front of the toilet using the lid as a desk; other times I sat on the closed lid using the counter as a desk. While my children played and splashed just a short distance from me behind the shower curtain or doors (depending on which house we lived in) I spent time with my Best Friend. I cried, I prayed, I read, I learned, I heard his voice and got to know him better.

Once the kids were too old for bathing together, I made a commitment to getting up before they did (or at least before they were allowed out of their rooms). I would make a cup of coffee and spend time with God at the kitchen table or in my favorite corner of the couch.

During one season of my life, my quiet time with Jesus happened at five thirty in the morning. I'd set my alarm for five, shower and get ready for my day, and then soak in his presence. I loved those quiet mornings. No phone rings that early, and rarely did a child rise before seven. By the time I had to wake the kids, the Holy Spirit had ministered to my soul, and I could face whatever the day held because I knew he would be with me through it all.

My morning routine was disrupted when I fell gravely ill a few years ago. I could no longer get up in the morning or stay awake for many hours at a time. I found reading difficult. I learned to give the first of every waking moment to the Lord. If I woke in the morning, afternoon, evening or anywhere in between, he'd get the first moments of prayer and praise. I kept my Bible close by in case I wanted to read something.

Another thing I started when my children were just little was not wasting my nights. There were nursing nights and up-with-sick-kids nights. Sometimes I just couldn't sleep. Occasionally a cup of coffee (leaded) would wake me up at night. I talked with Jesus about this after a string of nights where I hadn't slept well but had tossed and turned, getting increasingly frustrated that my tired body was not getting the sleep it needed. He reminded me of a verse that says God is in control of everything. So I asked him every night before I fell asleep to keep me asleep all night. I told him that if I woke up in the night, I would assume that he had woken me and that I would spend time with him cheerfully from my bed no matter what time it was.

It seems Jesus likes three o'clock in the morning. When I wake up at night, it is almost always the same time, no matter how late I've gone to bed. I check the clock and smile, then say, "Hi, God. You're on time again. So what do you want to talk about?" I might remember a friend, or a cause, or a child of mine. Sometimes I am impressed by his faithfulness and incredible love for me. Whatever comes to mind, that is what I pray about. There are some nights when I greet my Friend, ask him what he wants to talk about, and then hear him say, "Just wanted you to know I hadn't forgotten about you. I love you, now go back to sleep."

I've never woken up tired after a night with Jesus. Never. The joy of the Lord really can be your strength.

Make a commitment to make time for Jesus. Give him the freedom in your life to refresh your spirit, renew your mind, and restore your strength. Your circumstances will not necessarily change. But you will be a new person. The old, worn-out creation has passed away, and God will make you a new, vibrant creation as you spend time in his presence.

Chapter Eleven

Honoring the Man You Don't See Enough

Trent and I got to know each other over the phone. It was October 1, through the handset of my corded phone, that I heard him ask me if I would officially be his girlfriend. Yippee! I could hardly wait to tell my housemates that I was officially a "wanted woman." We had a long-distance dating relationship: he was in Toronto, Canada, and I was a twenty-four-hour drive west on the prairies.

Our dating consisted of all-night phone calls and letters through the mail (yes, snail mail). He came to visit me for the Thanksgiving weekend. Our conversations over the phone got so long that his phone company asked him for advance payments of his several-hundred-dollar phone bills! At Christmastime, just twelve short weeks after we started dating, he asked me to marry him.

It was a whirlwind Christmas week with him, planning our wedding and meeting his family for the first time, and not once did I think to ask him how his career might affect our marriage. Not once!

As I walked down the aisle in my only-to-be-worn-once, white satin gown, I was thinking of how amazing it would be to share my life with a man as incredible as Trent. It was plain to me that I had won the best man. I just knew it would never be hard to keep my vows with a man like him at my side.

It didn't take more than a week after the honeymoon to realize he wouldn't always be at my side. The wedding was over, the honeymoon had ended, and the struggle to honor and love the man I married had begun.

There are many reasons we choose to walk down the aisle: good looks, a heavy wallet, a promising career, a super family, the child you were carrying, a father for your children, and of course that illusive thing called love.

In the early days it was exciting, exhilarating even, to support your husband, live with him, respect him, and honor him. But loneliness and the eventual burdens of solo parenting become more difficult as time goes on. It gets harder and harder to love, honor, and respect the man you promised to cherish for better or for worse.

Recently I spoke with a woman who is now a grandma. She shared how she wanted to support her husband in the early years of their marriage. He wanted to change careers, which meant going back to school. It would be three years until his training ended. In order to make ends meet, he was also working. She willingly went into it, her eyes wide open. She knew it would be hard, that she'd get tired, and that there would be many sacrifices. She had not counted on how hard it would really be.

How could she keep herself vulnerable to the emotions of missing her husband and the loneliness that didn't end? She couldn't. It was just too hard. Instead she ground her feet into the dirt, sunk her teeth into the situation, and decided to become strong through it. She became fiercely independent. Hers was a character that grew stronger in adversity.

But the day came, when the courses were finished and a job had been secured, that she realized her solo-parenting days had not ended like they should have. Now the pressure to do well in a new career, to put in the hours needed for that next raise or promotion, and to build a good reputation tore her husband from his waiting family. She asked many questions, like all of us do. Can I learn to honor a man who is choosing not to pursue his wife and kids? Can this marriage survive?

Countless women have come to the conclusion that their marriages couldn't survive. I can only imagine how many have filed for divorce, hoping and praying that the man they married would be jolted to his senses and turn to pursue his wife and family with a Christlike love. I've met some of those women, no longer married solo parents but single moms. Most of them still wonder if things could have been different, what they did wrong, or why they and the kids weren't worth his time and effort.

Many married solo moms feel guilty because they want to support their husband's dreams and goals but find the sacrifice is much more costly than they believe they can afford. It makes no sense to us to support a spouse through school, a budding career, and life-altering decisions, when it means that it will jeopardize our marriage and family. It is even harder to learn how to honor and respect a man who is making harmful choices to continue in addictions, to waste time in hobbies, or simply to not come home.

Can a woman be a godly wife and honor her husband who, through his actions, asks her to carry the load alone—day after day after day?

> If your marriage is suffering because of your husband's absences, you are not alone. More than 97 percent of "married single moms" in a recent online survey indicated their marriages suffer at least some of the time. More than 78 percent say it suffers most of the time.

God alone has the answer to that. He says he hates divorce. The Bible says that nothing—nothing—should come between a man and his wife, nothing should "put them asunder" or separate them. So then what is happening when something has? Just because you live in the same house doesn't mean nothing is separating you. What is going on? Did God make a mistake?

Get a Biblical View

It is so important that we take the time to get a biblical view of who we are and what our marriage really is. Not what it seems to us that it is, but the reality of it that is found in the Truth of God.

God has pronounced husband and wife "one." The Message version of the Bible calls it a God-created, organic union. There is a connection between us and our husbands that we have with no other person. Even if you have sex with some other man, the union you have with your husband is still unlike anything else you will ever have.

This oneness is not in your personality, choices, character, or even your physical relationship. It is in a spiritual realm and at such a deep level of our souls that we rarely catch a glimpse of how intricate and complete the transformation on our wedding day was.

Some people may argue that it is the physical union or cohabitation that makes you married and therefore one. If that was the case, then Jesus made a mistake when he spoke to the woman at the well. We know he makes no mistake, so we will have to consider his words carefully. He said to her, "You're right! You don't have a husband—for you have had five husbands, and you aren't even married to the man you're living with now. You certainly spoke the truth!" (John 4:17–18). God told her that her sexual relationship and cohabiting arrangements did not qualify as marriage. But when a man and woman do become husband and wife, God himself knits them together, uniting them as one. It's a union deeper than our flesh, deeper than what we see, deeper than what we can easily understand. A union bound on earth and in heaven with your covenantal vow.

Because of that union, your oneness, whatever you do affects your husband. Whatever he does affects you. All of it.

We may not recognize the changes in ourselves or our spouses. That doesn't mean it hasn't happened. It simply means it is on a level that we are not aware of.

When we realize how connected we are to our husbands, we can finally begin to look at our situation in a new light. A perspective of hope can filter through the murky waters of our circumstances and begin to give us a new understanding of our role in marriage.

The choices our husbands make, whether we support them or not, affect our situations. The pain and distress caused by decisions made or a lifestyle lived can play havoc with our hearts and emotions. But in no way do these things render your "oneness" or marriage unstable. The unity between you and your husband can only be broken by death or by God himself. Your husband's actions, words said in anger, or the pain you live in cannot affect the strength of your union. Be encouraged! Although things may not look stable or seem reconcilable, the Truth has been declared, and God, who is the Redeemer of all things, says: With me all things are possible and I make all things beautiful in time.

Ecclesiastes 3:11 says: "Yet God has made everything beautiful for its own time. He has planted eternity in the human heart, but even so, people cannot see the whole scope of God's work from beginning to end."

Earlier I shared with you how God gave me a picture of my husband standing before him, giving an account of how he had spent his time, raised his family, and loved me. It has been a powerful picture for me to remember that what is happening now—however filled with junk and craziness, hurt and betrayal it might be—is not so much about today as it is about eternity.

Like the verse above says, God has planted eternity in our hearts. We all want to go to heaven. We want the beautiful to happen now. The passage also says that we cannot see the whole scope of God's work. We can't see how it is possible that God can turn our not-so-perfect marriages into something beautiful. It's out of our scope to see how he can redeem the time that's been lost.

There is more after this life passes, much more. When I enter that eternity, will I be thrilled to stand before a holy and righteous Judge, the God who sees all and knows all, confident that I have fought the good fight, and run the race well? Or will I hang my head because I didn't believe in the full work of redemption on the cross, because I didn't believe it meant my marriage, too?

God gave me a picture of my husband standing before God, giving him an account of his life. I watched as he lifted up our oldest daughter and offered her to the gentle King. God took her in his arms and asked Trent, "How did you worship me in the raising of this child?"

In the picture in my head, I saw Trent turn to look at me. I saw in his eyes regret, deep gratefulness, and a fuller understanding of what he had missed as a father. Then I hung my head. I hadn't done what God had called me to do—give Trent every opportunity to receive a reward from God for how he parented the kids and loved me.

The full weight of this view into eternity has never left me. It's been many years since God pressed on me the heaviness of eternity and the position he's asked me to fill. The significance of it has never lightened.

Once we understand that we are securely one with our husbands, that God has placed eternity in our hearts, and that he has given us an eternally significant role in our families—only then can we answer the question, "How can I honor the man I don't see enough?"

To honor someone means to respect the person and/or the position that he holds. Your husband holds a high position. God himself sacrificed his Son for your husband. He is created in the image of God. Whether or not your husband has any regard for God does not change the fact that Jesus loved him with his life. To honor your husband is to treat him in a way that acknowledges that truth.

We honor our husbands by living our lives in a way that gives them every opportunity to honor God. Our husbands don't always make good choices or do honorable things. And let's face it, we don't either. When we focus on what they've done, or not done, or the mistakes they've made, we take our eyes off God and miss what he is doing. We need to look through the lens of eternity that has been planted in our hearts and see the man who Jesus loves.

Just because you are solo parenting and living married life alone does not mean that your husband is the "bad" guy. You may even have a great marriage, having been able to establish a firm relationship within the turbulent lifestyle you lead. Some of what your husband is doing may be exactly what Christ has called him to.

I sometimes think about the wives of Jesus' disciples. They don't get much attention because Scripture says so little about them. Yet I'm sure they were women much like us. Did they ever go to God with complaints about their men like so many of us do? What if God had answered those prayers to "change their men" or "bring them home"? How much of the development of the early church and what we read today in the New Testament would have been lost?

Honoring your husband requires you to acknowledge that if your husband changes what he's doing to make you happy, he may very well be disobeying the Lord or sacrificing a reward in heaven. Of course, even if God *has* called your husband to whatever it is that is taking him away from home, that doesn't mean this lonely lifestyle is easy.

Your husband may not choose to or be able to clean up his act, come home, engage in family life, or make any change at all. God may not even want him to change. Regardless, God won't ask you if your husband made changes. He'll ask you what you did to set your husband up to succeed in the kingdom of heaven.

Philippians 2:5 says: "You must have the same attitude that Christ Jesus had."

Jesus came to serve us and die for us. Why? So that we could have every opportunity to stand blameless before his Father at the end of our lives on earth. He had eternity in mind!

How did he serve us? "He gave up his divine privileges; he took the humble position of a slave and was born as a human being. When he appeared in human form, he humbled himself in obedience to God and died a criminal's death on a cross" (Phil. 2:7–8).

I don't particularly like giving up privileges. Neither do I like feeling like I've been a slave all day. How about you?

God is not asking us to change our husbands or promising to change our situations. He is asking us to be obedient to him by following the example of Christ in our everyday lives and in our marriages.

Quite frankly, I'm a pretty selfish woman. I quite like being pampered. Trent is often better at serving me when he's home than I am at serving him. He has no problem giving me half his chocolate bar. I don't share chocolate unless I have to! And we all know that the one who gives up chocolate is truly being selfless. I've often wondered why we don't use chocolate as currency because it's that valuable, don't you agree? (Especially Hershey's Bliss with truffle centers . . .)

We can serve our husbands in many ways. By no means am I suggesting that you have to become his housemaid, nursemaid, and everyday doormat! Remember, serve him to honor him—serve him in the things that God directs you to in order to pave the way for him to win that prize in eternity.

Here are a few things to get your mental gears rolling and to give your prayers fodder as you approach the heavenly throne and ask Jesus what you should be doing. Trust me. He'll have many more ideas to add to this than I could ever come up with.

Stop Nagging

If you've told him over and over again, he's heard you. Saying it louder, more often, and with different words won't make him hear it any better. He may just tune you out. When we ask our husbands to join us, come home earlier, or help out a little more, and they don't respond to our requests, we need to stop nagging. You may have to ask more than once, but you don't have to nag!

I've always thought it funny to watch someone ask a question of a person who doesn't speak their language. When they hear a foreign language come back at them in a soft voice, they know they haven't been heard, so they repeat what they said. But the second time, they say it louder. Again they get a response they don't understand, so they raise their voice even more. Soon you have two people yelling at each other in frustration and anger. The repetition isn't helping any; things are only getting louder, and nobody is being heard.

That's kind of how nagging works. We can repeat ourselves until we're blue in the face, but if our husbands are not ready to move forward on our request, we might as well be speaking in some foreign tongue.

Remember the Good Things

Throughout the Old Testament when God did something really incredible (like part the Red Sea or bring down the walls of Jericho), he often instructed the Israelites to do one of two things. They were either to build an altar to remember the place and what God had done at that spot, or in a few cases, they were to hold a festival that would continue through the ages (like the Purim Festival celebrating the saving of the Jews through Queen Esther). The reason he did this was so that the Israelites would not forget the good things.

Alan D. Wright, author of *God Moments*, says, "Even mature, well-meaning Christians have an incredible ability to forget extraordinarily beautiful moments of God. The memory dulls. The moment loses its luster. And soon, its life-changing power is gone."[1] That's why we need to take time to record the amazing things God has done, the blessings in our life and all the moments that remind us of his faithfulness.

Sometimes it feels like there is little to remember that is good. Don't forget, though: the Jews still celebrate Purim, and that was a very long time ago! God doesn't mind if you go back a few years or decades in your memory and pull out some golden oldies.

Some people might say that taking pictures and scrapbooking is a waste of time and money. I beg to differ. As I've fingered through our boxes upon boxes of photos, making a feeble attempt to put some sort of reasonable record of our life together, I have found good things to remember. I remember the Greek dinner Trent brought to me in the hospital after I had my babies. How could I forget how we spent long hours after our honeymoon scraping and scraping at the goo on the top of the cupboards in the house we were renting? The photo of the smiling, baby-faced man with a sparkle in his eye and a scraper in his hand reminds me of the good.

I have a special candle and ikebana kenzan flower frog combination that Trent and I got on our tenth anniversary. I think I've only had flowers in it once. But I keep it out on our old piano. It reminds me of a good time. It brings back the memories of a time when hope was renewed for me.

When you experience the good things, write them down. You may even want to keep a "Good Things" notebook. The days come when no matter how hard you try it's a struggle to remember the good things without a prompt. That's when your written words will be concrete evidence to prove to you that there is good to remember.

Be a Philippians 4:8 Woman

This verse alone can keep me busy until the day I die! Memorize it. Post it up in the bathroom, by the kitchen sink, on your steering wheel. Wherever you spend your time, put the words of Philippians 4:8 there:

And now . . . one final thing. Fix your thoughts on what is true, and honorable, and right, and pure, and lovely, and admirable. Think about things that are excellent and worthy of praise.

It's just one verse, but it can smooth the path for you as you honor your husband. The next verse starts off: "Keep putting into practice all you learned." You need to do just that. Train your mind to keep practicing how you think honorable thoughts about your husband.

As a thought comes through your mind, weigh it against these guidelines. Is it true? Is it honorable? Is it right? Pure? Lovely? Admirable? Excellent? Praiseworthy?

As you train your mind to be renewed in the way you think about your husband, your actions and emotions toward him will change. You'll find yourself searching for the good instead of noticing the things that get you down. Your eyes will catch moments when he's being the dad you've dreamed of for your kids.

Speak blessing and life-giving words. The tongue is the most powerful tool you have. James 3:9–10 says: "Sometimes it praises our Lord and

Father, and sometimes it curses those who have been made in the image of God. And so blessing and cursing come pouring out of the same mouth. Surely, my brothers and sisters, this is not right!"

You have the choice to speak life-giving words or curses. As you train your mind and become a Philippians 4:8 woman, do the hardest thing of all and say those fabulous things out loud. Break the sound barrier in your home and speak up. There may be a lot of noise, but has encouragement and blessing had a voice recently?

This is particularly critical when you speak to your children. You may be disappointed in life as a solo mom. You may be hurt, angry, lonely, or tired. Don't forget, though, that your husband is also your children's father. Even if he dies and you remarry, no one else will ever be their father. As you speak negatively about your husband's characteristics and flaws, as you see them, remember that your children will be comparing themselves to him and wondering if they will fail to meet your expectations of them, as well.

They will ask questions like:

- Will Mom feel that way about me if I do such and such?
- I resemble my dad, does that mean Mom doesn't love me, either?
- I would love a job like Dad has, but does that mean my wife will feel about me like Mom does about Dad?

Guard your words and their hearts. It is your responsibility to train your children to love and honor their dad. It is a commandment. It's the first one with a promise. If you want to successfully raise your children to have every opportunity to succeed in a relationship with their father and with God, then guide them step by step through the process of honoring their dad.

They should honor you as well. Don't let them disrespect you. If you are consistently demonstrating speech and choices that are life-giving and grant blessing, then you are more likely to be respected yourself.

This applies not just when you speak to your children but also when you speak at all. There should never be a time when your friends or family hear you speak poorly about your husband. Now, that does not mean you cannot speak the truth. It means you need to speak truth saturated with love in a way that can bring life.

As you share your needs and life with your friends, a pastor, family members, or counselor, remember that all that you say should be to bring hope and life to whatever situation you are speaking about. If things are rough at home, it does no good to bash and complain about your husband. Complaining and whining to friends and family will only pit them against him and not provide you with the support you need. "Be as cunning as a snake, inoffensive as a dove" (Matt. 10:16 MSG).

At times you may need outside help to get through really tough things in life. If in your home you (or one of your children) are being physically hurt, abused, or threatened, then it is critical that you don't mince words but clearly state your urgent situation to a pastor or community worker.

As you communicate with others, remember that your words should not be like a trap set to snare prey. Words that come back to haunt you or that you wish you could take back are better left unsaid in the first place. In situations where friends, family, or co-workers are speaking poorly about their spouses, stand up for the true, noble, right, and pure things. Offer conversation that is excellent and worthy of praise.

Honoring your husband will give him reason to praise you like the husband of the Proverbs 31 woman praised his wife. Guarding your words, speaking blessing to your husband and over him will help you become a wife of noble character, more precious than rubies.

Pray for Him

I don't mean rattle off a "God be with him today, amen" kind of prayer. Use Scripture to pray for your husband. List off the areas of his life where you would like God to bless him. Don't just pray for God to change him, either!

When you pray, ask God to speak to your heart about what he would want you to pray for your husband. Quietly listen to what the Holy Spirit lays on your heart. Then pray that. It might have nothing to do with what you would normally have thought of or would even want to pray about, but be obedient to God. He knows your husband best.

As you pray for your husband, teach your children to pray for him also. Give them an opportunity to love their dad in the heavenlies. Throughout the day, whenever your husband comes to mind, turn your thoughts toward God and ask him to build character and pour blessing into your man.

Let Him Know You Are Still Choosing Him

Every woman wants her husband to pursue and choose her day after day. Men want to know that the woman they married is still madly in love with them and would say yes again if asked. Sometimes they don't ask because they can't tell by our actions what we'd say.

There have been days when I might have said no! But I have found a love for Trent that does not come from what he can offer me, who he may become, what he can earn, or how he makes my life better. I have been discovering a love for the man that God created, his unique personality, his kind heart, and the passion for godliness that he has been growing in.

Whatever the reason for your husband's absence, whether it seems noble or ignoble, forced or deliberate, you can honor him with your words and actions in a way that can affect him and your children for eternity. Your oneness before Christ is secure. Rise to the challenge of being a godly woman, wife, and mother even when you solo parent.

Chapter Twelve

I Have Needs Too, You Know!

Just after I graduated from college, I attended a wedding shower for some friends. They were both Christians and had decided to wait to make love until their wedding night when they would share their virginity with each other. The girls were in the basement opening gifts and talking about plans for the wedding. The guys were all upstairs doing what guys do at wedding showers—eating all the good snack food!

I had to go upstairs to use the bathroom, which was right beside the dining room where they were all sitting and talking (and eating). While I was in the bathroom, I overheard the groom say something I'll never forget.

"Being engaged is just like being married without any of the benefits." Sometimes solo parenting can feel exactly the same way: all the restrictions of married life with none of the benefits. Yes, there are those times when it's actually a relief not to have your husband around. His absence means you don't have to say no or be intimate when you are not in the mood. Then again, maybe you miss those intimate moments of love making. Married solo moms run the risk of becoming starved of emotional intimacy, of physical touch and affection, and of sexual intimacy. When this happens, it becomes tempting to look elsewhere to have our needs met. Emotional and physical affairs are a very real and constant danger for women who solo parent. We never intend to break our marriage vows, but it creeps up on us if we're not careful, standing guard over our hearts, minds, and actions.

Emotional Needs

Women love emotions. We laugh, we cry, we hurt, we agonize, we rejoice, we mourn, we sob, we guffaw, we romanticize, and we vocalize—about everything.

Solo moms have to carry the burden of all those emotions by themselves when their husbands are not around. When he is home, he listens, laughs, grunts when she pauses, and generally makes her feel like she's been heard and her heart has been shared. When he's gone, it builds up inside until she's ready to burst.

When those emotions finally have a chance to flow (or flood) past the dam, there is often a "Mother Goose, Baby Goose" imprinting effect that takes place. Let me explain how that works.

A gosling imprints on the first thing it sees after it is born. It assumes that is its mother. No matter who or what it is, no matter how strange or ridiculous, the gosling will follow it. Studies were done where a gaggle of goslings imprinted on Conrad Lorenz, an early behavioral therapist. As young geese, they followed him everywhere he went. They became sexually attracted to him as adults.

As solo parents we have to be very careful with whom we share what. It is our natural tendency as women to gravitate toward those who help us feel secure, validated, and valued. When we share our emotions, feelings, and personal thoughts with someone other than our husbands, we risk having our hearts "imprint" or attach to the one who gives credence to what we've shared. It will become easier and easier to share our thoughts, emotions, and desires with someone other than our husband—so much so that, like the goslings, we can too quickly find ourselves sharing our emotions intimately with another man, thinking about him when we're apart, and eventually becoming sexually attracted to him.

Countless women have found themselves in compromising situations, just like I did, wondering how it happened. Although women do appreciate the physical characteristics of a nice-looking man, the most alluring feature for a solo mom is not his looks but the attention he pays to her. Naturally there are exceptions, and every woman will have a plethora of reasons for why she is susceptible to an emotional affair. But we need to be aware that each one of our unmet needs becomes an opportunity for another man to fill the bill.

You have needs. You miss your husband's attention. As a married woman who is trying to follow God in her life and impact her family for eternity, you need to take responsibility for how, with whom, and when you allow your heart to be seen by others.

We teach our daughters about modesty. I hope you are leading by example in this area, covering up your breasts and cleavage, wearing tops, skirts, and outfits that do not draw attention to yourself in a sexual way, especially when your husband is not around. But have you taught your daughter modesty of the heart? Are you revealing a modest heart emotionally when you are around other men?

If you are sharing your problems (especially about your marriage and kids) with someone other than your spouse, your guard should be way up. If you are seeing a male counselor, be sure that he has checks and systems in place to protect his integrity. If at all possible, see a counselor who is a woman. We tend to share openly with our close friends, but even with them, we need to exercise caution. There are plenty of women who, after many years of marriage, have found themselves emotionally attached to another woman and have chosen to leave their husbands for her.

Guard your heart. Your marriage needs your attention, time, and safekeeping.

I have a friend with whom I can safely "vent." We've been friends for more than twenty years. Sometimes I don't even have to say anything, she can tell by my voice or tone that things are rough. When we get together, we often talk until the wee hours of the morning, sharing, crying, and laughing. I know I am safe with her because she always pushes me to work a little harder at my marriage and search for what God is doing. She never lets me settle for second best.

Sharing with a friend who can direct your emotions back toward building your marriage and growing as a woman and Christian will be beneficial. Ultimately, you want your heart to be ready for your husband—a soft, pliable, sensitive heart, full of love, compassion, and everything about you that makes you incredible. A friend who can keep you on that path or help you get back on it when you slip off is a gift from God.

Encouragement is something we all long for, and although we don't walk around asking people to encourage us, we often subconsciously wait for it.

It is incredible how far a little encouragement will go. We cheer our kids and they run faster. We clap at the end of a performance, and they are spurred on to keep practicing. Encouragement from others is a good thing if it is done with honesty and a pure heart.

Sometimes we ask for it in the form of feedback. For example, at work you might ask your boss, "Is this what you were expecting in the report? Am I on the right track?" You are giving your boss a direct question to which he or she can make a direct answer. Even basic confirmations such as that can begin to build in your heart if there is no encouragement coming on a regular basis from your husband. You can easily gravitate toward behavior that wins you that feedback from your boss on a more regular basis.

I made dinner for a friend's family one time and found myself asking if the potatoes tasted burnt. When I dished them out there were some dark and crusty potatoes stuck to the bottom of the pot. My friend's husband said, "If *you* make potatoes, they could never taste bad!" I saw a twinkle in his eye and knew in my head he was joking. What took me aback was how closely I paid attention to what my heart interpreted as sweet words spoken.

Pay attention to your heart. When a male cashier or doctor, the mailman or carpet cleaner, a waiter or bus driver says a few encouraging words, do you find yourself soaking them up like a dry sponge? Then it's time to soak in the presence of the One who can give you all the love, acceptance, and pure encouragement you will ever need. Jesus is the only One who can confirm your value and provide you with unconditional security and love. You need to pursue this from him.

Compliments are simply wonderful, aren't they? We are a little more open and forward when asking for compliments than we are encouragement. "Did you like the pie?" "What do you think of the color I chose for the living-room walls?" "Do you like these earrings?" We beg our friends for them, we pry them from our kids, we rely on our mom to send a few our way, and we even give them to ourselves now and then: "This is pretty incredible, if I must say so myself!"

Even these everyday comments can be cause for caution. I remember when I was involved in my emotional affair how I waited to see whether my friend would say something about my outfit. Sometimes he would say something simple like, "You look nice tonight." Other times he would be more specific, "Your hair looks great like that." Then there were the times his eyes did all the talking for him. Those compliments kept me going for a long time.

They also kept me headed down a path I had never intended to take. I found myself choosing outfits according to what had produced the best response from him instead of what was comfortable or what Trent liked. There was a day I got dressed to go out, and Trent made a negative comment about the top I was wearing and suggested I change it. I refused, because it had become more important to me that my friend had complimented me on that same top. I'm ashamed to say that I hardened my heart that day and chose to not wear something my husband could compliment me on. I had become infatuated with another man's words.

When your heart begins to long for the encouragement and compliments of someone other than God and your husband, you have gone too far. It's past time to put up your shield. Now it's time to cut yourself off from that person and hold on to the things that are pure, honest, and true. You may not have been unfaithful yet, but you are preparing your mind and emotions for that likelihood.

We have often picked on the men in our church congregations, telling them that they are committing adultery when they even look at a woman with lust in their hearts. We base that on Matthew 5:28 which says, "But I say, anyone who even looks at a woman with lust has already committed adultery with her in his heart." The Message's version of this more clearly says to me what the meaning of the verse is. "You know the next commandment pretty well, too: 'Don't go to bed with another's spouse.' But don't think you've preserved your virtue simply by staying out of bed. Your heart can be corrupted by lust even quicker than your body. Those leering looks you think nobody notices—they also corrupt."

Guarding your heart is not just about saving your marriage. How you think in your mind and how you allow your emotions to run wild with passion, love, or lust for a man who is not your husband is adultery. It is sin. End of story. No matter what your reasons, no matter how long it's been since your husband has met your needs, when you begin to attach yourself through your emotions and thoughts to another man, even if no one else knows about it, you have become an adulterer.

How then do we encourage our husbands to support us with their words and compliments so that these temptations are more manageable? First of all, ask them outright! The bottom line is that if we're distancing ourselves from our husbands, they will distance themselves from us, too. Our husbands are often afraid to say anything nice to us because they haven't done it well enough for us in so long that they have stopped trying.

My husband hates it when I ask him certain questions such as, "Does this make me look fat?" If he says no, I'll tell him that it probably does make me look fat but that he's too afraid to tell me. This tells him I don't think he is "man enough" to tell me the truth. If he says yes, then I'll get upset because he's saying I look fat. It's a lose-lose conversation as far as he's concerned.

Talk to your husband in such a way that you set him up to win, while at the same time getting to hear the honest compliments you long for. When you get a new outfit, prance around in front of him like a runway model and ask, "So which do you love more, the shoes, the skirt, or the blouse?" Or "What do you think is the best feature of my outfit tonight?" You may find that he has been waiting to tell you that he loves the way the shape of your hips show in that skirt, or how your hair looks so silky. When I asked my husband one evening as we were going out what he liked best about my top, he pulled me close and tight and said under his breath that the best thing about my top was that all night he'd be looking at it and dreaming of taking it off!

That's a top I want to wear again!

Emotional faithfulness is one of the best gifts you can give your husband. We have put such an emphasis on physical faithfulness that we've missed the huge damage that is being done to Christian families as wives are unconsciously choosing to be emotionally unfaithful to their husbands.

Being emotionally faithful takes work. You can guard your speech and sharing of personal needs and emotions. We've touched on how you can set your husband up for success in complimenting you, keeping you from drying out emotionally. You know that spending time with God is paramount. There is one other, incredibly powerful step you need to take.

Your mind needs to become faithful to your husband so that your emotions can follow. The Bible talks about renewing our minds. To renew means to renovate or reconstruct, to make new again.

When I refresh my living room, I move the furniture around. Nothing ends up in the same place it was when I started. I will move accessories from one room in my house to another. Candles from the bedroom go into the living room. Flowers from the bathroom get brought into our bedroom. Pictures in the hall get taken down and replaced with a swag from above the door.

But what God is talking about here goes far beyond a simple refreshing. It's a renovation. A complete reconstruction deal. It should not look at all the same when it's done. Friends of ours have recently renovated their home, including making a huge addition. The kitchen is where the front porch used to be, and the dining-room patio doors are where a sink and counter used to be. There are bedrooms where there was nothing before (okay, there was a roof there before). I had to have a tour the last time I was there so I could find all the rooms. Everything is different. They have changed their colors, the flooring, the cabinetry, and the layout. It's like a brand new house.

That's what is supposed to happen with our minds. A whole new mental perspective.

Harlequin romances, soap operas, and romantic movies have captured the hearts of women for decades. Magazines with steamy articles, ads, and interviews are purchased by millions every day. As women we have bought hook, line, and sinker into the fairy-tale mentality that there really is a Prince Charming and he really will save the beautiful princess from her plight.

We want to have the front seat of that show. We're willing to give time and money to see it happen in every book, episode, and movie. We tell ourselves that we know this is fiction, it's just a story. We allow ourselves an adventure into a world of exciting love, passion, and heady romance because it is a cheap and easy way to escape the burden of today.

And it may be ruining your chances to have an incredibly intimate relationship with your husband.

Every time a handsome hero wins the heart of the woman in your book, he's won yours, too. As a matter of fact, if he walked out of the pages and into your arms you'd be hard pressed to say no. You experience the emotion, drama, and thrill of a newfound love at every kiss, shared look, and tender love scene. It's because your imagination and your emotions are uniquely engaged to bring you pleasure.

When your hubby comes in the door grubby from work with grime under his fingernails and body odor reaching you before he does, it will be impossible to see just the man you married. Alongside him, some part of you is picturing the last lover you read about or watched on-screen. No matter what your husband says or does, he will never measure up to the man in your head or some author's fictional character. It is just not possible.

Perhaps you know the dangers of the steamy romance fiction genre. That's why you've stayed away. No one will find anything higher than a G-rated movie in your home, and they won't find a romance book or sleazy magazine, either. Yet most women don't need paperbacks and video players, their imaginations provide all the excitement they need.

I know that it is common for women to "dream" or fantasize about imaginary men. We wonder about a life with a different man—sometimes the husband of a friend, an old boyfriend, a boss, a celebrity, or our mind's mix of a few gentlemen. Perhaps we imagine a life with a man who has a different career, a tender heart for children, or no addictions or bad habits. One woman mentioned to me that she's always dreamed of a man who is self-employed, able to manage his own schedule to accommodate her fantasy of a steamy, lunchtime rendezvous, or show up early from work to cook dinner in the kitchen with her. She made sure that in her imagination she never named him or even gave him a face because she said, "Otherwise it would feel almost like an affair."

Whether you've created this fantasy yourself or you enjoy the creations of authors or screenplay writers, you are setting your husband up for failure. It is time to stop. Now.

Any woman whose husband is addicted to pornography knows the pain that comes from having a husband whose mind is obsessed with someone other than her. It affects her complete sense of who she is. It's not just about the act of sex. It's about who is in his mind. Few women would ever want to find out in the midst of a passionate love-making session that the reason her husband is enjoying himself is because he's pretending she's not there and some other woman is.

So then why do we tell ourselves that our own imaginations and fantasies don't really matter? Because we're afraid that if we don't provide for ourselves the kind of relationship we are looking for, it will never happen. Even if it is "just" in our minds.

You need to stop believing that lie. If you have engaged in fantasy relationships of any kind—short-term, long-term, paperback, soap opera, chick flick, or one of your own making—they need to end. For the sake of your marriage, for the sake of beautiful intimacy with your husband and your relationship with God, you need to renew your mind.

Make that commitment to be a Philippians 4:8 woman. Fill your mind with thoughts, words, and pictures that are pure, right, true, admirable, excellent, praiseworthy, and noble. Fill your mind with Scripture. Read true stories and biographies of men and women whose lives can encourage you to press on toward that beautiful eternity planted within you. It's okay if you become the only one on your block or in your friendship circle who watches mostly G-rated movies. Make a commitment to watch only what is edifying and life-giving. Fill your mind with praise and worship music, talk radio that honors the Lord, and inspirational audio teaching books or CDs that will assist you as you renew your mind.

Your mind is a filter over your heart. Whatever is allowed in will settle its way down and take root. And out of your mouth comes what is in your heart. If your mind has planted seeds of love for other men in your heart, critical and judgmental words, comparisons, and dissatisfaction will leak out with a slip of the tongue during a moment of anger.

Give your husband, your marriage, and yourself every opportunity to succeed. There is great joy in being freed from the bondage of your secret relationships and affairs of the heart in order to be ready for the love of your God and the husband he's given you.

MEET WILLOW

Name: Willow Pemelton

Location: Illinois

Kids: Four (10-year-old twins, 7, 5)

Married: ten years

Husband: Steve is a staff sergeant in the National Guard. He is gone for drills one weekend a month and two weeks of the year for further training. He's spent time in Iraq, and there's a chance he'll be going again.

Favorites: I'm a country girl at heart so it won't be a surprise that home-grown rib-eye steak, baked potato with the works, country music, and horseback riding are my top picks. But I also love volleyball so much I play and coach whenever I can.

Longest time hubby's been away: Steve was gone fifteen months during 2006–7.

My reality: It felt like we were just getting good at being physically intimate. I felt like I was missing out. I wanted to keep myself sexually pure. We hadn't been sexually pure before our marriage, and it took us six years to work through that. It wasn't until he left for Iraq that we were finally figuring out how to make things work in the bedroom.

There were lots of questions about what is biblically allowed in my husband's absence. The best thing I did for him was get the books *Romancing Your Husband* and *Romancing Your Wife* by Debra White Smith. In her books she had ideas from others—like King Solomon for instance. One example was to write a sexually explicit letter to him. It connects you in a way that couldn't be any other way with distance between you. My husband's response? "Send me more!" It helped that his visualization was about me and not someone else. And I avoided men at all costs because I didn't want the possibility of an emotional affair or anything else.

My struggle: I didn't want to even have the conversation about what would happen if Steve died. The worst was talking about what to do with the insurance money if he died. He had enough to pay off the mortgage, and I could live on some for a while. What do I do if he dies? Pay off house, get a job, sell the house, and move back to family. Do it. At least if something happens you won't wonder what he would say or do. Get his advice in advance.

My strength: Best thing I ever did was teach my kids early to clean up after themselves. By the time my kids were between two and three years old, they could clean up after themselves. I also keep a calendar of events. Because I tend to lose appointment cards, I write everything down on that calendar. I love my house clean, but I learned that the whole thing doesn't have to be clean at the same time.

My hope: When Steve's not there and that sense of him is gone, I know that God is there. I had to learn to give over control. I had to give over control of my husband because he was in another country and I couldn't help him even when there were people trying to kill him. I really learned to rely on God and grow. I finally realized you can just talk to God and not have to pray a certain way.

Physical Intimacy

One of the reasons women fantasize about relationships with men is because the reality of their physical relationship has lost the sparkle and there is nothing left to write home about. There's no sizzle or zing. The slow-burning passion has been replaced with an emotionally detached "quickie." As North American women we've been deceived into believing that unless there's plenty of action in the bedroom we're missing out on the "real thing."

The truth is that although a passionate sexual relationship within the bounds of marriage is a healthy, beautiful, and biblically desirable thing, your physical relationship with your husband needs first of all to be pure.

Second Corinthians 10:5–6 (KJV) says we should be "casting down imaginations, and every high thing that exalteth itself against the knowledge of God, and bringing into captivity every thought to the obedience of Christ." Many times, our imaginations, critical thoughts, and pride keep us from obeying Christ in the way we love our husbands and allow them to love us.

We all long to be touched, hugged, kissed, and loved. When the boy you had your first crush on sat just a little closer than usual, your tummy did flip-flops and your heart raced. Do you remember the first time a boy kissed you on the lips? And when your body responded for the first time to a man's touch? Suddenly, love was awakened, and the physical needs and urges that God created in you were brought to life.

From that moment on, we expect a replay. We want the thrill, the chills, and the experience of the physical act of love like it once was or like we've read it could be. And when the bedroom becomes humdrum and the time between moments of passionate love between us and our lover grows too long, we feel cheated. Cheated out of our dreams and expectations, cheated out of the kind of love we feel we deserve. We're not sure we'll ever get it, and we certainly don't want to talk about it or work at it. So we settle for less.

Pornography has become a women's addiction issue even though many would claim it is a man's problem. It's because women wonder if there could be more. Could it be better? Why don't I have the mountain-high experience that others talk about? Is it me? So a quick peek into a website here or there—just to check it out—becomes a snare and secret substitution for what they think they can never have with their husbands.

Along with pornography is the almost never talked about act of masturbation. As our imaginations run wild, or we fill our eyes with images that excite and stimulate our senses, we find our bodies hungering for the ecstasy of the moment. Quickly masturbation becomes a habitual substitute for the gentle, tender, and passionate love of a husband for his wife.

A woman sat at my kitchen table and explained to me that no man could be as great as her fantasy, or have the patience it would take to give her the kind of orgasm she could achieve on her own. She had convinced herself that she could divorce herself from him emotionally and become the "tool" on which he could release his physical needs and she'd be content with that as long as she could be her own lover. She will never experience the true love of her husband as long as she maintains that position.

Building a godly marriage means commitment to a relationship that points to Jesus Christ as the sole Provider of all our needs, the ultimate example of a lover and the Redeemer and Restorer of everything. That includes your sexual relationship with your husband.

One of the most difficult tasks a solo mom can put her hand to is freeing herself from the bondage of fantasy and masturbation. For many women it becomes a quick way to relax at the end of an exhausting day and an easy way to pull your mind away from the worries and unfinished to-do lists. Women also give themselves false reassurance that the ease of reaching orgasm through masturbation can free them up to give their husbands permission to have sex with them without the pressure of climaxing at all during the act of love.

Women have believed the lie that fantasy and masturbating can be a part of the pure marriage bed that Scripture talks about.

God gently taught me that in order to love my husband well, I had to prepare myself for encountering him in a physical way with much greater strategy and intention. I had to allow my body to long for him. I had to train my body to respond to his touch and not my own.

That meant a renewal of my mind! I confess that it was no easy task. There were many stops and starts. At first there were more failures than successes as I got started on this path toward marital purity. I made changes to what I read. Although I had never read secular romance novels, I felt God prompting me to cut out even the Christian romances—most of the heroes were handsome, hard-working, and passionate with the added bonus of being godly! The next step I felt God asking me to take was to seriously increase the censorship on the kinds of movies I watch. To this day I will almost never see anything that has a rating beyond "G." I have learned how to put a filter on my eyes and ears. You will need to spend time before the Lord, asking him to reveal to you if there is anything in your life that needs changing. It may not be movies or romance novels for you, but perhaps there are other areas the Lord would like to help you with in order to bring greater intimacy to your marriage bed.

Harder, though, is putting a stop to the movie of the mind. The only way to combat images and memories is to replace them with something new every time they come up. I purposely read before bed to keep my mind off things that could draw me into an imaginary situation. After the lights are out, I review Bible verses in my head. This may sound strict, but I must be. My relationship with my husband is not one I am willing to sacrifice for a few moments of pleasure without him. My choices will impact his eternity, and that of my children. So I do not allow myself a moment where my mind could wander down old trails.

As you embark on the task of renewing your mind, remember that you must replace everything you take out. You can't just remove something. You must replace it. You do not want to leave an "empty house."

When an evil spirit leaves a person, it goes into the desert, seeking rest but finding none. Then it says, "I will return to the person I came from." So it returns and finds its former home empty, swept, and in order. Then the spirit finds seven other spirits more evil than itself, and they all enter the person and live there. And so that person is worse off than before. That will be the experience of this evil generation. (Matt. 12:43-45)

I am not using this passage to imply that masturbation and fantasy are indications of demon possession. Not at all. But I am suggesting that the Devil will send his cohorts, his demons, to distract and dissatisfy you in every way possible to destroy you and your marriage. There's no question that Satan wants your marriage to fail. He wants you to be lonely, depressed, and feeling as sexually deprived as possible in the hopes that you will lose sight of the eternity that has been planted in you and thus lure you to his side. It is Satan's desire to make sure any intimate moments you have with your husband are robbed of the glory for which they were created. Satan does not want you to have a good sex life.

Put up a fight! Don't let him get another moment.

And he will do exactly what that passage says. You may have seen this work in your life or the lives of others. You get your act together, clean it up, and sweep it clean. Things go really well for a few days, weeks, or even months. Then all of a sudden there is a relapse like nothing you've ever seen. The grip it has on you is stronger than ever. The hope and freedom you once had is so far gone, you are not even sure it is worth the fight.

That strong relapse is this Bible verse in action.

You need to take this seriously and pursue, chase down, engage in, and establish habits and thought patterns that are pleasing to God—holy, pure, and acceptable. Nothing else will do.

Confess your sin to God and accept his forgiveness. He will rejoice over you and extend forgiveness—full and free. That is a promise. He is a God of healing and hope. I have learned that God's forgiveness is complete and refreshing. He is so tender in his love for us and so gentle in how he pursues us.

He wants more for you than just forgiveness. He also wants to bring you freedom and abundance in even this area of your life. Yes, God wants you to have a fulfilling and passionate sexual relationship with your husband. Forgiveness is just the first step.

Every physical relationship we have with a man connects us to him in some way. It is mysterious to me, yet it is so evident in the broken lives of women all over the world. Every time we allow a man to love us physically, we are opening a bit of our souls to them. I didn't understand that for years. I had no idea. All I knew was that I wanted freedom.

It took some time for me to break my bad habits of fantasizing and masturbation. As I did, I found a freedom I didn't know existed. I felt stronger. I was more confident in the power of God and his Word. I knew God was healing me. The change in me was spectacular, and I felt like a new woman. Except for one thing.

I couldn't enjoy my relationship with my husband in a way that would allow me to be free to climax or even initiate love-making with him. I felt stuck. I would get up in the morning and try to talk myself into the mood. I would set the stage, wear sexy little numbers, and get rid of the kids. (We've had a few awkward interruptions!) The time would come, and I would feel like a rock. A lump of ugliness and cold, hard emotion would form in the pit of my stomach. No soothing music or candlelight could soften my seemingly hardened heart. Yet I so desperately wanted to show Trent my love physically.

Following another failed attempt at engaging fully with my husband, I spent the day fasting and praying. I begged God to give me emotion and a soft heart toward my husband. For hours I cried out to God to bless me with the reality of a beautiful and intimate relationship with Trent. Finally God gave me a picture in my mind. It was almost like a movie.

On the screen of my mind was a stage with a life-sized marionette. She was dancing this way and that way, as if an amateur puppeteer was handling her, or if she was trying to dance on her own, out of sync with the puppeteer. The marionette was me. I had strings attached to my hands, wrists, head, shoulders, knees, feet, and waist. There were more strings than I had ever seen on a puppet.

All at once from stage left, a different puppet entered. Although in my picture he looked just exactly like I did, I knew in my heart that this new marionette represented Trent. So I went toward him to give him a hug.

A simple hug, yet the marionette failed. All my strings got tangled up with each other and his. I could hardly even get close to him because the strings were all in the way. I was holding my arms out as if to hug him when he asked me to dance.

I danced as well as any marionette can dance. I went this way and that, but I could never get close enough to Trent's marionette to hold onto him, embrace him, or move in sync with him. I plunked to the floor of the stage in a defeated heap of failure.

I was alone on the stage when God spoke to me. He explained how each of those strings were actual heart-ties I had accumulated over the years of my life. That I would never be able to love Trent fully with those strings attached. I leaned over and lay on the floor, sobbing. I didn't even look up as I wailed at God, "Then how am I ever going to be the wife he needs? How will I ever feel the love of my husband?"

Gently the words of the Lord rolled over me as he said, "Get rid of the strings."

"How? How do I get rid of the strings? How?"

"Confess each string to me, and I'll cut it. I'll set you free."

As he said those words to my hungry soul I saw that each string was attached not to the sticks in the puppeteer's hand but to men in my life. There was my first boyfriend. A co-worker. Another boyfriend. A guy I had liked and really wanted to date, but never had. A fantasy man. A boss. The man from my extramarital relationship. I saw then how each one of them was somehow tied to my inability to love Trent completely.

Although I had never slept or had sex with any other man, I had built relationships with them in my mind. God revealed to me how a man I had dated for only ten days had always been available for an imaginary rendezvous. It became apparent to me that even those that I had broken up with because of painful situations still had redeeming qualities that I could use to compare Trent to.

When we date, have a crush on someone, or engage in fantasy, we rarely (dare I say, never) allow our minds to linger on the terrible. When was the last time you fantasized about a dead-beat dad or a man who ignored you? Doesn't happen. We remember the good times. We concentrate on the moments that allow us to relive the excitement and dazzle. It is those moments that keep us from being fully released to love our husbands.

You may have broken up with them years, even decades ago. But the effects on your heart have not been erased. Every heart tie to another man is like an open door to an adventure in real life or fantasy that your husband is not a part of and can never measure up to.

God wanted to release me from those heart ties. He heard me as, one by one, I named for him each person that I had ever liked, loved, or wanted to love me. I asked him to break the tie that bound me to that person and set me free from the deceptive feelings of excitement that came with the memories of that relationship. I watched as the strings on my marionette were cut, removed. One by one, limb by limb, I was being freed until there was one left.

I asked God if that string belonged to Trent and he said it didn't.

Slowly, and gently, God reached down into my heart and mind and brought to my memory the one person I had thought was hidden. I actually had convinced myself that he had never really been an issue. But God sees all things. I did not want God to cut this string. I asked him to please allow me just one attachment. He said nothing. I was so afraid that if I let God cut that string and there was no change in my relationship with Trent that I'd never feel love again. I sobbed and sobbed. Finally the pain became so overwhelming that I said, "Okay, God, you can cut it. I want to dance freely, no strings attached. I want that more than anything." So he cut the string.

I lay there motionless as a marionette on the stage. I had no life left in me. "God," I cried out, "don't leave me here, useless and dead. Can I connect to you? Can you give me a connection that has life?"

I felt energy surge through the marionette that was me. As my head was pulled up I realized that God had attached me not to a cross of sticks from which to control me, but to his heart from where he could love me. And I danced. The stage in my mind became a place full of beautiful motion, grace, and exuberant joy. My arms and legs were moving freely.

Trent, the marionette, entered stage left once again, and I connected with him freely as we twirled around the stage. We entered each others arms and floated out again. He could come and go as he pleased, dance where he wanted to, but my dance steps never faltered because God, my heart-attached puppeteer, was leading in the dance.

It is this kind of freedom that I hope and pray for you. As a solo mom you are lonely and you long for the loving arms of a man who cherishes you. Your husband cannot and will not always (or ever) be able to meet your physical needs the way that the books, movies, or shows portray. As you remove all impurity from your mind and heart and allow God to cut the ties that bind, you will be free to dance a dance of love with Jesus and fully engage with your husband when the time is right.

Don't settle for anything less. Press on toward the prize set before you. God has planted eternity in your heart. Live for it with passion!

Chapter Thirteen

The Father Your Kids Need

We had had a fabulous day together, the kids and I. They had enjoyed a day in the pool at a friend's house, playing at a park, and a gourmet lunch of Costco samples (a highlight for my kids). To top it all off, I took them to Denny's for supper and our favorite waiter served us and gave the kids each a little something extra. I had the sense of having provided my children with an almost perfect day. There had been few to no squabbles. The bedtime routine was going smoothly, and my happy, tired children were almost all tucked into bed. I was ready for some precious quiet time of my own. So as I tucked in the last sleepy child, I had no idea what could possibly worm its way into our content little family and destroy those beautiful moments.

To tuck Aethan into his bed, I had to stand on the rails of the bottom bunk. Then I leaned way over to hug him. After praying for him, I said, "Okay, Aethan, now it's time for you to pray."

"I don't want to."

"Well, why don't you want to? At least tell Jesus thank you for the great day we had."

"I'm not talking to Jesus anymore."

"That's not very nice," I said with a quick answer to hide my shock that this child had decided to give God the silent treatment. I had anticipated this might happen during the teen years, not when he was six. "You wouldn't like it if your friends didn't talk to you."

"No, I'm not talking to Jesus."

"Just say thank you to him for at least one thing, honey." I wondered in my heart who I could ask that would know if it was wrong to force a child to pray. I didn't get very far in thinking of someone though, because with the force of an anger deeply held, he sat up in bed, looked me straight in the face, and spoke his mind.

"I'm not talking to God because he didn't do a good job today!"

I quietly spoke to him, reminding him of all the fun of the day, the friends he'd seen, how God had provided enough for us to go for supper, and that there had been extra samples at Costco that day. He kept shaking his head.

"None of that counts." He was an angry kid.

"What would God have had to do in order to do a good job today?"

He balled up his fists, flung himself onto his back, and with clenched teeth and tears in his eyes he said, "If God had done his job properly today he would have brought Papa home."

It was all I could do to keep from sobbing so hard I couldn't comfort him. Deep inside I knew this was not something a hug and a kiss would fix. I could hold him, cry with him, let him know that I also wished God had brought Trent home today, and pray.

Then anger filled me. I was more than upset at Trent. Why did he have to have a job that rarely allowed him to be home? Why had we ever thought this would be a good thing? Where was he when all the pain of his absence was being directed at me and at God? Did he not realize that his absence was making it more difficult for his son to choose a heavenly eternity?

I carried my weeping son to my bed. Trent was in another time zone, but I called his cell phone anyway. Aethan talked to him and told him what he had told me. My pain doubled when I spoke with Trent and heard him say how "cute" it was that Aethan missed him so much.

He either had no idea or, like me, had no way to make it better, so was at a loss for words and emotion.

> Every "married single mom" that responded to an online survey reported that she doesn't believe her husband understands how his absence affects her and the kids. Every one.

Our oldest daughter told a counselor, through play therapy for an emotional disorder, that she thought we were divorced and just hadn't told her. Trent would come home so late and leave so early she wouldn't see him. Or he was on trips for weeks at a time. When he did come home, it was Christmas or another holiday. Sometimes she'd see him arrive and me leave. She couldn't understand, and logically reasoned that I was taking advantage of having the car home and another adult in the house while I shopped for groceries and ran other errands in the middle of the night (there are great reasons for twenty-four-hour shopping). She thought we were divorced and that he was arriving to babysit and would leave when I got home.

When Trent and I moved our family to Canada to live a slower-paced life and have a little more opportunity for him to be home, we still had no idea how much stress the kids had been under. Then we saw them relax. Trent set up a home office just off our kitchen and worked from there much of the first year. When he did go away for business meetings, he'd often leave early and the kids would assume that he was in the office, not realizing he wasn't home.

One day though, several months after living under this new arrangement, Trent had to go for a lunch appointment. He got ready to leave, put his jacket on, and the kids started crying and acting out. The stress in our home escalated quickly. The good-bye kisses and hugs went on until we had to force them to stop so he could leave. Our youngest son sat on the stairs wailing. He cried for hours. No matter what I did, I couldn't calm him. He told me he was going to stay there until Papa came home. I told him it would be a long time, thinking a few hours. He understood a long time to be what they had experienced before—months. So his wailing got louder, and he didn't move from the stairs.

School work was a waste that day. The kids couldn't think straight and were fighting and angry with each other and me. They talked about Trent as if they'd never see him again and would burst into tears just thinking about him. So I announced a day off school.

There was no celebration. They moped around the kitchen. Later in the afternoon, Trent arrived home. McCaellen was still on the stairs. Trent was mobbed by four children who had grieved his absence for the entire four hours he was gone. That taught us to tell the children the day before if Trent was going to be leaving, where he'd be going, and approximately what time he'd be home. He made a point of calling from the road to let them know where he was and how things were going. It helped them begin to trust that he would indeed be coming home.

We've also learned how to express our playful love for each other in front of them. This encourages them. It reminds them that we are still choosing to love each other and that we are not divorced or even thinking about it.

We told our children the story of something that happened on our honeymoon. Because I had not worn my wristwatch on my wedding day and had forgotten to pack it into my suitcase, I was constantly asking Trent what time it was. For some reason I didn't realize before I married him that Trent doesn't wear a watch. He hates them! So the only time I could find the time was when we were in the car or in the bedroom of our cabin. Every time either of us checked the time—every single time—during our whole honeymoon, it was eleven minutes after the hour. It became our private joke. We would begin guessing. If it was close to suppertime, we would ask if it was six eleven. And we'd be right!

After our honeymoon ended, we would sometimes just happen to look at a clock when it was eleven past the hour, and it would remind us of our honeymoon. If Trent was around, he would lean over and say, "Honeymoon time!" and kiss me. The trouble was he hadn't been around enough for them to see that.

One day when he was home at 11:11 a.m., I noticed the time and called Trent to come out of his office. I called in such a tone that he thought it was an emergency! I grabbed him and said, "Eleven eleven, honeymoon time!" And we smooched. When we came up for breath, he looked at the clock and it hadn't changed yet—so we went in for round two! I took a quick break to tell the kids to let us know when the time changed. We kept kissing with an audience of four wide-eyed observers. When 11:12 came, we stopped, he went back to work, and I explained the story of honeymoon time to the kids.

Rarely does a day go by when Trent is home that the kids don't at least once come running to tell one of us that it is honeymoon time. If he's not home, I'll try to call him or he'll call me with a quick call that says, "It's honeymoon time. I love you!"

Not only does this keep us on our toes with our own relationship, but it has had an incredibly healing effect on our children. Your children and mine all need to know that Mom and Dad are in love. They need to know that their parents' marriage is safe and stable. You've heard it before, but it bears repeating: the best gift you can give your children is to love their dad.

Handling Your Children's Hurting Hearts

Those deep hurts my children suffered have healed some over the years. But even now there is still significant suffering in their hearts over the sense of abandonment they felt from their dad. Every business trip stirs up old hurts and reopens wounds. When Trent is home but has not participated in family life due to choices of work or excessive time in hobbies (such as computer gaming) or just poor time management, they begin to feel burdened with questions that beg answers. Why does he not want to spend time with me? Why do I have to beg for a date with Dad? Is there something wrong with me? Am I not good enough? Does he wish I'd never been born and think that I'm just in the way?

As a solo-parenting mom, you cannot heal the hurt in your children's hearts. Grieve that fact and then turn your attention to what you can do. You can lead them to places where they might experience hope and healing.

Children with absent dads—and I don't necessarily mean deadbeat dads—all need to be introduced to God as the one and only Father who will never leave them, abandon them, or hurt them. There is no other way for them to receive the healing their hearts need. You cannot be their savior. You will never be their dad. When you attempt to be their healer, to cover up for him to soften their pain, to continue to spoon-feed false hopes to them, or attempt to help them to expect less in an effort to avoid disappointment, then you hurt them. You will be stunting their growth as individuals by not empowering them to become strong in character and faith.

Life is hard. For some it is harder than others. You don't know what God's future is for your children. You cannot protect them from difficult times. Take them by the hand and walk with them through it. Lead them to the places where they can be nourished with the love, acceptance, and security that their very souls crave.

Let's say your son comes to you with his decision to compete in the Ironman Triathlon. First of all, your jaw might drop to the floor, especially if he huffs and puffs running to the basement for a load of laundry! After your initial shock wears off, you decide to support him the best way you can. You tuck him into a nice comfy bed to stay there for a few months to save his energy. You bring him his meals on a tray and serve him whatever his heart desires: pizza, smokie dogs, ice cream, hot wings, fried chicken, and Kraft dinners. You move the TV into his room and attach the remote to his wrist with a strap. He looks up to you from his pillow and with content-ment in his eyes says, "Thanks, Mom. I love you."

Your heart will melt, and you may be able to convince yourself that you are really doing the best for him. After all, things are going to be really hard on him during that race, and he needs to be as rested and ready for it as possible.

Yeah, right. You know as well as I do that to pamper him like that would guarantee failure for your son. Not just failure but possibly damaged mus-cles, torn ligaments, heart attack due to unaccustomed sudden exertion, and potentially even death. He won't be singing your praises then, will he?

Why, then, do mothers, especially solo moms, think we are helping our children by saving them from the pain of growing in character? We never want our children to suffer. If I could choose it, I would like to see my chil-dren grow in character and become incredible men and women without ever suffering a moment in their lives. But I can show you from Scripture that for them to become the kind of men and women we can eternally be proud of, we will have to allow them to hurt, grow, persevere, and learn to pursue God regardless.

> We can rejoice, too, when we [and our children] run into problems and trials, for we know that they help us develop endurance. And en-durance develops strength of character, and character strengthens our confident hope of salvation. And this hope will not lead to disap-pointment. For we know how dearly God loves us, because he has given us the Holy Spirit to fill our hearts with his love." (Rom. 5:3–5)

When our daughter was five, she was diagnosed with an emotional disorder called trichotillomania. It is an impulse-control disorder that is predominantly characterized by the urge (and consequent action) to pull out one's own hair. This devastated me. Our Christian psychiatrist told us he thought it was aggravated by her intense sense of abandonment by her dad and others in her life. There was nothing I could do. Seeing her come down the stairs with no eyebrows or eyelashes in those early days, and later whole bunches of hair missing from her head, crushed me. Sometimes it hurt me so badly I could hardly breathe.

The psychiatrist told me I could not beat myself up every time she pulled out her hair. He instructed me to allow her to take control of her own pulling and to make her responsible for it. He said I should only help her if she asked for it. I thought he was crazy! How could I stand by and watch this happen? Did he not understand how much I loved her and wanted to wipe away all trace of pain from her heart so that she would never pull again?

It took me many weeks to finally try his advice. I would only help her if she asked. It took many mornings of slipping away quietly to the bathroom to cry after seeing her face newly plucked that she began to ask for help. I have never felt so elated as when my little five-year-old, on her own accord, came asking, "Mommy, I feel like pulling again. Can I have oil?" With gentle fingers and a secret praise party happening in my heart I would put oil over her eyes so that she couldn't get a grasp of the lashes or brows.

I learned, through the painful process of letting go, that I cannot cure her pain. I have to rely on God to do that. My lifelong commitment is to bring her, and all my other children, to the throne of God, the Healer of all hearts. I am committed to giving them the freedom to feel the pain necessary to reach out to me and others who will point them to God when they can't find their own way there. That's what our role as mom is—to give our children every opportunity to encounter Jesus in every situation, in the pain, the joy, the suffering, and the blessing.

Maybe you think I'm too wound up in this Jesus stuff. Why not a different role model? Why not just redirect their energies to give vent to their frustration and anguish? Why Jesus?

I hope the words of Stephen Lawhead in my all-time favorite book, a novel called *Byzantium*, will set in your heart the answer to that question.

Aidan (Aeddan to the Vikings) is asking the same kind of hard questions we are asking. He is the first one speaking:

"We put our trust in the Lord God, and were proved fools for be-lieving. We endured slavery and torture and death, and God lifted not a finger to save us. I saw our own blessed Bishop Cadoc hacked to pieces before my eyes and God—the God he loved and served all his days—did not so much as lift a finger to ease his suffering."

Ruadh regarded me severely, his brow creased in disapproval. "As he did nothing when his beloved son died on the cross," my anamcara pointed out. "We are closest to Christ when sharing the world's misery. Think you Jesu came to remove our pains? Wherever did you get that notion? The Lord came, not to remove our suffering, but to show us the way through it to the glory be-yond. We can overcome our travails. That is the promise of the cross." . . .

Gunnar was quiet for a moment, gazing at the little stone cha-pel. "The people of Skania pray to many gods who neither hear nor care," Gunnar said. "But I remember the day you told me about Jesu who came to live among the fisherfolk, and was nailed to a tree by the skalds and Romans and hung up to die. And I remem-ber thinking, this Hanging God is unlike any of the others; this god suffers, too, just like his people.

"I remember also that you told me he was a god of love and not revenge, so that anyone who calls on his name can join him in his great feasting hall. I ask you now, does Odin do this for those who worship him? Does Thor suffer with us?"

"This is the great glory of our faith," I murmured, thinking of Ruadh's words to me—but changing them to reflect Gunnar's sentiment, "that Christ suffers with us and, through his suffering, draws us near to himself."

"Just so!" agreed Gunnar eagerly. "You are a wise man, Aeddan. I knew you would understand. This is most important, I think."

"You find this comforting?"

"Heya," he said. "Do you remember when the mine overseer

was going to kill us? There we were, our bodies were broken, our skin blackened by the sun—how hot it was! Remember?"

"Sure, it is not a thing a man easily forgets."

"Well, I was thinking this very thing. I was thinking: I am going to die today, but Jesu also died, so he knows how it is with me. And I was thinking, would he know me when I came to him? Yes! Sitting in his hall, he will see me sail into the bay, and he will run down to meet me on the shore; he will wade into the sea and pull my boat onto the sand and welcome me as his wayfaring brother. Why will he do this? Because he too has suffered, and he knows, Aeddan he knows." Beaming, Gunnar concluded, "Is that not good news?"[1]

Then Aidan remembers:

Everyone dies, Gunnar had said. All flesh is grass, said Cadoc. What did you expect, Aidan?

Did you really think that Christ would blunt the spear-points, deflect the lash, cause the chains to melt away when they touched your skin? Did you expect to walk in sunlight and not feel the heat, or to go without water and not grow thirsty? Did you think that all the hatred would turn to brotherly love the moment you strode into view? Did you think both storms and tempers would calm because of the tonsure on your head?

Did you believe that God would shield you forever from the hurt and pain of this sin-riven world? That you would be spared the injustice and strife others were forced to endure? That disease would no longer afflict you, that you would live forever untouched by the tribulations of common humanity?

Fool! All these things Christ suffered, and more. Aidan, you have been blind. You have beheld the truth, stared long upon it, yet failed to perceive so much as the smallest glimpse of all that was shown you. Sure, this is the heart of the great mystery: that God became man, shouldering the weight of suffering so that on the final day none could say, "Who are you to judge the world? What do you know of injustice? What do you know of torture, sickness, poverty? How dare you call yourself a righteous God! What do you know of death?"

He knows, Aidan, he knows![2]

Jesus is not "just" God. He is not out there somewhere. He is not distant from us. He is the God who walks with us. His presence in our lives is what gives hope, not to escape our circumstances or the effects we'll sustain from them, but to demonstrate that he is a God of power, love, and redemption. God with us. That is what the angels called him. Emmanuel. And that's "why Jesus."

Introducing Your Children to Jesus

Tell Them About Him. A surprising number of children and teens have no clue who Jesus is. They may know there is supposed to be some big deal about the dude, but they can't tell you what it is. That's because we're not telling them.

Tell them Bible stories. If they are young, you can get fabulous books that have beautifully illustrated Old Testament stories. Introduce them to the God of power. As they get older, you can find resources that encourage them to develop a fascination for God and his Word. Our family is particularly fond of the comic-strip-style Bible called *The Picture Bible.*[3]

Read the Bible with them and to them. There is a promise in the Bible that says: "So is my word that goes out from my mouth: It will not return to me empty, but will accomplish what I desire and achieve the purpose for which I sent it" (Isa. 55:11 NIV). That means that when you read God's Word (the Bible) it will never, ever be a waste. You may not see a difference today or next week, but God will never let the reading of his Word become a useless exercise.

Teach your kids to read the Bible themselves. Encourage them to come to you with questions, interesting facts, and comments about what they are learning as they read. Keep a Bible handy. It should be within easy reach at all times. I bought myself a cute little red one that fits easily into my small purse. I don't have very much of the Bible memorized, and it never fails that when I'm driving down the freeway someone will ask a deep theological question. If someone yells from the back of the van, "Hey, Mom, does the

Bible talk about dinosaurs?" I can flip through it at the next stop light or have them find the passages themselves because my Bible is handy.

Don't be surprised when your kids ask some interesting questions. Our young son and his friend were reading the Bible to find an answer to a question. I heard them laughing like crazy. Giggling actually. Finally my son came to me and said, "Mom, what's a prostitute? *He* won't tell me." I asked him why he wanted to know and he read Proverbs 30:20 to me out of the Message Bible.

"'Here's how a prostitute operates: she has sex with her client, takes a bath, then asks, "Who's next?"' Why does she have to take a bath after?" my son asked me. Such an innocent question, right?

You never know what they will read, but let them read. Give them permission to devour it. For many years we had a rule in our house that our kids were welcome to stay up past "lights out" time under one condition: they had to be reading their Bibles. At first they read just so they could stay up later. As time went on and the kids got older, we had to change that rule and limit how late they could stay up. They were able to find some riveting stories in that thick, old book, and I would occasionally find them still reading close to midnight.

Teach Them to Pray. I had never been taught how to pray. I had prayed, sure: grace before meals, a recited list of confessions every night, and a quick "bless all those I love" before I said, "Amen" and crawled into bed. Yet if you are like many people in North America, there are days, weeks, and maybe even months where you have wondered if praying is worth it. Your prayers never seem to get past the ceiling, and it has been a while since you can honestly say you've had a prayer answered. In order to teach your children, you need to learn to pray along with them.

Journal your prayers. Write out what you want to say to God and the questions you have for him. Learn to listen to what he is saying as you talk to him. Write that down, too. No conversation with God is one-sided unless we don't allow him to talk. He wants to communicate with you, share his secrets, and express his love. Be quiet long enough with him to hear him speak with a word, thought, or picture in your heart and mind. Then respond to him accordingly.

There are plenty of fabulous books on learning how to pray, by authors such as Dutch Sheets and Stormie Omartian. One of my favorites that talks about how to hear and understand what God is saying is called *The Power of a Whisper* by Bill Hybels. Take a look at appendix A for some other titles you can start with and pick up one or two of them. Make a point to get to know Jesus and learn how to talk with him. The best way to become great at praying is to pray.

The Bible says to pray continually. You can't spend all day on your knees. No one would eat, and you'd never get to work or even be able to make a move to obey what God's told you to do. Praying all the time means having an ongoing conversation with God in your head. As you make dinner, allow your mind to focus on the things you are thankful for. Talk to God about the person whose clothes you are folding. As you drive along, sing praise to God, focusing on how he has blessed you—because he has. As worries and concerns, stresses and frustrations enter your mind, turn them over to him. Make a point to use your entire mind, all day long, to talk to Jesus. In quiet moments throughout the day as you turn your attention to him, you will find him speaking to your heart, giving wisdom, direction, and encouragement because he loves you.

Pray out loud with and for your children. You can use the blessing prayers at the back of this book to pray for them each night if that helps. Touch your children when you pray for them. Ask them what their concerns, fears, and needs are. Then out loud, bring those needs before the Lord. Let your children observe you hand your concerns to God.

Allow them to pray for you, as well. Ask them to. The Bible says, "I also tell you this: If two of you agree here on earth concerning anything you ask, my Father in heaven will do it for you. For where two or three gather together as my followers, I am there among them" (Matt. 18:19–20). God hears children just as well as adults.

Teach your children to pray blessings for their dad. They are going to receive healing and forgiveness, hope and possibly restoration as they pray wholeheartedly for their father's success and God's blessing on him. You need to set this example. As you pray for your husband, pray not for God to change him but that God would shine his favor on him.

Go to Church with Your Family. If your husband joins you, praise God! If not, don't let that discourage you from providing yourself and your children the benefits for which God created the community of believers we call the church. Make sure the church you attend teaches that Jesus is the Son of God, fully man and fully God, born of a virgin; and that the only way to receive salvation is through him because of his death on the cross and his resurrection on the third day. It is critical that the church teach and live out the truth that the Holy Spirit is alive and working in our world and our lives, comforting us, empowering us, and teaching us. They must believe and teach that the Bible is the holy and inerrant Word of God.

Find a church where you all can make friends and where you feel comfortable with the style of worship and the amount of liturgy. Support and encourage your children to be active in the children's and youth programs. Get to know the leaders in the church. Volunteer and become active in using the gifts God has given you as you serve his people and his church.

We have been blessed with church leadership that loves our family. They pray for us. When my kids are struggling, their pastor and leaders pray with them, spend time with them, and lead them to Jesus in a way that I couldn't. I know that my kids are in a safe environment. I have gotten to know their leaders and their friends. I can give my children freedom and bless them by saying, "It's okay with me if you share tough stuff with your leaders." I love being able to empower them to seek out help, hope, and healing on their own in a godly environment.

Call on Help for Them When They Can't. Sometimes our kids need our help to walk the hard path to counsel, assistance, and freedom. When they are crying out for help, carry them to the Lord. Find biblical counselors, pastors, and leaders trained in prayer ministry, inner healing, and deliverance to help lead your child to Jesus.

Children from homes of all kinds suffer in today's world. It is not uncommon to have kids from good, solid, Christian homes make choices and experiment with lifestyles that are not healthy or safe. The children and youth of our culture are facing an uncertain future; the fear and insecurity that fills them each day cannot easily be dealt with, especially with their not-completely-developed understanding and maturity.

Let's face it—there are days even I worry about what tomorrow will hold. I've seen the news. It's no secret that the stock markets and economy in North America are not what they once were. We're on shaky ground. Instead of warning children about crossing the street safely, making sure they're wearing bike helmets, and the importance of completing high school, we're telling our grade school kids about drugs, sex, bullying, terrorism, and the global AIDS epidemic. Our children are not safe at school or on the Internet. They feel pressures we've never understood. If the world has gone so crazy, they wonder, then what's there to live for? Why do soldiers cross the ocean and die for this? Who will understand me? How can I live when I'm always so scared and lonely?

Now add to the mix a greater longing for significance because Dad is not around, building up their sense of identity. Our children carry an overwhelming burden.

Look out for them. Watch them. Touch them. Hold them. Talk with them. Listen to them. Pray for them.

Don't think that because you are a Christian, you go to church, or you've done so much to provide a good home for them that they won't look for a way to soothe their pain apart from God. They may try drugs, alcohol, sex, hooking up, cutting, bingeing and purging, violence, tagging, graphic music, body art or piercings, or any other number and combination of things.

Love them enough to be with them. I know that when our children hurt and act out it nearly breaks our hearts. This is not the time to show them anger and blame or to act out ourselves. We must wrap our arms around our children and show them that the unconditional love they are wondering about exists.

Do not blame your husband. It really doesn't matter whose fault is what. If an egg breaks on the floor, it makes a mess that needs to be cleaned up. How it broke will not make cleaning it up any easier. Let your child know that you will not lay blame, point fingers, or retaliate; then keep your promise.

Accept your part of the responsibility. Don't deny your part in your children's pain. When you have hurt your child or been part of a situation in which he or she was hurt, you need to acknowledge that truth and admit your mistakes. Then apologize and ask for forgiveness of your child. Ask God for forgiveness if you have, in fact, been part of the hurt your child bears. Then forgive yourself. Accept God's forgiveness and move on in the confidence that God allows nothing to happen that he cannot redeem.

Your children are a blessing from the Lord. Without his help, the path of parenting becomes a treacherous and dangerous journey. Give yourself and your children every opportunity for success. Lead them to encounter their heavenly Father so that they can rise to the challenge of living this hard life according to the eternity that has been planted in their hearts.

Chapter Fourteen

So Now You Want to Be a Part of This Family, Huh?

Every moment that our husbands are gone, we idealize the time when they will walk through that front door (or out of the TV room), throw their arms around us, and announce that they're home to stay, choosing to engage in family life and be the husbands and dads they were meant to be.

And when they do, we want to send them packing!

Learning to live as partners and parents together can be just as hard or harder than it was to adjust to the solo-parenting lifestyle you've wanted so long to be free from.

Each day you spent solo parenting was a day in which you grew stronger as a woman, more independent in your ways, more confident in your decisions, and less tolerant of not having things your way. You are less and less the woman you once were. Your character has grown, you've developed strengths and skills, and you have matured in your relationships with your children. You've created a home life that runs smoothly. Routines, schedules, and traditions have been set in place that do not include your husband. When he wants to participate again, there is no room.

You have changed. He has changed. Your situation has changed. The children have changed.

The kids forget his plate when they set the table. When arranging weekend social plans, you forget to see if they work for him because, well, because you are not used to including him. Your children balk and come running to you when he disciplines them because they are not used to being corrected by a "stranger" or with his style of discipline. When you come in from a busy day of shopping, doctor appointments, and a quick cup of coffee and he asks where you were, you feel offended that you have to give an account of your actions.

There are countless ways that adjusting to life as a family after a husband begins to reengage can be stressful. I recently spoke to someone whose sister-in-law was divorcing her husband. He had worked away from home for five years, a mutual decision they had made to help pay down debt and be able to save for their children's education. She managed the years apart. It was adjusting to life as a family afterward that was just too hard.

Let this be your warning: it will be hard. Be prepared for change and be willing to make the sacrifices necessary to learn to live and love as a family again.

All of what I've said in this book holds true here. Your role is to live according to the eternity planted in your heart. As your husband reenters family life, embrace him and give him every reason to be glad he did.

After all the time, perhaps years, that you have solo parented, you may feel like you deserve a break and that hubby had better be the one to serve it up on a silver platter. You may want to make life a little hard (or a lot hard) on him because he hurt you. This is one of the reasons dealing with the emotions from chapter 2 is so important. Only as your heart remains soft to him and ministered to by the Lord can you free your husband to learn to be the man that he wants to be, the man you need and that God created him to become.

Every payback you require from him, every punishment you deliver, every nettled comment will push him away. With experiences like that, he may be tempted to decide that coming home wasn't worth it and leave again, possibly for good. He may very well have a few things he needs to confess, apologize for, or provide for you, but you must allow God to reveal that to him. Don't try to be a human version of the Holy Spirit. You'll fail and your efforts will be lost, likely to backfire and hurt you both.

Decide to be the kind of woman he wants to come home to. You don't have to change your personality or strengths. Instead, take your attitude and fears to God. Don't let them slip between you and your husband.

MEET SAM

Name: Samantha Dodge

Location: Manitoba

Kids: two (ages 15, 9)

Married: fourteen years

Husband: Rick is a long-distance truck driver. He's actually an owner/operator. When he's not on the road with our truck, he's driving a cement truck locally. He's my absolute best friend, partner, and team player.

Favorites: I like to write poetry, the color blue, and I love the book *Meeting God at a Dead End* by Ron Mehl. Actually, Rick and I both like that book.

Longest time hubby's been away: Probably fifteen to sixteen days at one stretch. On average he's gone four to nine days at a time, but we never know how long he'll be home in between.

My choice: We always talk about our family as a team. The kids are a part of it, I am, and so is Rick. We all have to do our part, and sometimes that means filling in when another player is out of reach, so to speak. So when he's gone, the kids can mow the lawn (I hate that job!), or if I'm having a rough time, then Rick supports me. Because we have a common goal as a family, we are willing to do what it takes to reach it. We've asked the boys if they would rather that their dad get a job where he can be home every evening. They like the idea until they realize that it would mean I'd have to go back to work. They are supportive of Rick and his career because they understand their role and significance in our family.

I miss my husband when he's gone, but the decision to have this business was ours together. I support him in it, and I'm okay with what he does. I'm content knowing that we're in this together—it's not him against me.

My struggle: Because I have all boys, I see how much they miss a man around. They light up when they're with their dad. I don't know how to fill the needs like a dad or even how a guy should or does feel. I can't be both disciplinarian and nurturer, but I have to try.

My strength: We talk. A lot. We phone or e-mail all the time. Talking is one of the main ways we stay connected. I can call him just about whenever I want. We almost lost our marriage several years ago, so we know what we have to do to keep our marriage, and we do whatever it takes to never get to that place again. We have to talk about feelings and be open about everything. I've learned what he needs from me, and I give it to him. We talk like we're dating, and spontaneous PDA (public displays of affection) is something we're keeping!

My hope: When stuff happens—the truck breaks down or something else goes wrong—the kids and I pray for him. Just knowing that God's hand is in things helps. I know God knows the beginning and the end, but waiting in the meantime is where I learn trust. I picture us in a waiting room, patiently waiting our turn for an answer. God knows when the right time is, no matter how long the waiting gets. When you finally get that, it's easier to leave everything in God's hands.

Communication is every marriage counselor's favorite topic. That's because it really is important. When your husband is trying to reengage with you, it is even more so. Be very careful to keep the air clear and the communication lines open between you. How you handle things now will determine the rest of your lives together.

You have left each other to make certain decisions alone, pursue certain friendships or hobbies, and manage your own schedules. Don't assume that because he came home he automatically wants your input. You are not exactly begging for his, right? So why expect him to suddenly feel like he needs to report to you?

Step back and let things roll for a while. See how you naturally gravitate toward sharing information. As you notice things come up that are potential head-butting issues, stave them off by talking with him. Share with him how you have done things and how the changes are making you feel. Remember to honor him, show him love, and make even this conversation part of your effort to help him become God's man, fully and completely. Ask him for suggestions on how to make things work well. Take his suggestions seriously and consider how you could incorporate them, even if it seems like a bit of extra work. Not many men are interested in deliberately ruining their family's lives, especially not when they've just decided to "come home." Pray about what he's said, then follow the advice of the Holy Spirit.

It may take a few months to find even a shaky sense of stability. Be patient. Depending on how much he's been absent, it could take two years or more before you are fully reengaged as a family. The longer he's been gone, the longer it will take. The more flexible and obedient you are to Christ, the more smoothly and quickly it will happen.

Your children will struggle to adjust as well. They will come to you for everything because they always have. He could be sitting on the same couch they are, but they'll run two flights of stairs to ask you a question. They are doing this because it's what they've always done, not because they are purposely trying to hurt their dad. Your husband may not understand. Gently and respectfully become the liaison between them.

The times they come to you when they could have gone to their dad, send them back to him. Even if the answer is quick or it would take less time and effort for you to help them, if your husband is available and willing, encourage them to pursue him. "Go see what your dad says." One of the best gifts you can give your children is the freedom to have their dad be an active advisor in their lives. They may not want to offend you or make you feel like you've lost their allegiance. You will do them a great service by encouraging them to build a relationship with their father.

I often still respond to questions from my kids with, "What did Papa say?" Especially if I know they have not asked him. I am encouraging them to consider him a first-stop resource. If they say, "But Mom, can't you just tell me?" I often respond, "Absolutely! Just as soon as you find out what Papa says, I'll tell you what I think!" They usually grunt through a smile, go get his opinion, and come back for my answer. They have learned that whatever Papa says, I stand behind 100 percent. I will very rarely give an answer different than what he does. Not just because he gives good advice (because sometimes he doesn't, just like I don't), but because I want them to learn that doing things a different way or having a differing opinion is not necessarily a problem. Sometimes it's not about being right or wrong but about loving each other in spite of it all.

Create opportunities for your husband to succeed at home. Leave him with the kids, no matter how old, without cooking for him or leaving a written set of instructions for the day. If he can't cook (or won't), then the children will get to know the splurging side of a parent they may not have otherwise seen. If he orders in pizza, picks up a bucket of chicken, or treats them to McDonald's, thank him for giving the kids a day to remember. He may not do things the way you would. (Actually, it's quite likely that he won't.) That's okay. The house may be a disaster, and the kids might not be in bed when you get home at midnight. Relax. They are getting to know their dad in a way they couldn't if you were around.

As time goes on, you can share reasons for why you don't serve six bags of candy in a night or watch horror movies with the kids after dark. He may benefit from knowing the stress a sink full of dirty dishes and pretzels crunched into the carpet affords you. Remember, though, that he is not your housekeeper or nanny. Allow him to be the husband and dad he was created to be. Don't let chores or childcare get in the way of your relationship.

Take time away from each other. Wow! Did you ever think you'd need that? Give each other space. It's been a long time since you did everything together. Ease into it slowly. In the beginning, you may need more space than you will a few months down the road. Take it when you need it, and give him the permission he needs to get out, too.

You may actually need to kick him out for an evening now and then. If he's been on the road or had his time taken up with long hours at work, a hobby, or some other concerns, he also has not likely spent much time developing life-giving relationships for himself. He may have a whole host of business contacts or online gaming buddies, but lack face-to-face friends who care about him for who he is. Few things are scarier for a man than trying to make friends. Guys make friends when they play. Golfing, joining a sports team, or helping with a community project may be just what he needs. Don't be jealous of that. Instead, help him to ease into that and have your blessing as he does.

He may also be nervous about spending time away when he knows how difficult it is for you when he's gone. Encourage him to love you by growing as a person. As he develops friendships with other men, he will be refreshed and encouraged, ready to fulfill his role as the man in your life.

The number-one gift you can give your husband is freedom to spend time with God. Respect the quiet he may need to read his Bible and pray. When the men at church are going on a retreat, bless him as he joins them. Don't force him to go! But as you grow in godliness, pray that he will see Jesus in you and desire even more of that for himself.

Don't forget to compliment him. Thank him for being home. Share with him what you enjoy about him being home. Give him reasons to want to stay.

When things get hard (because they will) and he offends you, forgive quickly. You should also ask for forgiveness quickly when you know you've offended him. Pray continually and remember there's more to what is happening than what you see. The Devil is hoping you will let your guard down now that your husband is home. He wants to tear you apart, and if he can't tear you apart while you are living separate lives, he's going to fight with every trick at his disposal to keep you from coming together now.

There is one way—and only one way—to fight against this. Engage in spiritual warfare. Fight in the heavenlies for your marriage, your relationship, and the relationships of your children with their dad. Learn how to pray against the Enemy. Learn how to listen to the Holy Spirit and obey him.

It is possible to live as a happily married, godly couple with your husband away. It is possible to raise godly kids when Dad's not around. It is possible to bring all those parts together as a complete and unified family once again.

It is possible, but only with God's help.

I challenge you to this high calling. With God all things are possible. His glory can shine in your life. He wants to walk with you, to be Emmanuel in your situation, in your pain, in your joy, in your relationships.

You may be married, you may be a mom, you may be a solo parent. But you are first of all a daughter of the King.

Live out the passion of his love in your life. Live for the eternity planted in you.

Chapter Fifteen

From My Husband's Heart

It was June 5, 1993. I still remember the way my breath stopped as she walked toward me down the church aisle. I remember the earnestness of the vows I spoke and very little of what the pastor said. I was looking at my bride, and her beauty made me feel weak and strong at the same time.

I remember the tender awkwardness of our first kiss, and our second. We had saved them for that moment. I knew a great exhilaration, boldness, and peace as I walked out of that church holding the hand of my wife, the woman I knew God himself had selected for me.

I was absolutely confident.

I was utterly clueless.

Men Are Clueless

We had some things going for us. We both had solid roots in Jesus Christ and God's Word. We were both fully committed to a "till death do us part" kind of marriage. Both of our parents were married thirty years when we got married (and are still married today).

We were also starting our married life far away from family, which can be a great advantage in some ways. But it pulled Carla Anne out of her support network, leaving her for a time with only me to turn to. Unfortunately, I wasn't at all aware of how much and in what ways she needed me. Meanwhile, Carla Anne was convinced that she was being a good and supportive wife by not bothering me with her needs and struggles.

We lived like that for several years. With the help of a Christian marriage counselor, I slowly began to realize that I had some learning to do about my wife. She learned that she should be telling me much more and slowly began to realize that I needed and often really wanted to know.

We laugh about it now, but we missed out on so much of each other in those early years. It was also an incredibly lonely time for Carla Anne, particularly in that first year. She later told me how she once went through the talking yellow pages on the phone, starved for conversation.

One day she ran across an advertisement for St. Clair, the "Paint and Paper People." The advertisement said "call us to talk about it"—so she did. The ad clearly implied they wanted people to call about home renovation projects, but Carla Anne took advantage of their imprecision. She talked with someone at one extension for a while, then was transferred to another extension and talked to someone else for a while, then transferred again, and again. She probably chatted with most of their staff that day.

I would have never guessed my wife was so starved for my involvement in her life. It just simply didn't enter my mind.

There are many things that keep men from engaging with their families—some noble, some ignoble, and everything in between. They may be crippled in some way that prevents them from engaging. They may be constrained by circumstances outside their control. They may be choosing to invest themselves elsewhere for selfish reasons, or they may be investing themselves elsewhere because God has called them to do so. Often there is a combination of factors involved.

But the most common thing that keeps men from their wives and families is, quite simply, we are clueless. Husbands do not instinctively understand the nature and needs of their wives, nor do they easily comprehend when their wives try to tell them this. Add in a lack of good, observable role models and the bombardment of confusing and destructive messages in our culture and media, and what do you get? Whole generations of men who don't know what to do for their wives and families or how to engage with them. And they don't even know that they don't know.

This is an area where external help can be extremely effective.

External Help

I highly recommend finding a good marriage counselor. Many men when asked to see a marriage counselor will react negatively and defensively.

They may interpret the request as an attack or think you are trying to bring in someone else who will be on your "side." A good counselor must be on the husband's "side" as well. Finding a good counselor may take some time, but it is well worth the effort and investment.

The CEO of a company benefits from the counsel and involvement of a board of directors, and in a similar way, any married couple can be greatly helped by a good Christian marriage counselor. "Refuse good advice and watch your plans fail; take good counsel and watch them succeed" (Prov. 15:22 MSG).

I'm getting better, I think. And I'm still learning. These days I often have at least an inkling that I might be clueless about something. That helps me to be open to Carla Anne's suggestions, ideas, and comments.

Your husband may be clueless, too. You may have told him something a thousand times, but he still doesn't get it. That happens in our home, and it's often because Carla Anne and I aren't fluent in the same language. Oh, we both speak English, but I'm fluent in male or "blue" English and she's fluent in female or "pink" English. Unfortunately, the two languages share the same vocabulary, so it's rather easy to think we are speaking clearly yet be communicating something very different to each other.

For example, as I sit here and write, I'm aware that my gut is overhanging my belt a bit. It would be good for me to lose a few pounds. (Did I mention how great a cook Carla Anne is?) Now, if Carla Anne was to lovingly pick out a diet or exercise book for me and give it to me as a gift, I would probably appreciate it. If on the other hand I was to lovingly pick out a diet or exercise book and give it to her . . . what I say in *blue* is going to be heard very differently in *pink*!

Perhaps you have told your husband very little, expecting him to somehow know how to love and cherish you. That puts (and keeps) him at a disadvantage. He can't get better at something he doesn't know to do or know how to do.

Men are extremely achievement oriented and take pride in excellence. Give a man a clear blueprint for success, the tools he needs, and a push of encouragement, and watch him move mountains. Take those ingredients away and he will naturally disengage and look for them elsewhere.

Choose to believe in your husband's good will and intentions toward you even if you can't see them. Then tell him. Tell him what you need, what makes you tick, what you want. Keep telling him (in a non-nagging, loving way). Look for help in understanding each other. You may find you have been rather clueless about your husband, as well!

A good book can be an excellent source of help if both you and your husband go through it together. Carla Anne has read countless marriage books and has even bought a few especially for me to read. I've actually read a couple of these, but most I never even opened. That doesn't mean they can't be a great resource.

I recommend allowing your husband to pick a book and to take the lead in this area (you can ask him to do this), or your counselor may recommend some material. This is another pink versus blue language issue, much like the diet book example I mentioned earlier. If a man gives his wife a marriage book and says he would like to study it with her, she may go into shock, but she will certainly understand it as a loving act. But when a woman gives her husband such a book, it is likely to be understood *very* differently. What is being said in pink means something very different in blue!

It is difficult for most men to avoid taking offense when their wives suggest getting some kind of help for their marriage. While you may be trying to get closer to him, he will understand instead that you think he is a failure. Most men want a satisfying, happy, vibrant marriage, and so long as the boat isn't rocking, they believe the voyage is going well. It can be devastating to learn that their wives' hearts are bleeding with loneliness and hurt.

May I encourage you to be gentle with him?

Carla Anne and I have also gone on marriage retreats, attended marriage seminars and conferences, and watched marriage videos together. Some were fabulous, others didn't fit us well. From these shared experiences, however, we have been developing a much better understanding of each other. They have also allowed us to build a common language of understanding—those little phrases and references that are neither pink nor blue and that take us back to something we have shared and help to keep us on the same page. Two resources that stand out in our minds as having been extremely helpful are the Worldwide Marriage Encounter weekend[1] and the *Love and Respect* DVD series by Emerson Eggerichs.[2]

Let me encourage you to try some or all of these things and to do this with your husband as much as possible. If he seems closed to these ideas, do not lose hope. I haven't always been very gracious to Carla Anne when she has suggested getting help for our marriage. And that brings me to a very important detail.

Carla Anne has tried various things over the years to help me "wake up" to her needs and to encourage me to engage more with her and our family. I've been asked, What was the most effective? I'll tell you what it was: she prayed.

I remember one occasion where Carla Anne asked me to attend a marriage conference with her. I reacted to her in a way that shut her down and made her feel like there was no hope. In no uncertain terms I told her that I was not interested in going.

She took this heavy burden to a group of women she was meeting with regularly. They would encourage and pray for each other. She and they began to pray that my heart would soften and that I would be willing to attend this conference.

As I was driving along during the course of my work day several weeks later, I heard an advertisement on the radio for what sounded like a really neat marriage conference. I jotted down the info and went home, excited to tell Carla Anne all about it.

Needless to say Carla Anne agreed to attend with me. At the ladies' next meeting, they had a little praise session that the very retreat I'd adamantly said no to I'd come home excited to attend with my wife. Instead of nagging me, pouting, or complaining to others about me, Carla Anne did the best thing she could have ever done—she took her burden and desires to God. She knew that he was the only One who could change my stubborn heart.

But what should you pray about?

The best husband you can have is the man God intends your husband to be. So that's where you should focus your efforts in prayer.

Your Best Husband

There is a challenge of trust here—do you really believe that God's plans are for your best? Or are you partly convinced that he has cheated you, that he has given you the short end of the stick and you could do better for yourself going some other way?

The best husband you can have is the man God intends your husband to be.

Not the husband you think some other man could be. Not the man you think you would like your husband to be. The man God intends your husband to be.

This truth, this trust in God is foundational. The woman who doesn't really trust God in this will try to use God (and anyone or anything else) to make her husband into what she wants. But the woman who believes becomes available to be used by God to help her husband become all that God wants.

You may say, "That's easy to say, but I have to deal with the man my husband is!"

Yes, you do, but there is more to the man your husband is than you think.

Clear Vision

In Judges 6 we find the story of Gideon. For seven years Israel had been ruthlessly pillaged by the Midianites, who lived to the east of them. The Midianites repeatedly invaded to take all the livestock they could find and to destroy the crops in every field, pushing the people of Israel to the very edge of starvation.

> The angel of the LORD came and sat down under the oak in Ophrah that belonged to Joash the Abiezrite, where his son Gideon was threshing wheat in a winepress to keep it from the Midianites. When the angel of the LORD appeared to Gideon, he said, "The LORD is with you, mighty warrior."
>
> "But sir," Gideon replied, "if the LORD is with us, why has all this happened to us? Where are all his wonders that our fathers told us about when they said, 'Did not the LORD bring us up out of Egypt?' But now the LORD has abandoned us and put us into the hand of Midian."
>
> The LORD turned to him and said, "Go in the strength you have and save Israel out of Midian's hand. Am I not sending you?"
>
> "But Lord," Gideon asked, "how can I save Israel? My clan is the weakest in Manasseh, and I am the least in my family."

The Lord answered, "I will be with you, and you will strike down all the Midianites together." (Judg. 6:11–16 NIV)

So here's unremarkable Gideon, by his own admission the least of a weak family, hiding from the enemy in a winepress. Yet God addresses him as "mighty warrior"! Oh, really?

Yes, really.

God had a clear vision of Gideon and declared what he saw. Note that he does not say, "you will become a mighty warrior" or even, "do what I tell you and I will make you a mighty warrior." Gideon already was a mighty warrior—but God may have been the only one who was aware of it.

In the same way, God has a clear vision of your husband and is able to see great qualities in him that may be visible to no one else. He himself has put those qualities there and has matched them to his plans and purposes for your husband. As Ephesians 2:10 states, we are all "God's workmanship, created in Christ Jesus to do good works, which God prepared in advance for us to do" (NIV).

Of course, that's no guarantee we will accomplish those purposes. Gideon might have disobeyed God, no matter how mighty a warrior he was. Your husband may disobey God as well. Only God, however, has a clear vision of who your husband is, what is going on with him, and what God is doing and wants to do with him.

Start asking for his vision. There may be far more going on than you are aware of, and as you catch glimpses of God's plans, I pray that your hope strengthens and your trust in him grows.

Meanwhile, there is another level of activity going on around your husband you might not be aware of.

Would it surprise you to know that Satan has a strategic plan to ensure your husband never becomes the man God intends for him to be? I want to show you that plan and invite you to be just as strategic in how you battle for your husband in prayer.

Strategic Prayer Plan

I have come to love Jesus' parable of the sower. It is one of the few parables Jesus gave an interpretation for and it describes the process and pitfalls of growing in Christ. Using this parable as a plan for strategic prayer has made a difference in our lives, and can in yours as well.

Pray He'll Receive God's Word: The Shoot.

A farmer went out to plant his seed. As he scattered it across his field, some seed fell on a footpath, where it was stepped on, and the birds ate it. . . .

This is the meaning of the parable: The seed is God's word. The seeds that fell on the footpath represent those who hear the message, only to have the devil come and take it away from their hearts and prevent them from believing and being saved. (Luke 8:5, 11–12)

Satan's first strategy is to *defend the heart from the Word* so there is no shoot. One of the key things you can pray for your husband is that his heart becomes soft to the Word of God and that he will choose to follow Christ. A man's full potential can only be reached when his heart is yielded to God.

Pray He'll Grow in God's Word: The Root.

Other seed fell on shallow soil with underlying rock. The seed sprouted quickly because the soil was shallow. But the plant soon wilted under the hot sun, and since it didn't have deep roots, it died. . . .

The seed on the rocky soil represents those who hear the message and immediately receive it with joy. But since they don't have deep roots, they don't last long. They fall away as soon as they have problems or are persecuted for believing God's word. (Mark 4:5–6, 16–17)

Satan's second strategy is to *harden the heart to God's Word* so there is no root growth. If your husband is a Christian, pray that he will learn to handle God's Word constantly. Pray that he will have an increased desire to read the Bible. Pray that as he is reading, memorizing, and studying the Bible he will find joy and strength in it. Also pray that your husband will find other men who might encourage him in his walk with Christ and mentor him. These relationships are vital. Until God's Word is well-rooted in his heart, your husband will primarily be learning to follow God by "osmosis"—absorbing it from the examples of those around him.

Pray He'll Be Wholehearted in Obeying God: The Fruit.
> Other seed fell among thorns that grew up and choked out the tender plants so they produced no grain. . . .
> The seed that fell among the thorns represents others who hear God's word, but all too quickly the message is crowded out by the worries of this life, the lure of wealth, and the desire for other things, so no fruit is produced. (Mark 4:7, 18–19)

Once God's Word is rooted in your husband's life, he will be challenged more and more to obey it, and in this stage of life, his primary way of growing in Christ is through that obedience. As your husband obeys, the fruit of that obedience will eventually start to become obvious in his life.

Satan's strategy here is to *divide the heart from seeking and obeying God* so there is no fruit. Distractions of worry, wealth, and pleasure can derail your husband from becoming fruitful in what God intends for him. I know that I myself have struggled with and continue to battle on all three of these fronts. Pray against these distractions on behalf of your husband. Pray that he will learn to manage God's resources faithfully and grow in obedience. As your husband continues to spend time in Scripture, pray that as he reads, the Holy Spirit will move his heart to action.

At this point you may begin to encounter something new. Your husband will want to do things out of obedience that you are not accustomed to or that might require obedience of you as well. Become the kind of woman who prays these things for herself as you pray them for your husband so you will be ready at all times to stand in obedience with him.

Let me warn you: prepare yourself to face difficulties as your husband reaches this stage of his walk with Christ. No believer reaches maturity without learning obedience through some type of struggle. (Even Jesus himself had to learn obedience through suffering—see Heb. 5:8.)

Pray He'll Have Courage in Seeking God: The Pursuit.
Still other seeds fell on fertile soil, and they sprouted, grew, and produced a crop that was thirty, sixty, and even a hundred times as much as had been planted! . . .

And the seed that fell on good soil represents those who hear and accept God's word and produce a harvest of thirty, sixty, or even a hundred times as much as had been planted! (Mark 4:8, 20)

Once your husband has learned to walk in obedience to God, he will be reaching maturity in Christ. The fruit of that maturity will likely be evident in his life. He will be faced with challenges that go beyond obedience—where God shows himself in unusual circumstances and waits to see if we would dare pursue him outside of our comfort zone.

Note that in Jesus' parable, some mature plants bear much more fruit than others. At this point I believe Satan's main strategy is to *discourage the heart from pursuing God* in order to limit our fruitfulness. He will likely also redouble his efforts to get your husband out of the Word, and to distract him from seeking God. Pray against this and ask God to build a heart of passion in your husband. Pray that your husband would become surrounded with encouragers, other believers who are fervently pursuing God. Pray that he would become a man who would encourage others, you, and your children in their pursuit of God. Pray that he will have courage to chase after God in the areas and directions God reveals himself.

Hebrews 10:24–25 says, "Let us think of ways to motivate one another to acts of love and good works. And let us not neglect our meeting together, as some people do, but encourage one another, especially now that the day of his return is drawing near."

I've outlined the general growth process your husband may go through as you pray for him. But it is quite normal for changes to show up in some areas of a person's life long before they show up in other areas. You may see your husband mature quickly in some areas but still just "not get it" when it comes to family stuff. That doesn't mean he's not growing or that your prayers aren't being answered or that he's a hypocrite.

Also, there are differences between willingness, awareness, knowledge, and skill. A mature believer will have a willingness to care for and sacrifice himself on behalf of his wife and children. That will not, however, automatically clue him in to the needs of his wife. It certainly didn't in my case. Nor does it mean your husband will suddenly know what to do about those needs when he does become aware of them, or make him immediately skilled at doing the right things when he figures out what to do. It should mean that your husband, given even half a chance, is motivated to chase after these things with a desire to become skilled at doing the right things to care for you, to engage with you, and to communicate that he chooses you.

As you see this happen in your husband, pray that God would continue to fill you with grace so that you can freely offer it to him as well.

Without question, prayer is the most effective tool at your disposal in supporting your husband, keeping in mind again that you are aligning yourself with God in support of his plans for your husband, not trying to convince God to remake your husband more to your liking.

Prayer, however, is not the only tool you have available (although it can and should undergird everything else you do).

Let Him Know

I've already shared with you a little bit about letting your husband know about your needs and struggles and that you want him to be more engaged with you and your children. Letting him know these things in gentle, non-nagging ways that he can completely understand can be difficult.

I've sometimes been offended at what Carla Anne has had to say to me. Even if she said it nicely, the thought that I have not been good enough is never one I like to entertain. I would challenge you to wrap your words in respect and as many truthful compliments as you can. Every man likes to have his ego stroked! He'll be more receptive to your helpful suggestions if it feels like there's only one area you would like him to work on at a time. Don't make him feel that you're asking for a whole personality makeover!

I've mentioned the benefit of a Christian counselor, but I can't stress enough how important it is to find one you both trust. A good counselor will help you communicate and understand each other's needs with less misunderstanding and help you come up with effective ways to close the gap between what's happening now and the beauty of what your marriage can become.

Asking your husband to go see a marriage counselor is not likely going to be well received if it comes up out of the blue. Many times when my wife has asked me to go for marriage counseling, I have felt like running in the other direction. If you have just finished telling your husband that you have had it, are at the end of your rope, can't take this terrible marriage any more, and then deliver the demand to see a counselor—well, that's going to communicate with all the attractiveness of sticking one's hand in a meat grinder.

On the other hand, when Carla Anne has told me how committed she is to our marriage, and how she wants it to be the best ever, and then suggests that we go for a marriage tune-up every now and then with a marriage counselor, I am much more open to the idea. I understand the language of maintenance and tune-ups. Those are wise things to do. I'm willing to do wise things—at least I hope I am!

Carla Anne and I are committed to seeing a marriage counselor whenever one of us wants to go. It may simply be a desire to invest in our relationship, or one of us may sense a strain in or pressure on our marriage. At the time of this writing, we are partway through a year-long commitment to regular counseling. I like the idea of proactively strengthening our marriage and support network, and this is one great way to do that.

A Quiet Witness

Jesus taught that where our treasures are, there our hearts are also (Matt. 6:21; Luke 12:34). This principle applies as well to what we are talking about here—bringing a man's heart home to his wife. Is your husband able to see you as his treasure? Where a woman is treasurable, there is a natural draw and an appealing witness for God.

A nagging wife may push a man to react negatively toward her as well as toward God. When she becomes a treasure, however, her quiet witness may well heap burning coals of conviction on her husband's head.

Men are not idiots. We may act like it sometimes, but that's all it is—an act. We see what you do, we watch how you react toward others, the kids, and toward us. We see your acts of sacrifice—when you close your mouth at a time you would normally rather rant and rave. It may take us a while to catch on to exactly what is happening, but we see it.

When we see how you are growing and acting in Christlike ways rather than nagging, fighting, or complaining, it's likely we won't say anything about it. Conviction will begin to burn in our hearts as we see you doing what we know we should also be doing. Our admiration for you will grow over time. (You don't have to point out your good deeds to us, either, by the way. That won't make us feel very close to you.)

I've watched Carla Anne get up early and spend time in the Word and in prayer. Her example has often prodded me to grow as a Christian man. I hear the passion in her voice as she talks about what God is teaching her, how she's being convicted of things, and how much she longs to be called a good and faithful servant by God at the end of her life. Her example has been one of the things God has used to draw me closer to himself.

The conviction of the Holy Spirit is the best conviction there is. You don't need to do his job for him. But I'd like to warn you that although you might be living a perfect quiet witness in front of your husband, when God moves in his heart, he still has the choice to ignore or even turn his back on his Creator. This doesn't mean you've done anything wrong or that you should change what you are doing. It means you need to find your strength from God alone and keep obeying his Word to you.

Firmer Measures

At times, firmer measures need to be taken. When your situation includes physical abuse, severe mental health issues, or other circumstances that threaten the safety of you and/or your children, then you will need to take action and seek help.

Tough love needs to be demonstrated in some situations. This tough love will put boundaries in place to protect everyone involved. Carla Anne and I are not qualified to give you advice on how and when to do this.

But if you feel you fall into this category, don't give up hope. Keep praying for yourself, your husband, your marriage, and your family. Then take some or all of the following steps.

Find a group of women you can connect and pray with—perhaps a group in your church or through another Christian ministry. In a safe group of believers, you can share and pray together, thus obeying the command of Jesus to carry one another's burdens. This group will also provide support for you should firmer measures need to be taken.

Be in regular communication with the leadership of your church. Let them know what is going on. Talking about what is happening with safe church leadership is not gossip if it is for the purpose of protection and help.

Meet with a biblical Christian counselor on a regular basis—even if your husband won't attend with you or on his own. Your counselor will be better able to determine whether or not you need to remove yourself or the children from the situation, whether or not one or both of you might need to see a doctor to assess mental health concerns, and so on. Your counselor may advise that you take firmer measures, and he or she will help you to take them in the healthiest, most biblical way possible.

Consider talking with your parents and your husband's parents regarding what is happening in your family. They may be able to help support you in prayer and in other practical ways and may even be in a position to speak to your husband directly if God leads them to do that. This may or may not be appropriate, depending on your situation and your relationship with your parents. This is a wise step to take if it is an option for you.

Final Words

Solo parenting is still a reality for our family. There are seasons when I must travel a lot for work or must work extremely long hours, leaving Carla Anne to carry much of the burden at home alone. I'm still learning how to engage more with Carla Anne in meaningful ways, even in the midst of my busy seasons. God continues to challenge me to invest more of my life in things that really matter, and that includes my family. I've certainly not arrived at any finish line yet, if there is such a thing while I still live.

Our marriage is not perfect. We still misunderstand each other, still get angry with each other, and are sometimes slow to seek each other's forgiveness. Carla Anne still feels that her needs sometimes go unmet. I still sometimes get caught up in selfish endeavors and miss my opportunities to care for my wife and kids.

We are thankful that God has brought us to this good place. God has intervened far too many times for either of us to take credit for it. We see the healing and strength God has brought and continues to bring to us as we grow in this thing called marriage. We are learning how to live life sometimes together, sometimes apart, but more and more often with the grace that God extends to us.

Our prayer for you and your husband is that you would both fall in love with Jesus and allow him to transform your lives and your marriage, giving you hope and a renewed commitment to the beautiful plan and purpose he has for you.

May you be blessed by him.

Resources

Parenting and Disciplining Children

Chapman, Gary. *The Five Love Languages of Teenagers*. Chicago: Northfield, 2010.

Chapman, Gary, and Jennifer Thomas. *The Five Languages of Apology*. Chicago: Northfield, 2006.

Chapman, Gary, and Ross Campbell. *The Five Love Languages of Children*. Chicago: Northfield, 1997.

Cloud, Henry, and John Townsend. *Raising Great Kids*. Grand Rapids, MI: Zondervan, 1999.

Dobson, James. *Bringing Up Boys*. Carol Stream, IL: Tyndale, 2001.

Dobson, James. *The New Dare to Discipline*. Carol Stream, IL: Tyndale, 1992.

Welchel, Lisa. *Creative Correction*. Carol Stream, IL: Tyndale, 2005.

Marriage

Chapman, Gary. *The Five Love Languages*. Chicago: Northfield, 2010.

Cloud, Henry, and John Townsend. *Boundaries*. Grand Rapids, MI: Zondervan, 1992.

Dobson, James. *Love Must Be Tough*. Dallas: Word, 1996.

Eggerichs, Emerson. *Love & Respect: The Love She Most Desires, The Respect He Desperately Needs*. Nashville: Thomas Nelson, 2004.

Rosberg, Gary, and Barbara Rosberg. *6 Secrets to a Lasting Love*. Carol Stream, IL: Tyndale, 2006.

Smalley, Gary. *For Better or For Best: Understand Your Man*. Grand Rapids, MI: Zondervan, 1996.

Worldwide Marriage Encounter Retreats. http://www.wwme.org.

Freedom, Inner Healing, and Deliverance

Anderson, Neil T. *The Bondage Breaker, New Edition*. Eugene, OR: Harvest House, 2006.

Anderson, Neil T. *Victory Over the Darkness*. Ventura, CA: Regal Books, 2000.

Blessing Your Husband and Children

Trent, John. *Bedtime Blessings*, 2-volume set. Carol Steam, IL: Tyndale, 2009.

Trent, John, and Gary Smalley. *The Blessing: Giving the Gift of Unconditional Love and Acceptance*. Nashville: Thomas Nelson, 2004.

Encouraging Kids

Nappa, Tony, and Mike Nappa. *Lunch Box Laughs*. Cincinnati: Standard, 2000.

Stevans, Joy. *Hugs in a Lunchbox for Ages 5-7*. Cincinnati: Standard, 2002.

Stevans, Joy. *Hugs in a Lunchbox for Ages 8-12*. Cincinnati: Standard, 2002.

Prayer and Spiritual Growth

Bevere, John. *The Bait of Satan*. Lake Mary, FL: Creation House, 1994.

Bevere, John. *A Heart Ablaze*. Nashville: Thomas Nelson, 1999.

Bevere, John. *Under Cover*. Nashville: Thomas Nelson, 2001.

Hybels, Bill. *The Power of a Whisper: Hearing God, Having the Guts to Respond*. Grand Rapids, MI: Zondervan, 2010.

Omartian, Stormie. *The Power of a Praying Parent*. Eugene, OR: Harvest House, 2005.

Sheets, Dutch. *Authority in Prayer: Praying with Power and Purpose*. Bloomington, MN: Bethany House, 2006.

Sheets, Dutch. *The Beginner's Guide to Intercession*. Ann Arbor, MI: Vine Book, 2001.

Sheets, Dutch. *Intercessory Prayer*. Ventura, CA: Gospel Light, 2008.

Organization and Running a Household
Felton, Sandra. *Living Organized: Proven Steps for a Clutter-Free and Beautiful Home.* Grand Rapids, MI: Revell, 2004.
Felton, Sandra. *Organizing Magic: 40 Days to a Well-Ordered Home and Life.* Grand Rapids, MI: Revell, 2006.
http://www.flylady.net
http://www.organizedbydesign.com
http://www.messies.com

Bitty Breaks, Chuckles, and a Lighthearted Look at Life
Bolton, Martha, and Phil Callaway. *It's Always Darkest Before the Fridge Door Opens: Finding Joy in the Cold Places of Life.* Bloomington, MN: Bethany House, 2006.
Callaway, Phil. *Laughing Matters.* Colorado Springs: Multnomah, 2005.
Johnson, Barbara. *Fresh Elastic for Stretched Out Moms.* Grand Rapids, MI: Revell, 2003.
Johnson, Barbara. *Where Does a Mother Go to Resign.* Minneapolis, MN: Bethany House, 2004.
Linamen, Karen Scalf. *I'm Not Suffering from Insanity . . . I'm Enjoying Every Minute of It!* Grand Rapids, MI: Revell, 2002.
Linamen, Karen Scalf. *Just Hand Over the Chocolate and No One Will Get Hurt.* Grand Rapids, MI: Revell, 1999.
Linamen, Karen Scalf. *Sometimes I Wake Up Grumpy . . . and Sometimes I Let Him Sleep.* Grand Rapids, MI: Revell, 2001.
Linamen, Karen Scalf. *Welcome to the Funny Farm.* Grand Rapids, MI: Revell, 2001.
Meurer, Dave. *Boyhood Daze: An Incomplete Guide to Raising Boys.* Minneapolis, MN: Bethany House, 1999.
Meurer, Dave. *If You Want Breakfast in Bed, Sleep in the Kitchen.* Colorado Springs: Life Journey, 2005.
Meurer, Dave. *Out on a Whim: A Somewhat Useful Guide to Marriage, Family, Culture, God, and Flammable Household Appliances.* Minneapolis, MN: Bethany House, 2001.
Meurer, Dave. *You Can Childproof Your Home, But They'll Still Get In.* Grand Rapids, MI: Baker, 2005.

Blessings to Pray and Say

As you bless your children and husband with these Scripture verses, insert their names as appropriate. I've given you some reminders within the passages. Pray these in your quiet times, lay hands on your children and husband and pray the blessings out loud. Speak paraphrases of them in your everyday conversations. Scour the Scriptures to find other passages that you can pray and speak over your family. This is by no means an exhaustive list, just a little something to get you started.

> May the LORD bless you and protect you.
> May the LORD smile on you and be gracious to you.
> May the LORD show you his favor and give you his peace. (Num. 6:24–26)

> May God be merciful and bless us. May his face smile with favor on us.
> May your ways be known throughout the earth [in our family, home, and relationships], your saving power among people everywhere [in our family, home, and relationships].
> May the nations [we] praise you, O God. Yes, may all the nations [our entire family] praise you. (Ps. 67:1–3)

> The LORD keeps you from all harm and watches over your life.
> The LORD keeps watch over you as you come and go, both now and forever. (Ps. 121:7–8)

May God's peace be on this house. (Luke 10:5)

Peace be with you. (Luke 24:36)

May God, who gives us his peace, be with you all. Amen. (Romans 15:33)

May God our Father and the Lord Jesus Christ give you grace and peace. (1 Corinthians 1:3)

May what our Master Jesus Christ gives freely be deeply and personally yours, my friends [family, child, husband]. (Galatians 6:18 MSG)

O LORD, hear the cry of Judah [our family, husband] and bring them together as a people.
Give them strength to defend their cause; help them against their enemies! (Deuteronomy 33:7)

[Husband's or children's names] are loved by the LORD and live in safety beside him.
He surrounds them continuously and preserves them from every harm. (Deuteronomy 33:12)

May [my husband, child] be blessed by the LORD with the precious gift of dew from the heavens and water from beneath the earth;
with the rich fruit that grows in the sun, and the rich harvest produced each month;
with the finest crops of the ancient mountains, and the abundance from the everlasting hills;
with the best gifts of the earth and its bounty, and the favor of the one who appeared in the burning bush.
May these blessings rest on [my husband's, child's] head. (Deuteronomy 33:13–16)

There is no one like the God of Israel.
He rides across the heavens to help you,
across the skies in majestic splendor.
The eternal God is your refuge,
and his everlasting arms are under you. (Deuteronomy 33:26–27)

Peace be with you, dear brothers and sisters, and may God the
    Father and the Lord Jesus Christ give you love with faithful-
    ness. May God's grace be eternally upon all who love our
    Lord Jesus Christ. (Ephesians 6:23–24)

How joyful are those who fear the LORD and delight in obeying
    his commands.
Their children will be successful everywhere; an entire genera-
    tion of godly people will be blessed.
They themselves will be wealthy, and their good deeds will last
    forever.
Light shines in the darkness for the godly.
They are generous, compassionate, and righteous.
Good comes to those who lend money generously and conduct
    their business fairly.
Such people will not be overcome by evil.
Those who are righteous will be long remembered.
They do not fear bad news; they confidently trust the LORD to
    care for them.
They are confident and fearless and can face their foes
    triumphantly.
They share freely and give generously to those in need.
Their good deeds will be remembered forever.
They will have influence and honor. (Psalm 112:1–9)

Job 38–42

Then the LORD answered Job from the whirlwind:

"Who is this that questions my wisdom
  with such ignorant words?
Brace yourself like a man,
  because I have some questions for you,
  and you must answer them.

"Where were you when I laid the foundations of the earth?
  Tell me, if you know so much.
Who determined its dimensions
  and stretched out the surveying line?
What supports its foundations,
  and who laid its cornerstone
as the morning stars sang together
  and all the angels shouted for joy?

"Who kept the sea inside its boundaries
  as it burst from the womb,
and as I clothed it with clouds
  and wrapped it in thick darkness?
For I locked it behind barred gates,
  limiting its shores.
I said, 'This far and no farther will you come.
  Here your proud waves must stop!'

"Have you ever commanded the morning to appear
    and caused the dawn to rise in the east?
Have you made daylight spread to the ends of the earth,
    to bring an end to the night's wickedness?
As the light approaches,
    the earth takes shape like clay pressed beneath a seal;
    it is robed in brilliant colors.
The light disturbs the wicked
    and stops the arm that is raised in violence.

"Have you explored the springs from which the seas come?
    Have you explored their depths?
Do you know where the gates of death are located?
    Have you seen the gates of utter gloom?
Do you realize the extent of the earth?
    Tell me about it if you know!

"Where does light come from,
    and where does darkness go?
Can you take each to its home?
    Do you know how to get there?
But of course you know all this!
For you were born before it was all created,
    and you are so very experienced!

"Have you visited the storehouses of the snow
    or seen the storehouses of hail?
(I have reserved them as weapons for the time of trouble,
    for the day of battle and war.)
Where is the path to the source of light?
    Where is the home of the east wind?

"Who created a channel for the torrents of rain?
    Who laid out the path for the lightning?

Who makes the rain fall on barren land,
    in a desert where no one lives?
Who sends rain to satisfy the parched ground
    and make the tender grass spring up?

"Does the rain have a father?
    Who gives birth to the dew?
Who is the mother of the ice?
    Who gives birth to the frost from the heavens?
For the water turns to ice as hard as rock,
    and the surface of the water freezes.

"Can you direct the movement of the stars—
    binding the cluster of the Pleiades
    or loosening the cords of Orion?
Can you direct the sequence of the seasons
    or guide the Bear with her cubs across the heavens?
Do you know the laws of the universe?
    Can you use them to regulate the earth?

"Can you shout to the clouds
    and make it rain?
Can you make lightning appear
    and cause it to strike as you direct?
Who gives intuition to the heart
    and instinct to the mind?
Who is wise enough to count all the clouds?
    Who can tilt the water jars of heaven
when the parched ground is dry
    and the soil has hardened into clods?

"Can you stalk prey for a lioness
    and satisfy the young lions' appetites
as they lie in their dens
    or crouch in the thicket?

Who provides food for the ravens
  when their young cry out to God
  and wander about in hunger?

"Do you know when the wild goats give birth?
  Have you watched as deer are born in the wild?
Do you know how many months they carry their young?
  Are you aware of the time of their delivery?
They crouch down to give birth to their young
  and deliver their offspring.
Their young grow up in the open fields,
  then leave home and never return.

"Who gives the wild donkey its freedom?
  Who untied its ropes?
I have placed it in the wilderness;
  its home is the wasteland.
It hates the noise of the city
  and has no driver to shout at it.
The mountains are its pastureland,
  where it searches for every blade of grass.

"Will the wild ox consent to being tamed?
  Will it spend the night in your stall?
Can you hitch a wild ox to a plow?
  Will it plow a field for you?
Given its strength, can you trust it?
  Can you leave and trust the ox to do your work?
Can you rely on it to bring home your grain
  and deliver it to your threshing floor?

"The ostrich flaps her wings grandly,
  but they are no match for the feathers of the stork.
She lays her eggs on top of the earth,
  letting them be warmed in the dust.

She doesn't worry that a foot might crush them
 or a wild animal might destroy them.
She is harsh toward her young,
 as if they were not her own.
 She doesn't care if they die.
For God has deprived her of wisdom.
 He has given her no understanding.
But whenever she jumps up to run,
 she passes the swiftest horse with its rider.

"Have you given the horse its strength
 or clothed its neck with a flowing mane?
Did you give it the ability to leap like a locust?
 Its majestic snorting is terrifying!
It paws the earth and rejoices in its strength
 when it charges out to battle.
It laughs at fear and is unafraid.
 It does not run from the sword.
The arrows rattle against it,
 and the spear and javelin flash.
It paws the ground fiercely
 and rushes forward into battle when the ram's horn blows.
It snorts at the sound of the horn.
 It senses the battle in the distance.
 It quivers at the captain's commands and the noise of battle.

"Is it your wisdom that makes the hawk soar
 and spread its wings toward the south?
Is it at your command that the eagle rises
 to the heights to make its nest?
It lives on the cliffs,
 making its home on a distant, rocky crag.
From there it hunts its prey,
 keeping watch with piercing eyes.

Its young gulp down blood.
   Where there's a carcass, there you'll find it."

Then the LORD said to Job,

"Do you still want to argue with the Almighty?
   You are God's critic, but do you have the answers?"

Then Job replied to the LORD,

"I am nothing—how could I ever find the answers?
   I will cover my mouth with my hand.
I have said too much already.
   I have nothing more to say."

Then the LORD answered Job from the whirlwind:

"Brace yourself like a man,
   because I have some questions for you,
   and you must answer them.

"Will you discredit my justice
   and condemn me just to prove you are right?
Are you as strong as God?
   Can you thunder with a voice like his?
All right, put on your glory and splendor,
   your honor and majesty.
Give vent to your anger.
   Let it overflow against the proud.
Humiliate the proud with a glance;
   walk on the wicked where they stand.
Bury them in the dust.
   Imprison them in the world of the dead.
Then even I would praise you,
   for your own strength would save you.

"Take a look at Behemoth,
  which I made, just as I made you.
  It eats grass like an ox.
See its powerful loins
  and the muscles of its belly.
Its tail is as strong as a cedar.
  The sinews of its thighs are knit tightly together.
Its bones are tubes of bronze.
  Its limbs are bars of iron.
It is a prime example of God's handiwork,
  and only its Creator can threaten it.
The mountains offer it their best food,
  where all the wild animals play.
It lies under the lotus plants,
  hidden by the reeds in the marsh.
The lotus plants give it shade
  among the willows beside the stream.
It is not disturbed by the raging river,
  not concerned when the swelling Jordan rushes around it.
No one can catch it off guard
  or put a ring in its nose and lead it away.

"Can you catch Leviathan with a hook
  or put a noose around its jaw?
Can you tie it with a rope through the nose
  or pierce its jaw with a spike?
Will it beg you for mercy
  or implore you for pity?
Will it agree to work for you,
  to be your slave for life?
Can you make it a pet like a bird,
  or give it to your little girls to play with?
Will merchants try to buy it
  to sell it in their shops?

Will its hide be hurt by spears
  or its head by a harpoon?
If you lay a hand on it,
  you will certainly remember the battle that follows.
  You won't try that again!
No, it is useless to try to capture it.
  The hunter who attempts it will be knocked down.
And since no one dares to disturb it,
  who then can stand up to me?
Who has given me anything that I need to pay back?
  Everything under heaven is mine.

"I want to emphasize Leviathan's limbs
  and its enormous strength and graceful form.
Who can strip off its hide,
  and who can penetrate its double layer of armor?
Who could pry open its jaws?
  For its teeth are terrible!
Its scales are like rows of shields
  tightly sealed together.
They are so close together
  that no air can get between them.
Each scale sticks tight to the next.
  They interlock and cannot be penetrated.

"When it sneezes, it flashes light!
  Its eyes are like the red of dawn.
Lightning leaps from its mouth;
  flames of fire flash out.
Smoke streams from its nostrils
  like steam from a pot heated over burning rushes.
Its breath would kindle coals,
  for flames shoot from its mouth.

"The tremendous strength in Leviathan's neck

strikes terror wherever it goes.
Its flesh is hard and firm
   and cannot be penetrated.
Its heart is hard as rock,
   hard as a millstone.
When it rises, the mighty are afraid,
   gripped by terror.
No sword can stop it,
   no spear, dart, or javelin.
Iron is nothing but straw to that creature,
   and bronze is like rotten wood.
Arrows cannot make it flee.
   Stones shot from a sling are like bits of grass.
Clubs are like a blade of grass,
   and it laughs at the swish of javelins.
Its belly is covered with scales as sharp as glass.
   It plows up the ground as it drags through the mud.

"Leviathan makes the water boil with its commotion.
   It stirs the depths like a pot of ointment.
The water glistens in its wake,
   making the sea look white.
Nothing on earth is its equal,
   no other creature so fearless.
Of all the creatures, it is the proudest.
   It is the king of beasts."

Then Job replied to the LORD:

"I know that you can do anything,
   and no one can stop you.
You asked, 'Who is this that questions my wisdom with such
      ignorance?'
   It is I—and I was talking about things I knew nothing about,
   things far too wonderful for me.

You said, 'Listen and I will speak!
I have some questions for you,
and you must answer them.'
I had only heard about you before,
but now I have seen you with my own eyes.
I take back everything I said,
and I sit in dust and ashes to show my repentance."

After the LORD had finished speaking to Job, he said to Eliphaz the Temanite: "I am angry with you and your two friends, for you have not spoken accurately about me, as my servant Job has. So take seven bulls and seven rams and go to my servant Job and offer a burnt offering for yourselves. My servant Job will pray for you, and I will accept his prayer on your behalf. I will not treat you as you deserve, for you have not spoken accurately about me, as my servant Job has." So Eliphaz the Temanite, Bildad the Shuhite, and Zophar the Naamathite did as the LORD commanded them, and the LORD accepted Job's prayer.

When Job prayed for his friends, the LORD restored his fortunes. In fact, the LORD gave him twice as much as before! Then all his brothers, sisters, and former friends came and feasted with him in his home. And they consoled him and comforted him because of all the trials the LORD had brought against him. And each of them brought him a gift of money and a gold ring.

So the LORD blessed Job in the second half of his life even more than in the beginning. For now he had 14,000 sheep, 6,000 camels, 1,000 teams of oxen, and 1,000 female donkeys. He also gave Job seven more sons and three more daughters. He named his first daughter Jemimah, the second Keziah, and the third Kerenhappuch. In all the land no women were as lovely as the daughters of Job. And their father put them into his will along with their brothers.

Job lived 140 years after that, living to see four generations of his children and grandchildren. Then he died, an old man who had lived a long, full life.

Notes

Chapter 8: Make the Most of Mealtime

1. "Family Meals," Child Trends, http://www.childtrendsdatabank.org /archivepgs/96.htm (© 2003; accessed May 6, 2011). This is Child Trends' original analysis of data from the 2003 National Survey of Children's Health found at http://www.cdc.gov/nchs/slaits/nsch.htm.

2. Shirley Dobson, "Coming Home," Power to Change Ministries, http://power tochange.com/experience/family/cominghome/ (accessed May 6, 2011).

Chapter 11: Honoring the Man You Don't See Enough

1. Alan D. Wright, *God Moments* (Colorado Springs: Multnomah, 1999), 17.

Chapter 13: The Father Your Kids Need

1. Stephen Lawhead, *Byzantium* (New York: HarperTorch, 1996), 854, 861–62.

2. Ibid., 867–68.

3. Iva Hoth, *The Picture Bible* (Colorado Springs: David C. Cook, 1998).

Chapter 15: From My Husband's Heart

1. For more information on Worldwide Marriage Encounter, see http://www .wwme.org/.

2. I credit Eggerichs for both the "pink" versus "blue" language and diet/marriage book gift illustrations I have used here. *Love & Respect Live Marriage Conference*, Dr. Emerson & Sarah Eggerichs, Love & Respect Ministries, 2006, available at http://loveandrespect.com.

About the Author

After living the life of a married solo parent, Carla Anne Coroy feels compelled to encourage other women who feel like they're going it alone. A gifted teacher and communicator, she now shares her life, her mistakes, her passions, and her faith through speaking, writing, and mentoring.

Carla Anne's zeal for seeing others live godly, fruit-filled lives is no recent development. She worked with Youth for Christ for many years before going on to develop a successful music studio, teaching children and adults. She founded a MOPS (Mothers of Preschoolers) chapter and was involved in speaking for MOPS events. After a few years of volunteering with Crown Financial Ministries, she served full time as the Director of Crown Financial Ministries, Central Canada.

In 2003 Carla Anne began mentoring groups of preteens and teens, a ministry that has grown to include coaching of other mentors leading similar groups. She has also been a homeschooling mom for more than a decade.

Carla Anne writes for the online magazine *www.mentoringmoments.org*, and is an active blogger. Her website www.carlaanne.com allows her to stay connected with, and provide resources and support to, the many groups she ministers to, while allowing others to get to know her a bit and discover her passion for uncovering God's hope in everyday life. Her Married Single Moms blog provides a platform to reach and inspire many married women who live and parent alone.

Married for eighteen years, Carla and Trent live with their four children in Manitoba, Canada, where they try to stay warm in winter and mosquito-bite-free in summer.